Building C Libraries

Windows, Menus & User Interfaces

Building C Libraries

C Libraries

Windows, Menus & User Interfaces

Len Dorfman

 WINDCREST®

Windcrest books are published by Windcrest Books, a division of TAB BOOKS. The name "Windcrest" is a registered trademark of TAB BOOKS.

Published by **Windcrest Books**
FIRST EDITION/FIRST PRINTING

Library of Congress Cataloging-in-Publication Data

Dorfman, Len.
    Building C libraries : windows, menus & user interfaces / Len Dorfman.
      p.   cm.
    ISBN 0-8306-8418-2   ISBN 0-8306-3418-5 (pbk.)
    1. C (Computer program language) I. Title.
QA76.73.C15D67   1990
005.4'3—dc20   89-29127
                                          CIP

TAB BOOKS offers software for sale. For information and a catalog, please contact TAB Software Department, Blue Ridge Summit, PA 17294-0850.

Questions regarding the content of this book should be addressed to:

Windcrest Books
Division of TAB BOOKS
Blue Ridge Summit, PA 17294-0850

Stephen Moore: Acquisitions Editor
Patti McCarty: Technical Editor
Katherine Brown: Production
Jaclyn J. Boone: Book Design

Contents

Acknowledgments

Thank you Barbara, my wife, and Rachel our daughter, for your collective patience and loving support during the many hours of intense work required to complete this text. You're the best!

Introduction

Over the past few years, the C programming language's popularity has sky-rocketed for a variety of reasons. Although originally developed as a systems programming language, C has now moved into an eminent position for use in general-application programs. At work and home, professional and hobbyist programmers have taken C to heart.

The purpose of this text is to provide step-by-step instructions on how to build tools for, and create, your own specialized C language library. The library you develop using this book can improve the "look and feel" of your programs while drastically reducing development time.

This text is written at a level where it assumes that you will have a rudimentary knowledge of the C and assembly programming languages. If you don't have an assembler, I suggest that you consider buying one. TASM and MASM are both wonderful assemblers and have been seen in the $100 range.

The source code presented in the text is purposefully written in (what I feel is) simple C and assembly. I chose this style for two reasons. The first comes from force of habit. It is not uncommon for a programmer to write some code and then have to look at it, say, one year later. That has happened to me, and I could not print my puerile response when the code was not documented and easy to read. Code maintenance remains high on my priority list when developing a program. The second reason is that in my heart I'm a teacher (and forever a student!). Providing simple-looking code will facilitate your learning process.

For purposes of our tool and library creation theme I've chosen to demonstrate the building of a professional Window, Screen, and Keyboard Handling Library. If you wish, you may obtain all the routines presented in this book (and more!) by ordering the TSR 'C'erious library through the coupon located at the back of the book. The $59.95 price represents a 40 percent discount off list price. You will receive two diskettes containing the source code for all the function modules, the Small, Medium, and Large model libraries, many demonstration programs, all the source code presented in this text, and a comprehensive manual.

Although this book supports Turbo C (all versions), Microsoft C (all versions), Microsoft Quick C, Watcom C (all versions) and Watcom Express C, you should have little difficulty in applying these routines to another compiler. In fact, at the time of this writing, the C and assembly functions presented in this text were converted to the Zortech compiler in a few hours.

For assembly routines, two macro assemblers are supported. They are: Microsoft's MASM and Borland's TASM macro assemblers. As the Watcom C Optimizing Compiler by default uses different calling conventions from those of Microsoft C and Turbo C, special attention will be paid in describing the assembly bindings. Note that the Watcom Express Compiler compiles using the Medium Memory Model only, and that its calling conventions are the same as those of the Turbo and Microsoft compilers. If you own Watcom Express, that means that you should follow the instructions for using the Medium Model directives and the calling conventions of the Turbo and Microsoft compilers.

The assembly bindings are presented using the new directives made available with the introduction of MASM 5.0 (and on) and TASM. Directives such as .MODEL, .CODE and .DATA make assembly programming dramatically easier. They are a wonderful addition for beginning and intermediate assembly programmers.

When assembly routines start being presented, copious comments will infuse each function. This is done for those who aren't totally familiar with the new directives offered by the latest versions of MASM and TASM. The complete function description will be presented in all C and Assembly source. I chose to do this for those programmers wishing to type either the C or assembly source code, but not both.

Multiple compilers have been selected because one feature of a library is that it can make a program compiler-transparent. For example, I find Turbo C best for quick development of general-purpose programs. But, I like the code produced by the Watcom C compiler best. By having a specialized windowing library up and ready for both compilers, with the smallest of changes based on the differences between the standard compiler libraries, I can develop my program in a fast and elegant environment (Turbo) and produce final version code using the compiler that I feel produces the tightest and fastest code (Watcom).

What I'm saying is that no compiler is perfect for all situations. Compiler designers always must make trade-offs concerning speed of compile, algorithms for optimization, etc. Because the prices of C compilers have settled in the under $300 range, for the most part, it might make sense for enthusiastic programmers to have more than one compiler. Creating a series of specialized libraries would allow the programmer to go from one compiler to another when the need arises. When you finish this text you will understand what it takes to write a compiler transparent library.

HOW TO USE THIS BOOK

If you want to learn all the ins and outs of library building, I suggest that you start on Page 1 and read through the text in a page-by-page fashion. The material has been presented in such a way so that the reasoning behind all decisions is thoroughly explained. All good how-to books present material in a sequential fashion. This book does not deviate from that philosophy.

Do you want to know what considerations go into designing object modules for a specialized C language library? Do you want to know what criteria go into selecting functions to include in your library? Do you want to know when to code functions in C and when to code in those functions in assembly? Do you want clear instructions on how to use your compiler's library manager program? Enough said. My recommendation is to read the book through and not jump about.

One last note: I find programming great fun. If you have fun while working your way through the text, it will be icing on the cake.

1

Libraries

There are libraries filled with books and others filled with C language compiled object modules. One great feature of the C programming language is that it allows you to take your functions, package them separately, and then place them in a library. This is a wonderful feature.

When you need a book, you take that book off the shelf, but all the other texts in the library remain on the shelf. When you link your C object modules into an executable program, the linker automatically pulls only those functions that are requested by the object files produced by your compiler, and then links them into your executable program. This proves a very efficient way of managing C object modules.

By keeping your functions small and separate, they are very easy to maintain. You can easily modify one of your functions. You can then replace your old object module in the C library with the object module of the modified function. Dealing with a small individual source for functions is very convenient when compared to dealing with large multiple function source files.

In your public book library, titles of similar subjects are placed in the same section on the shelves. This is a very good way to manage information. The concept of having a specialized C function library, in a sense, has similar advantages. By placing similar functions in a specialized library it will prove easy to know where they are. If you ever need to take out a function and modify it, you will know exactly where to go to access that function.

One advantage of the C object library over keeping each object module separately is that the object library will (most of the time) consume less disk space. Another advantage is that linking using an object library means that your linker need perform only one opening procedure when it opens the library, as opposed to the repeated openings of many separate object modules. Opening and closing files is a time consuming operation.

Sometimes, the functions in a library are called tools. This is another good analogy. Functions (tools) that are related may be placed in a library. The library may then be called a 'tool box'. If the job calls for a widget, take the widget out and use it. The other tools remain in the tool box. For the purposes of this text, Tool Box and Library will be used in an interchangeable fashion. The following describes how to add a function to a library:

1. Write a function in C or assembly.
2. Compile the function using your compiler. The newly created .obj file is called the 'object module'.
3. Use you compiler's library manager, add your object module to the library, or replace an old object module with the new object module.

WHAT DOES YOUR LIBRARY MANAGER DO?

Your library manager program is a utility program included with your compiler. The Microsoft library manager program is called 'lib.exe', Turbo's library manager program is called 'tlib.exe', and Watcom's library manager program is called 'wlib.exe'. The library manager's functions are:

*   Create a new library of object modules.
*   Add an object module to an existing library.
*   Remove an object module from an existing library.
*   Replace an object module in an existing library.
*   Extract an object module from an existing library.
*   List the object module contents of a new or existing library.

When you create a library, it means that you add an object module to a library which does not exist. When the library manager detects that the target library doesn't exist, by default it creates a new library. The following describes the procedure for adding an object module to a library:

1. Compile your C function into an object module.
2. Use your library manager to add it to an existing library.

If a function with the same name already exists in the target library, you will get an error message. The object module that you are attempting to add to the library will not be added. When you remove an object module from a library, the object module is removed from the library and the .obj (object module file) is *not* placed on disk.

The object module replace function of the library manager allows you to replace an object module already existing in a library with an object module of the same name. For example, lets say that you decide to write a C function called vidInit( ) (which you will in a later chapter) and add it to your library. Then, at a later time, you decide to recode this function in assembly (which you will). Because I (and possibly you) like the assembly function better (smaller code—and I have a slight prejudice in the direction of assembly) you now want to replace the old C vidInit( ) function object module with the new assembly created vidInit( ) function object module. If you use your library manager's Add Object Module function you will get an error message. Instead, you must use the library manager's Replace function to fulfill your desire to replace the C created object module with your assembly created object module.

When you extract an object module from an existing library, you are removing the object module from the existing library and placing the .obj (object module) file on disk. This option proves useful if you need to grab an object module from, say, one library and stick it in another. For example, your TAB library, created by following the instructions in this book, will place the keyboard handling routines in the same library as the screen handling routines. If one day you feel that this library gets a tad too large, by using the extract object module library manager function you would be able to pull all the keyboard handling routines in the existing library and create a whole new library devoted just to keyboard handling. The following describes the procedure for moving an object module from one library to another:

1. Extract one keyboard object module from general TAB library.
2. Add extracted object module to new target library (new library will automatically be created).
3. Extract next object module from TAB library.
4. Add it to new library.

Creating a listing of your library means that an ASCII file will be created which displays all the names of the object modules in the library. A sample segment of a library listing is shown in FIG. 1-1.

Fig. 1-1. A sample segment of a library listing.

```
Publics by module

RESTSCRN      size = 4058
    _SCRN_MEM                    _restScrn

VIDINIT      size = 190
    _SCRNSEG                     _SPARKLE_FLAG
    _VID_PORT                    _crt
    _vidInit
```

Table 1-1. The Function Underscore
Convention for Compilers Discussed in This Text.

Function	Description
_restScrn	Microsoft, Turbo, and Watcom Express underscore naming convention for functions.
restScrn_	Watcom C underscore naming convention for functions
_SCRN_MEM	Microsoft, Turbo, Watcom Express and Watcom C naming convention for variables (char, int, etc.)

The first object module, RESTSCRN, has a size of 4058 bytes. There are two GLOBAL (C terminology) or PUBLIC (assembly terminology) names. _SCRN_MEM is one GLOBAL and _restScrn is another. Please note, that the preceding underscore (as in _restScrn) is automatically added by the Microsoft, Turbo, and Watcom Express compiler to your function. The Watcom C Optimizing compiler will add a post underscore. For example, the name _SCRN_MEM, might be declared in C as:

```
int SCRN_MEM;
```

TABLE 1-1 shows the underscore conventions for the compilers discussed in this book.

If the preceding section seemed a bit confusing to you, don't worry, the issue of naming conventions will be further clarified when we discuss adding assembly functions to your library. That section comes later in the text.

The second object module has five public names. Remember that there is no way to determine when you're using the Microsoft, Turbo, or Watcom express library what the PUBLIC names represent. You can't tell if _SCRN_SEG is a function in the library or a variable. You can make that distinction in the Watcom C library because variables will have a preceding underscore and functions will have a following underscore.

HOW WE PLANNED OUR 'C'ERIOUS LIBRARY

In this section I will loosely describe the process that we (the folks and TSR Systems Ltd., the consulting and software development company who are producing and marketing 'C'erious Tools—see coupon in back of book for more information) used in the development of a programmer's library for three compilers. The first part of this section, in a sense, will be anecdotal in nature and the second part will present concrete suggestions for library development.

The original mission of TSR Systems Ltd. was to produce terminate and stay resident programming (TSR) utilities for corporate clients. Our original development tools were Microsoft C 5.1 and the Blaise C Tools + Library.

Although our programs worked just fine using Microsoft's exemplary compiler and Blaise's first-rate library, our corporate clients always complained that, regardless of the size of our TSR programs, they had to be smaller. Smaller. SMALLER!

Smaller is a big word in TSR programming. The simplest way to keep a TSR program small is to write it in assembly and make it a .COM file. Although we could have written the programs in assembly, it seemed easier and faster to code the programs in C. As a start-up company we needed products "real soon" and C seemed the best way to go.

One afternoon Norm, my friend and TSR Systems Ltd.'s colorful business manager, noticed an advertisement in Dr. Dobbs, I believe, for a new C compiler from Watcom. The Watcom people claimed that their compiler produced tighter and faster code than either Microsoft C or Turbo C—a claim we had to check out.

We purchased a copy of Watcom C version 6.5 and ran some simple test programs. I was astonished that the executable code produced by Watcom C did indeed turn out to be about 20 percent tighter and ran faster than the code produced by Microsoft C. A 20 percent reduction in code size seemed enough incentive to port our TSR programs to Watcom C.

So I called Blaise and asked for the Watcom version of Blaise C Tools +. The folks at Blaise (at the time of my call) shared that they had made a business decision (based on sound judgment in my opinion) to continue supporting the Microsoft and Turbo Compilers in a big way. There simply weren't enough Watcom compilers on the market to justify the expense of converting Blaise C Tools to Watcom (programmer's time, advertising, manuals, etc . . .).

What to do? So I took on the responsibility of converting the Microsoft version of Blaise's C Tools + to Watcom C 6.5. At first I thought the job would be trivial, but then discovered that Watcom's default function calling conventions (how parameters are passed in the registers—more on that later) differed from those of Microsoft and Turbo. Groan! I understood that there was a way to mimic the Microsoft calling convention standards, but they just didn't seem to do the trick in all the memory models.

With patient technical support from Watcom, I finished converting 98 percent of the Blaise routines in the small, medium, and large memory models from Microsoft C to Watcom C. We recompiled and linked our commercial programs and—lo and behold—they ran a tad faster and were a full 20 percent smaller on disk and in the machine. Yeah for Watcom C!

But, during the conversion process I came to know the Blaise Library at a deep level. There were some function features that we just didn't need in our code. And, of course, there are many ways to approach coding a function. Also, there's a renegade aspect to my nature, and I thought "Gee, I wonder If I could do better?" So (for fun) I took a little time to produce a windowing library which had similar functionality to Blaise's C Tools +, but by coming from a different angle produced code a bit leaner and meaner.

A week or two later I replicated the Blaise menu demonstration program for the Watcom C compiler. The Blaise executable menu demonstration program weighed in at about 28,000 bytes and my functionally similar menu demonstration program weighed in at about 8,000 bytes. At that moment, the light bulb went on and we at TSR System's Ltd. said: "We've got a product here!"

I began the process of building the 'C'erious Tools library. First thing I did was have a glance at the list of functions in some other programmer's Windowing, Screen and Keyboard handling libraries. We talked: . . . let's code this function, but it will be better if we do it this way; . . . this function is just filler, let's not stick it in our library, . . . etc.

I began coding the 'C'erious functions in the Small, Medium and Large (more on memory models later) memory models using the Watcom compiler. Now, in another part of our little sweat shop, there were two utility programs set to the pace of our insanely frantic project development cycle. Of course, these utilities would be coded with our (at that time) in-house 'C'erious library. Wunderkind Jay, who codes the utility application programs (and continually reminds me that there are three zillion ways to optimize my code), kept the function requests coming. "Len, we need a real time clock; put it in the library; we need the function today; do it this way." Another set of functions was born from the demands of a bright, clear-thinking, demanding applications programmer.

Okay, now the Watcom library was taking shape. We initially felt that we should just produce a Watcom version of the library. Why? Our collective wisdom indicated that we could never compete successfully against the already established libraries. After all, they had a solid base of users and significant market share. Let's stick with Watcom. We'll be the first library on the Watcom block. We'll, for sure, get noticed then. Partially correct and partially fuzzy thinking on our part.

After our library demonstration programs were coded we shipped out the source and executable files to a few distributors and magazines. The distributors said: "Yes!" and were delighted. But, a consistent message came back from all the distributors: "If you want to make some money then make Turbo and Microsoft versions of your library. They have market share. Who knows how Watcom will do? By tying your product to Watcom . . ."

Let's think a moment here. We'd need a Small, Medium and Large model library for Microsoft C (3 libraries to manage), Turbo C (3 + 3 libraries = 6 libraries to manage), and Watcom C (6 + 4 libraries = 10 libraries). Oh no! It seemed that some serious thought would have to go into the organizational structure for our library development activities and management.

Once the Watcom 'C'erious library was in the Beta Testing stage I began working on the Turbo version. Once all the functions were converted, I compiled and ran our demonstration programs. I really like the Turbo programming environment. The Turbo-developed programs all ran fine, but were larger and slower.

The Microsoft 'C'erious version came next. The Microsoft compiler produced code somewhere between the Watcom Compiler and the Turbo compiler. Then, something serendipitous happened. I came to really enjoy working with the Turbo compiler. Its compile and link time felt faster than Microsoft or Watcom C. Turbo C had increased my programming productivity.

The executable code produced by the Turbo compiler wasn't my favorite, though. The Watcom compiler was my current darling. C has been touted as a language which will let you easily move your code from one computer and operating system to another with a minimum of effort. In a sense, that might be thought of as machine portability. Our libraries came to have a useful function we had never previously thought of: compiler portability. We could prototype our code in Turbo C and produce our commercial product with Watcom. We could avoid the slow (in comparison to Turbo) compile and link time of the Watcom development system during code generation, but use the Watcom compiler without tears for the final product version. We smiled as our productivity and final product quality increased.

Here are some guidelines using one method of library development:

1. Select a theme for your library (graphics, communications, math . . . etc.).
2. Choose your compiler(s) and macro assembler.
3. Use currently existing libraries as a starting point.
4. If possible, work in a group.
5. Place the library in a situation where ALL functions are continually tested in real world programming situations.

PLANNING YOUR OWN TAB LIBRARY

Finally, let's begin talking about developing the TAB Windowing, Screen, and Keyboard handling library. We'll follow the guidelines mentioned above.

Number 1. The theme in this text is declared by despotic proclamation. Your TAB library will be a Window, Keyboard, and Screen Handling library.

Number 2. I'll develop the library using the Turbo C as our main compiler. All the C source code will also compile using Microsoft's and Watcom's compilers. The few special-case differences for Watcom and Microsoft will be noted. Then for the most part, I'll develop the actual library in the SMALL memory model. I will however demonstrate how to develop code in the medium and large memory models so you may create your own medium and large libraries.

Also, we'll be using Turbo's TASM compiler in the Microsoft MASM (/jMSC51) emulation mode. Note that ALL assembly files for Turbo C will work as shown with Microsoft C. If you own Microsoft's MASM, simply assume that every time you see TASM we mean MASM.

Number 3. I'll start developing the TAB library by examining the 'C'erious Tools library. I know the code all too well (since I wrote it) and can take pot-shots at the library's author without worrying about being sued!

Number 4. Working in a group . . . um . . . You're never alone when you're a multiple . . ..

Number 5. All functions which are developed here will be demonstrated and tested with short utility programs. If you have it in the back of your mind to make a commercial library one day, or if your library will be used by other people, having demonstration programs will prove to be a real boon. Until you begin selling a library, it is hard to imagine the problems that will crop up with users. In truth, it was the demonstration programs which saved TSR's hide in the first look of 'C'erious Tools in Dr. Dobbs. Our first documentation didn't quite cut the mustard. Also, it is wonderful for product support to say: "Oh, just look at the demo program TESTKEY.C and you'll see how it works."

Now that we've followed our own rules for library development, let's FINALLY start the process. Here's a tentative list of what we'd like our library to do:

1. **A base of screen handling routines, using Direct Video Access:**

   - Determine the characteristics of the existing video adapter.
   - Put a character to the screen.
   - Combine a character's foreground color, background color, intensity level and blink into one CHAR.
   - Combine a character and it's foreground color, background color, intensity level and blink into an INT.
   - Put a character with its foregound color, background color, intensity level and blink to the screen.
   - Put a string to the screen controlling the foreground color, the background color, intensity level and blink to the screen.
   - Change the foreground color, background color, intensity level and blink of characters currently existing on the screen.
   - Clear the screen.
   - Save the existing screen image to memory.
   - Relocate a previously saved screen image from memory to the screen.
   - Draw a horizontal line controlling foreground color, background color, intensity level and blink.
   - Draw a vertical line controlling foreground color, background color, intensity level and blink.

- Read the character, its foreground color, background color, intensity level and blink from any location on the screen.
- Move the cursor on the screen.
- Draw a rectangle on the screen using the PC's character graphics and controlling the foreground color, background color, intensity level and blink.
- Save a rectangular segment of the screen to memory.
- Relocate a previously save segment of the screen from memory to the screen.
- Clear a rectangular area of the screen.
- Fill a rectangular area of the screen with a character.

2. **Keyboard read routines**:

- Wait and get a keystroke from the keyboard. We will need the SCAN code and CHARACTER code (more on SCAN and CHARACTER later).
- NO WAIT and get a keystroke from the keyboard. We will need the SCAN code and CHARACTER code (more on SCAN and CHARACTER later).
- Get a string of characters from the keyboard and return a pointer to that string.
- Get a LONG number from the keyboard and return the LONG (not ascii representation of the long).
- Get a FLOATING POINT number from the keyboard and return a float (not ascii representation of the float.

3. **Low level window routines using Direct Video Access**:

- Set a window's size.
- Set a window's default foreground color, background color, intensity level and blink.
- Select your window border (double line, single line, . . .etc.).
- Write a character with its foreground color, background color, intensity level and blink to the window.
- Write a character string with its foreground color, background color, intensity level and blink to the window.
- Alter window character's foreground color, background color, intensity level and blink without changing the character.
- Move the cursor in the window.
- Remove the window.

- Display the window.
- Destroy the window structure (more about structures later).

The preceding list of assessed needs for the TAB library provides a good starting point. Just as would happen in a real life library building situation, we will discover that we need a few more functions on the way to make things happen the way we want to.

In the text's subsequent chapters you will find source code for the many functions which will be contained in the TAB library. If you are planning to purchase the 'C'erious library using the discount coupon in the back of the book, you do not need to type in the listings. The routines presented in this book are duplicated in the 'C'erious library although they are more heavily documented in this text for instructional purposes.

Now, on to the fun part: actually getting our hands dirty and building the library.

SUMMARY

Libraries provide programmers with an efficient organizational structure for managing many function object modules. Two advantages of using the library technology available to C programmers are:

- In most instances, libraries will use less disk space than the separate function object modules would.
- Linking with libraries takes less time than linking with separate object modules.

The library manager program is used to create and maintain libraries.

2

Getting Started

In order to facilitate development of the TAB library building process, it will simplify things dramatically if you first type in the header files shown in the upcoming figures. Begin with FIG. 2-1 to define ASCII symbols. Of course, if you're planning to purchase the 'C'erious library using the discount coupon in the back of this book, then just look over the listings and continue reading. Selected sections of these listings will be explained in detail when germane to the content of the text.

It is essential to have KEYBOARD.H, shown in FIG. 2-2, prepared before any of the library functions are coded or any of the demonstration programs are compiled. All keyboard equates used by the TAB library come from KEY-BOARD.H.

TSTRUCT.H presents the C structures for rectangles, windows, etc . . . Certain PC and DOS defines are also presented. Each structure and define are carefully documented in the listing for TSTRUCT.H presented in FIG. 2-3.

TPROTO.H, shown in FIG. 2-4 is a listing that includes all the names for the TAB library function prototypes. These function prototypes are, in a sense, a wish list. If there are some you see that are not coded, then they are in 'C'erious Tools version 1.0, but not in this text. The advantage of prototyping all the functions here is that you now have a "paint-by-number" situation. Once you've coded all the functions in this text, then you have a direction on what to code next.

Fig. 2-1. A listing of the ASCII.H header file.

```
/*
 * Start of source file
 *
 * File name: ASCII.H
 *
 * Definitions for ASCII symbols.
 * Note that each definition
 *    begins with the letter 'a'
 */

#define   aNUL     0        /*        null \0 delimeter    */
#define   aSOH     1        /* ^A - start of heading       */
#define   aSTX     2        /* ^B - start of text          */
#define   aETX     3        /* ^C - end of text            */
#define   aEOT     4        /* ^D - end of transmission    */
#define   aENQ     5        /* ^E - inquiry                */
#define   aACK     6        /* ^F - affirm acknowledge     */
#define   aBEL     7        /* ^G - audible bell           */
#define   aBS      8        /* ^H - backspace              */
#define   aTAB     9        /* ^I - horizontal tab         */
#define   aLF      10       /* ^J - line feed              */
#define   aVT      11       /* ^K - vertical tab           */
#define   aFF      12       /* ^L - form feed              */
#define   aCR      13       /* ^M - carriage return        */
#define   aSO      14       /* ^N - shift out              */
#define   aSI      15       /* ^O - shift in               */
#define   aDCE     16       /* ^P - data link escape       */
#define   aDC1     17       /* ^Q - device control 1       */
#define   aDC2     18       /* ^R - device control 2       */
#define   aDC3     19       /* ^S - device control 3       */
#define   aDC4     20       /* ^T - device control 4       */
#define   aNAK     21       /* ^U - neg acknowledge        */
#define   aSYN     22       /* ^V - synchronous idle       */
#define   aETB     23       /* ^W - end of transmission    */
#define   aCAN     24       /* ^X - cancel                 */
#define   aEM      25       /* ^Y - end of medium          */
#define   aSUB     26       /* ^Z - substitute             */
#define   aESC     27       /*        escape               */
#define   aFS      28       /*        file sererator       */
#define   aGS      29       /*        group seperator      */
#define   aRS      30       /*        record seperator     */
#define   aUS      31       /*        unlinked seperator   */
#define   aSPC     32       /*        space                */

#define   aCODE    94       /* ^character indicating
                               printer command follows */
#define   aHCR     aEOT     /* Hard carriage return        */
#define   aCENTER  'C'      /* code to center line         */
#define   aDOUBLE  'D'      /* double strike toggle        */
#define   aEXPAND  'E'      /* emphasize toggle            */
#define   aSUPERS  'S'      /* superscript toggle          */
#define   aITALIC  'I'      /* italics toggle              */
#define   aBOLD    'B'      /* bold toggle                 */

#define   aTRUE    1        /* true                        */
#define   aFALSE   0        /* false                       */
```

```
/*
 * End of source file
 */
```

Fig. 2-1 ends.

Fig. 2-2. A listing of KEYBOARD.H.

```
/*
 * Start of source file
 *
 * File Name: KEYBOARD.H
 *
 * Keyboard Scan and ASCII codes
 *
 * These defines are useful in
 *    evaluating keypresses
 *    returned from gtKey()
 */

#define INSERT        0x5200
#define DELETE        0x5300
#define SPACE         0x3920
#define ESC           0x011b
#define ESCAPE        0x011b
#define PGDN          0x5100
#define PGUP          0x4900
#define PERIOD        0x342e
#define TAB           0x0f09
#define RT_SQUARE     0x1b5d
#define LT_SQUARE     0x1a5b
#define RT_BRACKET    0x1b7d
#define LT_BRACKET    0x1a7b
#define CNTL_HOME     0x7700
#define CNTL_END      0x7500
#define HOME          0x4700
#define END           0x4f00
#define s_BS          0x0008
#define BS            0x0e08
#define BACKSPACE     0x0e08
#define s_CR          0x000d
#define CR            0x1c0d
#define ENTER         0x1c0d
#define UP_ARROW      0x4800
#define RIGHT_ARROW   0x4d00
#define LEFT_ARROW    0x4b00
#define DOWN_ARROW    0x5000
#define F1            0x3b00
#define F2            0x3c00
#define F3            0x3d00
#define F4            0x3e00
#define F5            0x3f00
#define F6            0x4000
#define F7            0x4100
#define F8            0x4200
#define F9            0x4300
```

Fig. 2-2 continued.

```
#define F10             0x4400


#define SHIFT_TAB       0x0f00
#define SHIFT_HOME      0x4737
#define SHIFT_END       0x4f31
#define SHIFT_INSERT    0x5230
#define SHIFT_DELETE    0x532e
#define SHFT_INSERT     0x5230
#define SHFT_F1         0x5400
#define SHFT_F2         0x5500
#define SHFT_F3         0x5600
#define SHFT_F4         0x5700
#define SHFT_F5         0x5800
#define SHFT_F6         0x5900
#define SHFT_F7         0x5a00
#define SHFT_F8         0x5b00
#define SHFT_F9         0x5c00
#define SHFT_F10        0x5d00
#define SH_R_ARROW      0x4d36
#define SH_L_ARROW      0x4b34
#define SH_U_ARROW      0x4838
#define SH_D_ARROW      0x5032


#define CNTL_F1         0x5e00
#define CNTL_F2         0x5f00
#define CNTL_F3         0x6000
#define CNTL_F4         0x6100
#define CNTL_F5         0x6200
#define CNTL_F6         0x6300
#define CNTL_F7         0x6400
#define CNTL_F8         0x6500
#define CNTL_F9         0x6600
#define CNTL_F10        0x6700
#define CNTL_LEFTA      0x7300
#define CNTL_RIGHTA     0x7400

#define ALT_F1          0x6800
#define ALT_F2          0x6900
#define ALT_F3          0x6a00
#define ALT_F4          0x6b00
#define ALT_F5          0x6c00
#define ALT_F6          0x6d00
#define ALT_F7          0x6e00
#define ALT_F8          0x6f00
#define ALT_F9          0x7000
#define ALT_F10         0x7100

#define ALT_A           0x1e00
#define ALT_B           0x3000
#define ALT_C           0x2e00
#define ALT_D           0x2000
#define ALT_E           0x1200
#define ALT_F           0x2100
#define ALT_G           0x2200
#define ALT_H           0x2300
```

Fig. 2-2 continued.

```
#define ALT_I          0x1700
#define ALT_J          0x2400
#define ALT_K          0x2500
#define ALT_L          0x2600
#define ALT_M          0x3200
#define ALT_N          0x3100
#define ALT_O          0x1800
#define ALT_P          0x1900
#define ALT_Q          0x1000
#define ALT_R          0x1300
#define ALT_S          0x1f00
#define ALT_T          0x1400
#define ALT_U          0x1600
#define ALT_V          0x2f00
#define ALT_W          0x1100
#define ALT_X          0x2d00
#define ALT_Y          0x1500
#define ALT_Z          0x2c00

#define CNTL_A         0x1e01
#define CNTL_B         0x3002
#define CNTL_C         0x2e03
#define CNTL_D         0x2004
#define CNTL_E         0x1205
#define CNTL_F         0x2106
#define CNTL_G         0x2207
#define CNTL_H         0x2308
#define CNTL_I         0x1709
#define CNTL_J         0x240a
#define CNTL_K         0x250b
#define CNTL_L         0x260c
#define CNTL_M         0x320d
#define CNTL_N         0x310e
#define CNTL_O         0x180f
#define CNTL_P         0x1910
#define CNTL_Q         0x1011
#define CNTL_R         0x1312
#define CNTL_S         0x1f13
#define CNTL_T         0x1414
#define CNTL_U         0x1615
#define CNTL_V         0x2f16
#define CNTL_W         0x1117
#define CNTL_X         0x2d18
#define CNTL_Y         0x1519
#define CNTL_Z         0x2c1a

#define K_0           0x0b30
#define K_1           0x0231
#define K_2           0x0332
#define K_3           0x0433
#define K_4           0x0534
#define K_5           0x0635
#define K_6           0x0736
#define K_7           0x0837
#define K_8           0x0938
#define K_9           0x0a39
```

Fig. 2-2 continued.

```
#define ALT_0        0x8100
#define ALT_1        0x7800
#define ALT_2        0x7900
#define ALT_3        0x7a00
#define ALT_4        0x7b00
#define ALT_5        0x7c00
#define ALT_6        0x7d00
#define ALT_7        0x7e00
#define ALT_8        0x7f00
#define ALT_9        0x8000

#define K_SPACE      0x3920
#define K_EXCLAM     0x0221
#define K_QUOTE      0x2822
#define K_POUND      0x0423
#define K_DOLLAR     0x0524
#define K_PERCENT    0x0625
#define K_AND        0x0826
#define K_APOST      0x2827
#define K_LPAREN     0x0A28
#define K_RPAREN     0x0B29
#define K_STAR       0x092A
#define K_PLUS       0x0D2B
#define K_COMMA      0x332C
#define K_MINUS      0x0C2D
#define K_PERIOD     0x342E
#define K_FSLASH     0x352F


#define K_COLON      0x273A
#define K_SCOLON     0x273B
#define K_LESS       0x333C
#define K_EQUAL      0x0D3D
#define K_GREAT      0x343E
#define K_QUEST      0x353F
#define K_AMPER      0x0340

#define K_A          0x1E61 - 0x20
#define K_B          0x3062 - 0x20
#define K_C          0x2E63 - 0x20
#define K_D          0x2064 - 0x20
#define K_E          0x1265 - 0x20
#define K_F          0x2166 - 0x20
#define K_G          0x2267 - 0x20
#define K_H          0x2368 - 0x20
#define K_I          0x1769 - 0x20
#define K_J          0x246A - 0x20
#define K_K          0x256B - 0x20
#define K_L          0x266C - 0x20
#define K_M          0x326D - 0x20
#define K_N          0x316E - 0x20
#define K_O          0x186F - 0x20
#define K_P          0x1970 - 0x20
#define K_Q          0x1071 - 0x20
#define K_R          0x1372 - 0x20
#define K_S          0x1F73 - 0x20
#define K_T          0x1474 - 0x20
```

```
#define K_U              0x1675 - 0x20
#define K_V              0x2F76 - 0x20
#define K_W              0x1177 - 0x20
#define K_X              0x2D78 - 0x20
#define K_Y              0x1579 - 0x20
#define K_Z              0x2C7A - 0x20

#define K_LBRACK         0x1A5B
#define K_BSLASH         0x2B5C
#define K_RBRACK         0x1B5D
#define K_KARAT          0x075E
#define K_UNDER          0x0C5C

#define K_a              0x1E61
#define K_b              0x3062
#define K_c              0x2E63
#define K_d              0x2064
#define K_e              0x1265
#define K_f              0x2166
#define K_g              0x2267
#define K_h              0x2368
#define K_i              0x1769
#define K_j              0x246A
#define K_k              0x256B
#define K_l              0x266C
#define K_m              0x326D
#define K_n              0x316E
#define K_o              0x186F
#define K_p              0x1970
#define K_q              0x1071
#define K_r              0x1372
#define K_s              0x1F73
#define K_t              0x1474
#define K_u              0x1675
#define K_v              0x2F76
#define K_w              0x1177
#define K_x              0x2D78
#define K_y              0x1579
#define K_z              0x2C7A

/*
 * End of source file
 */
```

Fig. 2-2 ends.

Fig. 2-3. A listing of TSTRUCT.H.

```
/*
 * Start of source file
 *
 * File Name: TSTRUCT.H
 *
 * Structures and definitions
 *    used by the library
 */

/*
```

Fig. 2-3 continued.

```
 * definitions
 */

#define IMAGE unsigned int

/*
 * WIND structure
 *
 * This structure holds all the
 *    data needed by the window
 *    routines to display the
 *    window properly
 */

typedef struct {
    int ul_row;                      /* upper left row     */
    int ul_col;                      /* upper left column  */
    int lr_row;                      /* lower right row     */
    int lr_col;                      /* lower right column */
    unsigned int img_size;           /* window img size    */
    unsigned int far *img_ptr;       /* pointer scrn image */
    unsigned int far *wind_ptr;      /* pointer scrn image */
    int box_type;                    /* border selection   */
    int attr;                        /* window attribute   */
    int visible;                     /* window on          */
    int top_offset;                  /* col offset title   */
    int top_length;                  /* length title str   */
    int show_top;                    /* display title      */
    int bot_offset;                  /* col offset title   */
    int bot_length;                  /* length title str   */
    int show_bot;                    /* display title      */
    char *t_title;                   /* ptr to t title str */
    char *b_title;                   /* ptr to b title str */
} WIND;

/*
 * DSKINFO structure
 *
 * This structure holds all the
 *    data which describes the
 *    disk status
 */

typedef struct {
    unsigned char media_descr;     /* media descriptor byte  */
    unsigned int clust_avail;      /* # of free clusters     */
    unsigned int clust_total;      /* total # of clusters    */
    unsigned int sec_p_clust;      /* # of sectors per clust */
    unsigned int bytes_p_sec;      /* # of bytes per sector  */
} DSKINFO;

/*
 * VIDEO structure
 *
 * This structure holds all the
 *    data concerning information
 *    about the video mode.
```

Fig. 2-3 continued.
```
 */

typedef struct {
   int mode;                    /* video mode           */
   int row_width;               /* columns per row      */
   int page;                    /* video page           */
   unsigned int far *scrn;      /* pointer to video RAM */
} VIDEO;

/*
 * RECT structure
 *
 * This structure holds all the
 *    data needed by the screen
 *    rectangle routines
 */

typedef struct {
   int ul_row;                  /* upper left row       */
   int ul_col;                  /* upper left column    */
   int lr_row;                  /* lower right row      */
   int lr_col;                  /* lower right column   */
   unsigned int *image;         /* pointer to scrn image */
} RECT;

/*
 * CUR_LOCATION structure
 *
 * This structure holds row
 *    and column of the saved
 *    cursor location
 */

typedef struct {
   int row;                     /* cursor row           */
   int column;                  /* cursor column        */
} CUR_LOCATION;

/*
 * LIGHT_PEN structure
 *
 * This structure holds all the
 *    concerning the light pen status
 */

typedef struct {
   int status;                  /* pen down or up       */
   int pix_col;                 /* pixel column         */
   int pix_row1;                /* pixel row            */
   int pix_row2;                /* pixel row            */
   int ch_row;                  /* character row        */
   int ch_col;                  /* character column     */
} LIGHT_PEN;


/*
 * Definitions for WRBOX.C
```

Fig. 2-3 continued.

```
 *
 */

/*        T B L R  #       */
/*        - - - -  -       */
#define S_S_S_S  0
#define S_S_D_D  1
#define D_D_S_S  2
#define D_D_D_D  3

/*
 * Definitions for MKATTR.C
 */

#define BLACK     0
#define BLUE      1
#define GREEN     2
#define CYAN      3
#define RED       4
#define MAGENTA   5
#define BROWN     6
#define WHITE     7
#define NORMAL    7
#define REVERSE   112

#define ON_INTENSITY  8
#define OFF_INTENSITY 0
#define ON_BLINK      128
#define OFF_BLINK     0

/*
 * Definitions for scrollint routines
 */

#define UP_SCROLL    6
#define DOWN_SCROLL 7

/*
 * Definitions for printer routines
 */

#define PRINT_TIME_OUT  1
#define IO_ERROR        4
#define PRINT_SELECTED  8
#define OUT_OF_PAPER    16
#define ACKNOWLEDGE     32
#define PRINT_NOT_BUSY  64

/*
 * Defines for flush kb buffer and get char
 */

#define ON_ECHO_CTRL     1  /* on char echo and ctrl-c enabled */
#define OFF_ECHO_CTRL_C 7  /* off echo and ctrl-c disabled    */
#define OFF_ECHO         8  /* off echo and ctrl-c enabled     */

/*
```

```
 * Defines for kb shift status
 */

#define RIGHT_SHIFT 1
#define LEFT_SHIFT  2
#define CLRL_PRESS  4
#define ALT_PRESS   8
#define SCROLL_LOCK 16
#define NUM_LOCK    32
#define CAPS_LOCK   64
#define INSERT_ON   128

/*
 * End of source file
 */
```

Fig. 2-3 ends.

Fig. 2-4. A listing of TPROTO.H.

```
/*
 * Start of source file
 *
 * File Name: TPROTO.H
 *
 * Function prototypes for
 *   library
 */

/*
 * Include files for all library definitions
 */

#include <keyboard.h>
#include <ascii.h>
#include <tstruct.h>

/*********************/
/*                   */
/* Disk Routines     */
/*                   */
/*********************/

long diskFree(void);
DSKINFO *diskInfo(DSKINFO *);
int getdrive(void);
void setdrive(int);

/*********************/
/*                   */
/* String Routines   */
/*                   */
/*********************/

void delChar(char *);
int findChar(int, char *);
void insChar(char *, char);
void insNum(char *,int);
```

21

Fig. 2-4 continued.

```
void strCjust(char *);
void strEnul(char *);
void strLjust(char *);
void strRjust(char *);
int strAnal(int *,int *,char *);


/**********************/
/*                    */
/* Keyboard Routines  */
/*                    */
/**********************/


char gtChar(void);
int gtKey(void);
char gtScan(void);
int gtKBstat(void);
int gtKBflag(void);
int inpflt(float *,int);
int inpnum(long *,int);
int prompt(char *,int);


/**********************/
/*                    */
/* Cursor Routines    */
/*                    */
/**********************/


void gtCur(int *,int *);
void mvCur(int, int);
void rmvCur(int, int);
void offCur(void);
void onCur(void);
void ssizeCur(void);
void rsizeCur(void);
void sizeCur(int, int);
void sCloc(void);
void rCloc(void);


/**********************/
/*                    */
/* Rectangle Routines */
/*                    */
/**********************/


RECT *setRect(RECT *, int, int, int, int);
void addRect(RECT *, RECT *);
void subRect(RECT *, RECT *);
void dupRect(RECT *, RECT *);
void dsyRect(RECT *);
void offRect(RECT *, int, int );
void boxRect(RECT *, int, int);
void clrRect(RECT *);
void fillRect(RECT *, int);
void saveRect(RECT *);
unsigned int sizeRect(RECT *);
void restRect(RECT *);
void scUp(RECT *, int, int);
```

Fig. 2-4 continued.

```
/*********************/
/*                   */
/* Sound Routines    */
/*                   */
/*********************/

void beep(void);
void bleep(void);
void offSound(void);
void onSound(int);

/*********************/
/*                   */
/* Print Routines    */
/*                   */
/*********************/

int prChar(int,char);
int prScrn(int);
int prScrnFF(int);

/*********************/
/*                   */
/* Screen Routines   */
/*                   */
/*********************/

void putChr(char);
void putCRLF(void);
void putLF(void);
void putCR(void);
void putStr(char *);
int rdChar(void);
void vdAttr(int, int, int, int);
void vdChar(int, int, int);
void vdStr(int, int, int, char *, char);
void vdWrite(int, int, int, char *, int);
void vidInit(void);
int vrdChar(int, int);
void wrChar(char, int);
void vdHoriz(int,int,int,int);
void vdVert(int,int,int,int);

void saveScrn(void);
void restScrn(void);

/*********************/
/*                   */
/* Window Routines   */
/*                   */
/*********************/

void dispWind(WIND *);
void dsyWind(WIND *);
void rdImg(WIND *);
void rdWind(WIND *);
void remvWind(WIND *);
```

Fig. 2-4 continued.

```
void scrnClr(void);
void setAttr(WIND *, int);
void setBord(WIND *, int);
void setTitle(WIND *,char *);
WIND *setWind(WIND *, int,int,int,int);
void strtWind(WIND *);
unsigned int sizeImg(WIND *);
void wmvCur(WIND *, int, int);
void wrBox(WIND *);
void wrImg(WIND *);
void wrWind(WIND *);
void wvdAttr(WIND *, int, int, int, int);
void wvdHoriz(int,int,int,int);
void wvdVert(WIND *,int,int,int,int);
void wvdStr(WIND *, int, int, int, char *, char);
void wvdWrite(WIND *, int, int, int, char *, int);
int wvrdChar(WIND *, int, int);


/**************************/
/*                        */
/* Miscellaneous Routines */
/*                        */
/**************************/

int mkToken(int,int);
int mkAttr(int, int, int, int);
void ascup(int, int, int, int);
void gtMode(int *, int *, int *);
void rLpen(LIGHT_PEN *);
int ramSize(void);
void exit_bad(char *);


/**************************/
/*                        */
/*  Intervention Routines */
/*                        */
/**************************/

long getvec(int);
void setvec(int,long);
void setCE(void);
void set16(int,int,int,int);
void set9dos(int,int,int);
int tsrfind(int);
int dosfind(int);
int tsrremv(void);
int dosremv(void);
void tsr(int);
void tsr9(int);
void setPSvec(void);
void tsrps(int);

void DispErr(void);
void ErasErr(void);

void tsrtime(int);
void setTimer(void);
```

```
void tsrgtime(void);
void setClock(int,int,int);

/*
 * End of source file
 */
```

Fig. 2-4 ends.

Now that you've looked through these files let's take a moment to briefly explore each one.

The header file ASCII.H holds definitions for standard ASCII functions. I have included a lowercase 'a' before each definition as a naming convention particular to this file and so far, I've never encountered a duplicate label.

The header file TSTRUCT.H holds the structure definitions used by the library. A *structure* is a wonderful concept that allows programmers to access data in an organized and conscious way. More about structures when we discuss the vidInit( ) function later in the text.

The header file KEYBOARD.H lists all the SCAN and CHAR portions of every keypress. The SCAN code occupies the MSB (most significant byte) of the define and the CHAR code occupies the LSB (least significant byte). For example, let's take a look at the SCAN and ASCII key code for the lowercase 'a':

```
#define  K_a  0x1e61
```

The scan code for lowercase 'a' is 0x1e and the character code for lowercase 'a' is 0x61. If you look at the ASCII character set in the appendix you will see that the ASCII value for lowercase 'a' is 0x61. All the function keys have a CHAR value of 0. Having both the scan and CHAR values available at keypress time makes it *very* simple to construct keyboard handlers that respond to both function keys and alphanumeric keys.

The header file TPROTO.H includes the previously mentioned header files and lists the function prototypes. The function prototypes are used by the compiler to help it understand how parameters will be passed between functions.

Correct prototyping became important to me when I developed a library module for the Watcom C compiler which used the standard library malloc (. . .) function. The program compiled fine (I neglected to have my warning messages set to the highest level – W3) but didn't work correctly. Why?

I forgot to include the malloc.h header file, which has the function prototypes. Because the Watcom C compiler will assume an INT is returned when no function prototype is offered, and that my malloc should have been returning a FAR * in the large model, the compiler got confused. And I got a massive headache figuring out why the function wasn't working properly.

There are many ways to organize a hard drive to facilitate library development with a variety of compilers. I will share with you the method I use. It seems to work just fine for me.

DISK ORGANIZATION

These header files will work with each compiler supported by this text. I have Microsoft C, Turbo C, and Watcom C all installed on my D: drive. I have created three batch files which I may invoke at any time to set the DOS environment variables to support the compiler I wish to use. For example, FIG. 2-5 is a listing of the TURBO.BAT file.

Fig. 2-5. A listing of the TURBO.BAT file.

```
prompt $p$g
path D:\TASM;D:\TC;C:\BRIEF;C:\DOS;C:\
set INCLUDE=D:\TC\INCLUDE
set LIB=D:\TC\LIB
```

As you can see I've put D:\TASM, D:\TC, C:\BRIEF, C:\DOS and C:\ all in my path. \TASM holds the Turbo Macro Assembler. \TC holds all of the Turbo C files and directories. C:\BRIEF holds my beloved text editor. \DOS allows me to use FORMAT.COM, etc. from the current directory.

Now that I've set the environment variables to the specifications required by the Turbo C compiler, it's time to present a sequence of DOS commands to create disk subdirectories which will facilitate development of your TAB library. This sequence of commands is shown here:

1. cd \tc Change to the turbo C directory.
2. md src Create a subdirectory to hold your library C source.
3. md asm Create a subdirectory to hold your library assembly source.
4. md tab Create a subdirectory to hold your demonstration programs.

Now that you've got a copy of the header files previously described, copy them into your Turbo C \INCLUDE directory. FIGURE 2-6 is a listing for the Microsoft C batch file.

Fig. 2-6. My MSC50.BAT file, which sets DOS environment variables for the Microsoft compiler.

```
prompt $p$g
PATH=D:\MSC\BIN;D:\MASM;C:\BRIEF;C:\DOS
set LIB=D:\MSC\LIB
set INCLUDE=D:\MSC\INCLUDE
set TMP=D:\TMP
```

In this case you would copy the header files to D:\MSC\INCLUDE. You would go into the \msc subdirectory and create your \src, \asm, and \tab subdirectories. FIGURE 2-7 provides a listing for the Watcom C batch file.

Fig. 2-7. A listing of my SETW65.BAT file which sets the DOS environment variables for the Watcom compiler.

```
prompt $p$g
path D:\wat65\bin;C:\BRIEF;C:\DOS;C:\;D:\MASM;
set include=D:\wat65\h
set lib=D:\wat65\lib
```

In this case you would copy the header files to D:\WAT65\H. You would go into the \WAT65 subdirectory and create your \src, \asm, and \tab subdirectories.

LIBRARY DEVELOPMENT PROCEDURE

There are as many ways to create a program development environment as there are programmers. The methods and habit patterns I describe in this text reflect my inclinations. Of course, yours may differ. But for those not familiar with library development, the habits presented in this work can provide some initial direction. The following is a summary of the procedure I use to add new routines to an existing library:

1. Write the C Source code for the function in the \src directory.
2. Using the Turbo C compiler, compile the source code in the small model using the highest level warnings invoked.
3. Add the new function to the small TAB library.
4. Switch to the \tab directory and write a test program to see if the function works. If it doesn't work GOTO 1.
5. Return to \src. Compile the function in the medium model. Add the function to the medium TAB library. Compile the function in the large model. Add the function to the large library.
6. Return to \tab. Compile and link the test program in the medium model. Run it. Compile and link the test program in the large model and run it.

Once I'm satisfied that the function is working up to snuff, I then copy the source code to my Microsoft's \src directory. I invoke my MSC50.BAT file and follow the above procedure. Once I'm satisfied that all is well in Microsoft land, then, you guessed it, I follow the same procedure for Watcom C.

CREATING YOUR FIRST
SCREEN HANDLING OBJECT MODULE

All of the direct video functions require that they have access to the video mode. For purposes of a text library, there are basically two choices: Monochrome and Color. Let's start our library by getting the video mode. The source code listing for GTMODE.C is presented in FIG. 2-8.

Fig. 2-8. The source code listing for the gtMode function.

```
/*******************
 * Source Code Start
 *
 * File Name:    GTMODE.C
 *
 * Synopsis:     gtMode(&mode,&col,&page)
 *
 * int *mode     pointer to mode
 *
 * int *col      pointer to # of cols pre row
 *
 * int *page     pointer to active video page
 *
 * Description: gtMode receives pointer to
 *               the three integers and returns
 *               the mode, the number of
 *               columns per row, and the
 *               active video page (in the
 *               case of color).
 *               This is an int 0x10
 *               function 0x0f (Get
 *               current display mode.
 *               A mode=7 means mono.
 *
 * Returns:      Nothing
 */

/*
 * Include files
 */

#include <dos.h>
#include <tproto.h>

/*
 * gtMode function
 */

void
gtMode(mode,c_p_line,page)
int *mode,*c_p_line,*page;
{
union REGS ir,or;
ir.h.ah = 15;
int86(0x10,&ir,&or);
*mode = or.h.al;
*c_p_line = or.h.ah;
*page = or.h.bh;
}

/*
 * End of Source
 ***************/
```

Change to the \src directory. Create the file GTMODE.C. Now that we have the source file we need to compile it into an object module, which will then be added to our newly created library. I use an identical command line for all of the different compilers. The batch file I use to compile is called CC.BAT. FIGURE 2-9 presents the listing for the Turbo C compile batch file.

Fig. 2-9. The Turbo version of CC.BAT.

```
tcc -c -w3 -m%1 %2.c
```

The −c switch invokes the compiler only; the −w3 switch sets the warning level to its highest setting; −m%1 switch sets the model; and %2.c appends a .C at the end of your source name.

Once you have created your CC.BAT file in the \SRC directory you may then compile GTMODE.C. To compile GTMODE.C type:

```
cc s gtmode
```

and press Enter.

Your function will compile into your small model object module. Now we need to create a new library and add this function to the library. To do this we will write a batch file called DOLIB.BAT. FIGURE 2-10 presents the listing for the Turbo library manager batch file.

Fig. 2-10. A listing for DOLIB.BAT.

```
tlib \tc\lib\%1 %2 %3 %4
```

This batch file will allow you to use Turbo's library manager to operate on the library specified by %1. Let's use the following naming convention for our libraries. Let the first three letters of the library start with TAB, followed by an underscore, then we'll use the first letter of the compiler, compiler version number, and then memory model. For example, a sample list of TAB library names for the Turbo compiler is shown in TABLE 2-1.

Table 2-1. Possible TAB Library Names for the Turbo Compiler.

Name	Description
TAB_T2S.LIB	Stands for (T)urbo (2) (S)mall Library
TAB_T2M.LIB	Medium model
TAB_T2L.LIB	Large model

To create our new Small library type:

dolib tab_t2s + gtmode

and now press Enter. As tab_t2s.lib doesn't exist, the library manager will automatically open up this new library file and then add GTMODE to it.

Following the suggested procedure, we now need to demonstrate and test the function. First switch to the \tab subdirectory. Let's call the program to test the gtmode function SHOWMODE.C., shown in FIG. 2-11.

Fig. 2-11. The source listing for SHOWMODE.C.

```
/*
 * Source Code Start
 *
 * File Name:   SHOWMODE.C
 *
 * Description: Demonstration program for]
 *              gtMode
 */

/*
 * Include files
 */

#include <stdio.h>
#include <tproto.h>

void main(void);

void
main()
{
int mode, row_width,page;

/* get the video mode */
gtMode(&mode,&row_width,&page);

/* if mode == 7 then print MONO */
if(mode==7)
        printf("\nThe video mode is: MONOCHROME\n");
/* mode != 7 then print color */
else
        printf("\nThe video mode is: COLOR\n");

/* print number of chars per row */
printf("The number of chars per row is: %d\n",row_width);

/* if COLOR then print video page */
if(mode!=7)
        printf("The active display page is: %d\n",page);
}

/*
 * End of Source
 */
```

The final step is to compile and run the program. We've created another batch file to compile and link the test program with the appropriate library. The DOSMALL.BAT batch file will accomplish the task, and its listing is presented in FIG. 2-12.

Fig. 2-12. A listing for the DOSMALL.BAT file.

```
tcc %1.c tab_t2s.lib
```

To invoke DOSMALL.BAT type:

```
dosmall showmode
```

and press Enter. SHOWMODE.EXE will now be in your directory. FIGURE 2-13 shows the results of running SHOWMODE.EXE.

Fig. 2-13. The results of SHOWMODE.EXE's execution.

```
The video mode is: COLOR
The number of chars per row is: 80
The active display page is: 0
```

Now that the gtMode function works fine let's return to the \src subdirectory. Here we will use our CC.BAT file to compile GTMODE.C in the medium model. Simply type:

```
cc m gtmode
```

and press Enter.

To create the new TAB_T2M.LIB and add the medium model GT MODE.OBJ simply type:

```
dolib tab_t2m +gtmode
```

and press Enter. Now the TAB_T2M.LIB library has been created. Return to \tab subdirectory.

To compile SHOWMODE.C and link SHOWMODE.EXE we need to modify DOSMALL.BAT. The medium model compile and link batch file is called DOMED.BAT, shown in FIG. 2-14.

DOLARGE.BAT, shown in FIG. 2-15, is the compile and link batch file for the Large Model.

Fig. 2-14. A listing of DOMED.BAT.

```
tcc -mm %1.c tab_t2m.lib
```

Fig. 2-15. The DOLARGE.BAT file for the large model.

```
tcc -ml %1.c tab_t21.lib
```

Once you know that the program is working in the medium model, follow the established procedure to create the TAB_T2L.LIB. Once that's done compile and test SHOWMODE.C in the large model.

Finally, we are finished with the Turbo gtMode function. Now, we need to include the batch files for the Microsoft and Watcom C compilers. FIGURE 2-16 through FIG. 2-20 will do the trick.

Fig. 2-16. The batch files for the Microsoft compiler.

```
The CC.BAT file for the Microsoft compiler is:

cl /A%1 /c /%2.c

The CC.BAT file for the Quick C compiler:

qcl /A%1 /c /%2.c
```

Fig. 2-17. The DOLIB.BAT file for the Microsoft compiler.

```
lib \msc\lib\%1 %2 %3 %4 %5 %6;
```

Fig. 2-18. The DOSMALL.BAT file for Microsoft C.

```
cl /AS %1.c tab_m5s.lib
```

Fig. 2-19. The DOSMALL.BAT file for Quick C.

```
qcl /AS %1.c tab_m5s.lib
```

Fig. 2-20. The CC.BAT file for the Watcom compiler.

```
wcc %2.c -m%1 -w3
```

The CC.BAT file would be invoked for GTMODE.C by typing:

cc S gtmode

and pressing Enter. Notice that the 'S' for small memory model is capitalized. To compile in the medium memory model simply change the S to M. Or L for the large memory model.

The DOLIB.BAT file would be invoked for GTMODE.C by typing:

dolib tab_m5s + gtmode

and pressing Enter. Note that the new library name is: TAB, Microsoft, 5, Small.

To create your executable program with the Microsoft compiler you need a new DOSMALL.BAT file. FIGURE 2-18 provides such a listing.

Note that the /AS stands for small memory model; /AM stands for the medium memory model; and /AL stands for the large memory model.

The DOSMALL.BAT file would be invoked by typing:

dosmall showmode

and pressing Enter.

The Watcom Batch files are presented in FIG. 2-20 through FIG. 2-24.

The /o option tells Watcom Express to create an object file and /dl says do not include any debugging information.

Fig. 2-21. The CC.BAT file for the Watcom Express compiler.

```
wcexp %1 /o /dl
```

Fig. 2-22. The DOLIB.BAT file for the Watcom compiler and Watcom Express.

```
wlib \watcomc\lib\%1 %2 %3 %4 %5 %6
```

Fig. 2-23. The DOSMALL.BAT file for Watcom C.

```
wcl %1.c -ms tab_w7s.lib
```

Fig. 2-24. The DOSMALL.BAT file for Watcom Express C.

```
wcexp %1 /o /dl
wlink file %1 library tab_wex
```

The CC.BAT file would be invoked for GTMODE.C by typing:

`cc s gtmode`

and pressing Enter.

By default, Watcom Express compiles in the medium memory model. For Watcom C, to compile in the medium memory model simply change the s to m. Or 1 for the large memory model.

The DOLIB.BAT file for Watcom C would be invoked for GTMODE.C by typing:

`dolib tab_w7s +gtmode`

and pressing Enter. Note that the new library name is: TAB, Watcom, 7, Small.

Note that the /AS stands for small memory model; /AM stands for the medium memory model; and /AL stands for the large memory model.

The DOSMALL.BAT file would be invoked by typing:

`dosmall showmode`

and pressing Enter.

SUMMARY

In this chapter we typed in our header files first, in order to facilitate library development. The source code for GTMODE.C was presented. This file was compiled into an object module; the object module was used to create a new library called TAB_T2S.LIB (Turbo Library names will be used from now on. If you are using a different compiler assume the appropriate name when the Turbo name is mentioned). The source code for testing GTMODE.C and SHOWMODE.C was presented. SHOWMODE.C was compiled and then linked to the newly created library. Next the medium model library (TAB_T2M.LIB) and the large model library (TAB_T2L.LIB) were created.

Batch files to compile, link and manage the libraries were suggested in order to facilitate library development. These batch files also lend an air of transparency to the development of libraries for more than one compiler.

Microsoft C object modules are interchangeable with Quick's files. Watcom Express compiles, by default, in the medium memory model. The Watcom Express calling conventions are the same as the Microsoft and Turbo memory models. This will become clearer in the next chapter.

The Batch files for Microsoft C and Watcom C were also presented. With the exception of the memory model specifier required by the CC.BAT file for the Microsoft compiler being capitalized, the batch files are invoked in an identical fashion for each of the supported compilers.

The following provides a quick summary of the recommended library development process. This process is referred to in Chapter 3:

1. Write function source.

2. Compiler to object module using highest warning level.

3. Add module to appropriate library.

4. Write test program source.

5. Compile and link test source with appropriate library.

6. Run program.
   If function check out Okay, then
     add the function to the other
     memory models
   Else
     GOTO to step 1

Hold on to your seat belts! Chapter 3 talks of hardware, rings the Assembly bell, and explores some Assembly versus C programming considerations.

3

Screen Handling Routines

All PCs have a set of built-in routines which are burned into ROM (Read Only Memory). These built-in routines are called the BIOS. BIOS stands for *Basic Input Output System*. The BIOS takes care of interfacing with devices such as: the video display, the keyboard, the disk drives, etc.

A programmer can access BIOS functions from C and assembly. As the C and assembly bindings to the BIOS require the programmer to load various registers with values, it makes sense to present a brief look at the 8086 architecture before presenting the code. Do not be frightened if you don't have a deep understanding of the register and segment scheme of the 8086 chip. Read the following pages before you look at the assembly or C BIOS interface code. After going through a few routines presented later in the text, reread these few pages again. I must admit it took me a while before I became fluent in 8086 assembly. If you are a beginner assembly programmer be patient with your speed of learning. You'll understand the scheme of things in time—guaranteed.

The discussion of the 8086's architecture is very basic and not intended to be anything more. If the discussion leaves you in the total dark, it might make sense to pick up a beginning assembly text for added information.

The 8086 has general registers, pointer registers, index registers, segment registers and the flag registers. Each of these registers is composed of 16 bits, although, certain 8086 instructions allow you to deal with two 8-bit registers instead of the one 16-bit register.

The general registers are named AX, BX, CX and DX. These registers are 16 bits, but each can be divided into two 8-bit registers. The 8-bit registers are named AL, AH, BL, BH, CL, CH, DL, DH.

AX is the *Accumulator register*. This 16-bit register is divided into two 8-bit registers. Bit 0 of AL is equivalent to bit 0 of AX. Bit 0 of AH is equivalent to bit 8 of AX. Some arithmetic operations use this register by default. The components of the AX register are represented in FIG. 3-1.

Fig. 3-1. Components of AX Register.

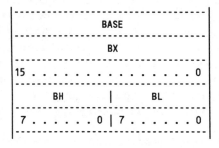

BX is the *Base register*. This 16-bit register is divided into two 8-bit registers. Bit 0 of BL is equivalent to bit 0 of BX. Bit 0 of BH is equivalent to bit 8 of BX. The BX register is the only general purpose register which can be used in an address calculation. The components of the BX register are represented in FIG. 3-2.

Fig. 3-2. Components of the BX register.

```
---------------------------------
|              BASE             |
---------------------------------
|               BX              |
---------------------------------
| 15 . . . . . . . . . . . . . 0 |
---------------------------------
|      BH       |      BL        |
---------------------------------
| 7 . . . . . . 0 | 7 . . . . . . 0 |
---------------------------------
```

CX is the *Count register*. This 16-bit register is divided into two 8-bit registers. Bit 0 of CL is equivalent to bit 0 of CX. Bit 0 of CH is equivalent to bit 8 of CX. The CX register is used as an iteration counter in the 8086's set of looping instructions. The components of the CX register are represented in FIG. 3-3.

DX is the *Data register*. This 16-bit register is divided into two 8-bit registers. Bit 0 of DL is equivalent to bit 0 of DX. Bit 0 of DH is equivalent to bit 8 of DX. The DX register is used in instructions for multiplication and division. This register is also used to specify the port address whenever the I/O port

Fig. 3-3. Components of the CX Register.

```
--------------------------------------
|              COUNT                 |
|--------------------------------------|
|               CX                   |
|--------------------------------------|
| 15 . . . . . . . . . . . . . . 0   |
|--------------------------------------|
|       CH       |       CL           |
|--------------------------------------|
| 7 . . . . . . 0 | 7 . . . . . . 0   |
--------------------------------------
```

address is in the range of 100 Hex to FFFF Hex. The components of the DX register are represented in FIG. 3-4.

Fig. 3-4. Components of the DX Register.

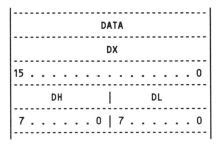

```
--------------------------------------
|              DATA                  |
|--------------------------------------|
|               DX                   |
|--------------------------------------|
| 15 . . . . . . . . . . . . . . 0   |
|--------------------------------------|
|       DH       |       DL           |
|--------------------------------------|
| 7 . . . . . . 0 | 7 . . . . . . 0   |
--------------------------------------
```

There are two pointer registers in the 8086 chip. They are named **SP** and **BP**. These 16-bit registers are generally used to access data in the Stack. Use of these registers is especially important in interfacing assembly code with your C code because the C function parameters are held in the Stack. The components of the Stack Pointer and Base Pointer registers are represented in FIG. 3-5.

The 8086 has two Index registers. These registers are named **SI** and **DI**. Although these registers can be used in arithmetic and logical operations their major use is in the 8086's string functions. The components of the SI and DI registers are represented in FIG. 3-6.

The 8086 has four segment registers—named CS, DS, ES, and SS.

The **CS**, or *Code Segment register* is used in conjunction with the instruction pointer to determine the address of the 8086 instruction to be executed. The components of the CS register are represented in FIG. 3-7.

The **DS**, or *Data Segment*, points to the segment where data are located. The components of the DS register are represented in FIG. 3-8.

Fig. 3-5. Components of the Stack and Base Pointers.

```
--------------------------------------
|              STACK POINTER          |
--------------------------------------
|                   SP                |
--------------------------------------
| 15 . . . . . . . . . . . . . . . 0  |
--------------------------------------
```

```
--------------------------------------
|              BASE  POINTER          |
--------------------------------------
|                   BP                |
--------------------------------------
| 15 . . . . . . . . . . . . . . . 0  |
--------------------------------------
```

Fig. 3-6. Components of the SI and DI registers.

```
--------------------------------------
|              SOURCE INDEX           |
--------------------------------------
|                   SI                |
--------------------------------------
| 15 . . . . . . . . . . . . . . . 0  |
--------------------------------------
```

```
--------------------------------------
|            DESTINATION INDEX        |
--------------------------------------
|                   DI                |
--------------------------------------
| 15 . . . . . . . . . . . . . . . 0  |
--------------------------------------
```

Fig. 3-7. Components of the Code Segment register.

```
--------------------------------------
|              CODE SEGMENT           |
--------------------------------------
|                   CS                |
--------------------------------------
| 15 . . . . . . . . . . . . . . . 0  |
--------------------------------------
```

Fig. 3-8. Components of the DS register.

```
-------------------------------------
|          DATA SEGMENT             |
-------------------------------------
|                DS                 |
-------------------------------------
|15 . . . . . . . . . . . . . . . 0 |
-------------------------------------
```

The **ES**, or *Extra Segment*, register is used in the memory address calculations for string operations. The components of the ES register are represented in FIG. 3-9.

Fig. 3-9. Components of the ES register.

```
---------------------------------------
|            EXTRA SEGMENT            |
---------------------------------------
|                 ES                  |
---------------------------------------
|15 . . . . . . . . . . . . . . . 0   |
---------------------------------------
```

The **SS**, or *Stack Segment*, register is used in the memory address calculations using the BP and SP pointer registers. The components of the SS register are represented in FIG. 3-10.

Fig. 3-10. Components of the SS register.

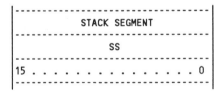

```
-------------------------------------
|          STACK SEGMENT            |
-------------------------------------
|                SS                 |
-------------------------------------
|15 . . . . . . . . . . . . . . 0   |
-------------------------------------
```

The 16-bit Flags register contains many status bits. As this is a brief description of the 8086's architecture, only the names of the flags are presented. When germane to the assembly bindings, the appropriate flags will be discussed more thoroughly. TABLE 3-1 presents a list of the Flag register bit names.

Table 3-1. Flag Register Bit Names.

FLAGS EXPLANATION

O-	Overflow
D-	Direction
I-	Interrupt
T-	Trace
S-	Sign
Z-	Zero
A-	Aux. Carry
P-	Parity
C-	Carry

SEGMENTS AND OFFSETS

There are two ways of viewing memory in the PC. The first way is to visualize the memory as one continuous block. Using this first method of viewing memory, we refer to addresses in memory as the *Physical Address*. Based on the original design of the 8086 chip, this physical address space is limited to 20 bits. The range of physical addresses can go from 00000 Hex to FFFFF Hex. In other words, the 8086 is limited to addressing 1 megabyte of physically addressed memory.

The second way is to visualize memory as a series of 64K blocks. This is a programmer's view. The *Segment* points to the *Start* address of the 64K block, and the *Offset* refers to the distance from the start of the 64K block.

The reason for using 8086's segment registers is that the 8086 must not address memory larger than 64K blocks. By adding the Segment concept, the 8086 chip designers allowed programmers, in truth, to access all of the memory addresses of the 1 megabyte permitted by the 20-bit addressing of the 8086. Set the Segment register to point to the start of the 64K block and the Offset can access any memory within that 64K block.

For example, let's take the physical address b8000 Hex. This address just happens to be the physical address at the start of the display RAM for direct color video text access. Direct video access will be discussed later in the text, for now let's look at how this physical address may be converted into the Segment and Offset way of viewing memory. FIGURE 3-11 shows how physical

Fig. 3-11. How the Physical Address relates to the Segment register and Offset register.

```
-------------------------------------------------
     PHYSICAL ADDRESS (b8000 Hex)
-------------------------------------------------
 b      80                  00
-------------------------------------------------
 1 0 1 1   1 0 0 0 0 0 0    0 0 0 0 0 0 0 0
-------------------------------------------------
     SEGMENT  b800 Hex      OFFSET  0000 Hex
-------------------------------------------------
```

addresses may be converted into Segment and Offset information.

Recapitulating, to access the memory at physical address b8000 Hex you simply set the Segment Register to b800 Hex and the Offset register to 0000 Hex and the 8086 takes care of combining the 16-bit Segment and 16-bit Offset into the all important 20-bit physical address.

My first programming experience began with assembly on the 6502 chip. Because this chip was limited to 64K of addressing there was no need for the Segment and Offset concept. I then migrated to the 68000 chip where you could address any memory directly. When I finally arrived into the land of 8086, the issues of 20-bit addressing using segments and offsets seemed cumbersome. Now, I'm used to it and it seems as normal as can be. Once again, if you're not quite grounded in the world of Segments and Offsets, don't give up. There will be more discussion of segments and offsets in the assembly routines. Be patient.

You're almost ready to begin the TAB library's initial routine. But first, let's flush out the idea of memory models a bit. For purposes of this text, only three memory models are discussed. They are: 1) the Small Model, 2) the Medium Model and 3) the Large Model.

The *Small Memory Model* means that all the code for the computer instructions will fit within the 64K Code Segment. All the Data will fit within the 64K Data Segment. In the Small Memory Model all the calls are *Near calls*, that is, calls within the one Code Segment. The Small Memory Model can be said to have Small Code and Small Data characteristics.

The *Medium Memory Model* means that the code for the computer instructions can use many 64K Code Segments. All the Data will fit within one 64K Data Segment. In the Medium Memory Model all the calls are *Far calls*, that is, calls must use the Code segment and Code Offset. The Medium Memory Model can be said to have Big Code and Small Data characteristics.

The *Large Memory Model* means that the code for the computer instructions can use many 64K Code Segments. Data will also be held in many 64K Data Segments. In the Large Memory Model all the calls are Far calls, that is, calls must use the Code segment and Code Offset. The Large Memory Model can be said to have Big Code and Big Data characteristics. In order to access any Data, the programmer must have access to the Data Segment and Data Offset. TABLE 3-2 summarizes the characteristics of each model.

In this text the primary library will be built in the small model. The first assembly routine, however, will be coded in the Small, Medium and Large

Table 3-2. Memory Model Characteristics.

Memory Model	Code Model	Data Model
Small	Small	Small
Medium	Big	Small
Large	Big	Big

models. Once assembly for the three models has been introduced, the rest of the text will deal with the Small Memory Model exclusively.

MOVING THE CURSOR IN C OR ASSEMBLY?

First, look at a simple BIOS interrupt routine that moves the cursor to a specified location on the video display (the screen), as shown in TABLE 3-3. BIOS interrupt 0x10, function 2 moves the cursor.

Table 3-3. Register Values for BIOS Cursor Move.

AH	register with function number 2
BH	register with video page (always page 0 for TAB library)
DH	register with the desired row
DL	register with the desired column

Moving the cursor is very simple to accomplish in C and assembly. Let's have a look at the code. FIGURE 3-12 lists the source code for MVCUR.C.

Fig. 3-12. The C source listing for MVCUR.C.

```
/******************
 * Start Source File
 *
 * File Name:    MVCUR.C
 *
 * Synopsis:     mvCur(row,column)
 *
 * int row       move cursor to this row
 *
 * int column    move cursor to this column
 *
 * Description: mvCur uses BIOS int 10h,
 *              function 2, to move the curor
 *
 * Returns:     Nothing
 */

/*
 * Include files
 */

#include <dos.h>
#include <tproto.h>

/*
 * mvCur function
 */

void
```

```
mvCur(row, column)
int row,column;
{
union REGS ir,or;
ir.h.ah = 2;
ir.h.dh = row;
ir.h.dl = column;
ir.h.bh = 0;
int86(0x10,&ir,&or);
}

/*
 * End of Source
 ***************/
```

Fig. 3-12 ends.

As you can see, using the union REGS, which is defined in the DOS.H header file, allows you to load any register with any value and call any BIOS interrupt. Now follow these steps:

1. Type in the source now and place it in your \src directory.

2. Compile the source using your CC.BAT file in the small model.

3. Add your new object module to your small memory model library using DOLIB.BAT.

4. Change directory to you \tab directory.

Now create your executable file for TESTCUR.C, shown in FIG. 3-13, using your DOSMALL.BAT file. When TESTCUR.C is compiled and linked, the result shown in FIG. 3-14 is displayed on the screen. The file sizes are shown in FIG. 3-15.

Fig. 3-13. Source code for mvCur(...) test program.

```
/********************
 * Source Code Start
 *
 * File Name:    TESTCUR.C
 *
 * Description: Demonstration program for
 *              mvCur
 */

/*
 * Include files
 */

#include <stdio.h>
#include <tproto.h>

void main(void);
```

```
void
main()
{
int row,col,count;

/* print diagonal 'TEST MVCUR.C' message on screen */
for(row=0,col=0,count=0; count<22; row++,col++,count++)
        {
        mvCur(row,col);
        printf("TEST MVCUR.C");
        }
}

/*
 * End of Source
 ***************/
```

Fig. 3-13 ends.

Fig. 3-14. Screen display for TESTCUR.EXE screen output.

```
TEST MVCUR.C
 TEST MVCUR.C
  TEST MVCUR.C
   TEST MVCUR.C
    TEST MVCUR.C
     TEST MVCUR.C
      TEST MVCUR.C
       TEST MVCUR.C
        TEST MVCUR.C
         TEST MVCUR.C
          TEST MVCUR.C
           TEST MVCUR.C
            TEST MVCUR.C
             TEST MVCUR.C
              TEST MVCUR.C
               TEST MVCUR.C
                TEST MVCUR.C
                 TEST MVCUR.C
                  TEST MVCUR.C
```

Fig. 3-15. File sizes.

MVCUR.OBJ	C version	417	bytes
TESTCUR.EXE	C mvCur	6848	bytes

Now let's try code MVCUR in assembly and see what happens to the code size. First we'll have a look at the object listing for the C code produced by the Turbo C compiler. You can get the object listing the MVCUR.C by typing:

    tcc -c -ms -S mvcur.c

and then press Enter. FIGURE 3-16 presents the assembly source code listing which Turbo C's compiler generated for the MVCUR.C source code file.

Fig. 3-16. Turbo C assembly source to create MVCUR.OBJ.

```
        ifndef    ??version
?debug    macro
    endm
    endif
    ?debug    S "mvcur.c"
_TEXT    segment    byte public 'CODE'
DGROUP    group    _DATA,_BSS
    assume    cs:_TEXT,ds:DGROUP,ss:DGROUP
_TEXT    ends
_DATA    segment word public 'DATA'
d@    label    byte
d@w    label    word
_DATA    ends
_BSS    segment word public 'BSS'
b@    label    byte
b@w    label    word
 ?debug C E9066057120760766375722E63
 ?debug C E900101D1113443A5C54435C494E434C5544455C646F732E68
 ?debug C E9555F3C1216443A5C54435C494E434C5544455C7470726F746F2E+
 ?debug C 68
 ?debug C E9AE03431118443A5C54435C494E434C5544455C6B6579626F6172+
 ?debug C 642E68
 ?debug C E90543020F15443A5C54435C494E434C5544455C61736369692E68
 ?debug C E9FD9C230 17443A5C54435C494E434C5544455C74737472756374+
 ?debug C 2E68
_BSS    ends
_TEXT    segment    byte public 'CODE'
;    ?debug    L 30
_mvCur    proc    near
    push    bp
    mov    bp,sp
    sub    sp,32
;    ?debug    L 34
    mov    byte ptr [bp-31],2
;    ?debug    L 35
    mov    al,byte ptr [bp+4]
    mov    byte ptr [bp-25],al
;    ?debug    L 36
    mov    al,byte ptr [bp+6]
    mov    byte ptr [bp-26],al
;    ?debug    L 37
    mov    byte ptr [bp-29],0
;    ?debug    L 38
    lea    ax,word ptr [bp-16]
    push    ax
    lea    ax,word ptr [bp-32]
    push    ax
    mov    ax,16
    push    ax
    call    near ptr _int86
    add    sp,6
@1:
;    ?debug    L 39
```

```
    mov    sp,bp
    pop    bp
    ret
_mvCur    endp
_TEXT    ends
    ?debug    C E9
_DATA    segment word public 'DATA'
s@  label    byte
_DATA    ends
_TEXT    segment    byte public 'CODE'
    extrn    _int86:near
_TEXT    ends
    public    _mvCur
    end
```

Fig. 3-16 ends.

Because the Turbo code doesn't interest me too much, let's have a look at some simple assembly code. FIGURE 3-17 presents the source code for MVCUR.ASM. Go to your \asm directory and enter create MVCUR.ASM. You can assemble this file using the A.BAT file shown in FIG. 3-18.

Fig. 3-17. Source code for TAB MVCUR.ASM.

```
;******************
; Start Source File
;
; File Name       MVCUR.ASM
;
; Synopsis:       ret = mvCur(row,column)
;
; int row         move cursor to this row
;
; int column      move cursor to this column
;
;
;
; Description     moves the cursor via BIOS
;                 int 10h to the position
;                 specified by row and column
;
;
;
; Small model off defined at 4
; Medium model off defined at 6
;
off      equ    4   ; Small Model offset
;
; set row to parameter 1
; set column to parameter 2
;
row      equ    BYTE PTR [BP+off]
column   equ    BYTE PTR [BP+off+2]
;
; Enable DOS segment-ordering at link time
```

Fig. 3-17 continued.

```
;
        DOSSEG
;
; Set the memory model for simplified segmentation
; directives
;
        .MODEL SMALL
;
; Declare the function as GLOBAL
; so it will be recognized by your
; C functions.  Note the underscore
; preceding the function.  This is
; a standard function naming convention
; for the MICROSOFT and TURBO compilers
;
        PUBLIC _mvCur
;
; Defines the start of the code segment
;
        .CODE
;
; Set the start of the function
;
_mvCur PROC NEAR
;
; Save BP
;
        push    BP
;
; Prepare BP to get arguments off the stack
;
        mov     BP,SP
;
; The row goes to DH
;
        mov     DH,row
;
; The column goes to DL
;
        mov     DL,column
;
; Set cursor position function 2
;
        mov     AH,2
;
; Move cursor on page 0
;
        mov     BH,0    ; 0 -> BH
;
; Invoke BIOS int 10h
;
        int     10H     ; BIOS video int
;
; Restore BP
;
        pop     BP
;
```

```
; Return to calling function
;
        ret
;
; End of procedure
;

_mvCur ENDP

;
; End of assembly source file
;

        END

; End Source Here
;****************
;
```

Fig. 3-17 ends.

Fig. 3-18. Source for A.BAT.

```
tasm /MX %1
```

The /MX directive tells the assembler to make all PUBLICs (GLOBALs) case sensitive. Because C is a case sensitive language it is ALWAYS wise to use this option. Some linkers use case sensitivity ON as default and other linkers use case sensitivity OFF as their default. By using the /MX option you will never mess up with using your assembly routines with C. So type:

```
a mvcur
```

and then press Enter. Your MVCUR.ASM file will assemble in no time flat. Now let's replace the old MVCUR.OBJ with the new assembly MVCUR.OBJ in your TAB_T2S.LIB. Use the DOLIB.BAT file. Type in:

```
dolib tab_t2s − +mvcur
```

and then press Enter. The − +mvcur tells the Turbo library manager to take out the old MVCUR.OBJ and replace it with the new MVCUR.OBJ.

Now return to the \tab subdirectory and use DOSMALL.BAT to create a new TESTCUR.EXE file. The results are compared in FIG. 3-19. So here we get a glimpse of Assembly magic. There is a 50 percent reduction in the object code for MVCUR and that savings is reflected in the TESTCUR.EXE file.

Reducing the size and increasing the speed of TESTCUR.EXE is discussed in another section in this chapter. But first, there needs to be a slightly different listing for the Watcom Express compiler.

Fig. 3-19. File comparison.

	Before				After		
MVCUR.OBJ	C version	417	bytes	MVCUR.OBJ	Assembly Ver	205	bytes
TESTCUR.EXE	C mvCur	6848	bytes	TESTCUR.EXE	C mvCur	6608	bytes

"Why?" you ask. Because Watcom Express uses the Medium Memory Model by default, and it also uses the standard Microsoft and Turbo calling conventions. The MVCUR.ASM file for the Medium Memory Model using the Microsoft and Turbo C parameter passing conventions is presented in FIG. 3-20. FIGURE 3-21 shows the MVCUR.ASM file for the Large Memory Model.

Fig. 3-20. Assembly source for MVCUR.ASM in the medium memory model.

```
;*******************
; Start Source File
;
; File Name      MVCUR.ASM
;
; Synopsis:      ret = mvCur(row,column)
;
; int row        move cursor to this row
;
; int column     move cursor to this column
;
;
;
; Description  moves the cursor via BIOS
;              int 10h to the position
;              specified by row and column
;
;
; Small model off defined at 4
; Medium model off defined at 6
;
off  equ  6    ; Medium Model offset

row  equ  BYTE PTR [BP+off]
column    equ  BYTE PTR [BP+off+2]


     DOSSEG

;
; Set the memory model for simplified segmentation
; directives
;
```

```
        .MODEL MEDIUM

        PUBLIC _mvCur
;
; Defines the start of the code segment
;
        .CODE

_mvCur PROC NEAR
        push BP
        mov  BP,SP
;
; The row goes to DH
;
        mov  DH,row
;
; The column goes to DL
;
        mov  DL,column
;
; Set cursor position function 2
;
        mov  AH,2
;
; Move cursor on page 0
;
        mov  BH,0
;
; Invoke BIOS int 10h
;
        int  10H
        pop  BP
        ret
_mvCur ENDP
        END
; End Source Here
;****************
;
```

Fig. 3-20 ends.

Fig. 3-21. The source to MVCUR.ASM for the Large Memory Model.

```
;*******************
; Start Source File
;
; File Name      MVCUR.ASM
;
; Synopsis:      ret = mvCur(row,column)
;
; int row        move cursor to this row
;
; int column     move cursor to this column
;
;
;
; Description  moves the cursor via BIOS
```

```
;              int 10h to the position
;              specified by row and column
;


;
; Small model off defined at 4
; Medium model off defined at 6
; Large model off defined at 6

off   equ  6   ; Medium Model offset

row   equ  BYTE PTR [BP+off]
column     equ  BYTE PTR [BP+off+2]

      DOSSEG
;
; Set the memory model for simplified segmentation
; directives
;
      .MODEL LARGE

      PUBLIC _mvCur
;
; Defines the start of the code segment
;
      .CODE
_mvCur PROC NEAR
      push BP
      mov  BP,SP
;
; The row goes to DH
;
      mov  DH,row
;
; The column goes to DL
;
      mov  DL,column
;
; Set cursor position function 2
;
      mov  AH,2
;
; Move cursor on page 0
;
      mov  BH,0
;
; Invoke BIOS int 10h
;
      int  10H
      pop  BP
      ret
_mvCur ENDP
      END
; End Source Here
;****************
```

Fig. 3-21 ends.

As the compiler designers of Watcom C 6.5 decided to use, as default, a different parameter passing convention between functions than the passing-on-the-stack method which has become the industry standard, we need to present a different assembly routine for MVCUR.ASM. By default, Watcom passes parameters in registers instead of passing them on the stack like Microsoft and Turbo.

At first, deviating from the industry standard seems potentially foolish, but in truth, it actually permits the writing of tighter and faster code. Watcom C does allow the programmer, though, to customize the calling conventions for any C function on an individual basis. This means that the programmer may use the "on the stack" method by utilizing some of Watcom's Pragmas. However, it is not within the scope of this book to delve more deeply into Watcom C's many features.

I'll stop here. FIGURE 3-22 lists the revised assembly binding for MVCUR.ASM, which may be used with Watcom C. As you can see, a few lines of code were saved. A few lines of code means a few bytes. A few bytes on, say 200 functions, could mean 1K which would speed things up a bit. In time-critical routines those bytes can suddenly become *big*.

Fig. 3-22. The Watcom version of MVCUR.ASM.

```
;******************
; Start Source File
;
; File Name      MVCUR.ASM
;
; Synopsis:      ret = mvCur(row,column)
;
; int row        move cursor to this row
;
; int column     move cursor to this column
;
; Description  moves the cursor via BIOS
;                  int 10h to the position
;                  specified by row and column
;
; No stack passing of parameters
; Parameter 1 comes in on AX
; Parameter 2 comes in on DX
;
; set row to parameter 1
; set column to parameter 2
;
row        equ  AL
column     equ  DL
;
; Enable DOS segment-ordering at link time
;
     DOSSEG
;
; Set the memory model for simplified segmentation
; directives
```

```
        .MODEL SMALL
;
; Declare the function as GLOBAL
; so it will be recognized by your
; C functions.  Note the underscore
; after the function.  This is
; a standard function naming convention
; for Watcom C compiler
;
        PUBLIC mvCur_
; Defines the start of the code segment
;
        .CODE
;
; Set the start of the function
;
mvCur_ PROC NEAR
;
; No need to:              push BP
; or:                      mov BP,SP
;
; Row goes to DL from AL
;
        mov  DH,row
;
; Column is already in DL
; so there is no need to:    mov DL,column
;
; Set cursor position function 2
        mov  AH,2
;
; Move cursor on page 0
        mov  BH,0
;
; Invoke BIOS int 10h
        int  10H
;
; No need to restore BP
; so:                       pop BP
;
; Return to calling function
;
        ret
mvCur_ ENDP
;
; End of assembly source file
;
        END
; End Source Here
;****************
```

Fig. 3-22 ends.

There are now two functions in our library. One function allows you to get information about the video adapter and the other allows you to move the cursor about the screen. If you could write a string of characters to the screen, then you could replace the slow (although sometimes indispensable) 'printf' function with something a bit faster and more elegant.

Before presenting that string write function, let's stop and talk about different ways to write to the screen.

ACCESSING THE SCREEN

A programmer can write to the screen using standard C library functions. For example, putchar, sends an INT to the standard output, which is often the screen. The way that happens, is that the compiler for the PC knows how to access the PC's BIOS. It is the BIOS that does the work. More on the BIOS in a moment.

The advantage of using standard screen functions for screen access is that your code will be able to run on *any* computer that has a C compiler. That is a decisive advantage for many programs. One big disadvantage of using standard C library, though, is that screen writes are slow compared to other methods of writing to the screen. Why are the standard C library screen output functions slow? First, the standard C library function must send appropriate information to the PC's BIOS, then the BIOS must assess the display hardware, and lastly, must alter the display RAM so that there will be the appropriate change on the monitor. Using standard C functions for screen output is a multi-level process.

The PC has a Basic Input Output System (BIOS) that permits the programmer to access peripherals with a certain sense of uniformity. For example, if the programmer uses a BIOS call for a screen write, the screen will be written whether it is CGA, EGA, MONO, VGA. By directly accessing the BIOS for screen output, the programmer eliminates the outer DOS layer of the standard C library.

The advantages of using the BIOS are that the screen output is faster than that of using the standard C library, and that the programmer is insulated from the display RAM. Disadvantages are that the code will lose its portability; in other words, the code will become PC (with a very close BIOS, that is) specific, and that the code will not be the fastest.

Going directly to display RAM is the fastest method of accessing the screen for writes. You will get very professional looking results. But there are hazards: 1) If the display RAM's address ever changes your code will fail 2) On some very aged PC CGA boards there will be an annoying sparkle 3) The code is not portable. But, alas, the results are so good that the TAB library will take the direct video route.

There are a variety of considerations one must consider when writing direct video routines. The way your video adapter displays the character in the text mode is to write the character code and attribute-byte next to each other in the display RAM. This is the same display RAM written to by the BIOS. But, your 8086 (etc.) also has access to this display RAM. The physical addresses for the Color Display RAM and the Monochrome Display Ram are different.

The video adapter interprets each byte in display RAM in an interesting way. One byte contains the character value. The next contiguous byte contains the attribute for that character. The attribute describes the character's foreground color, background color, foreground intensity (on/off), and foreground blink (on/off). The attribute bit pattern is presented in TABLE 3-4.

Table 3-4. The Bit Arrangement for the Attribute Byte.

BIT	Controls
7	Blink
6	
5	Background Color
4	
3	Intensity
2	
1	Foreground Color
0	

Instead of presenting bit patterns and color, I thought that it would prove more useful to you to present equates for the Controls in the attibute's bit pattern. These equates are defined in the header file TSTRUCT.H which you created earlier and are presented in FIG. 3-23.

Fig. 3-23. Color equates.

```
#define BLACK      0
#define BLUE       1
#define GREEN      2
#define CYAN       3
#define RED        4
#define MAGENTA    5
#define BROWN      6
#define WHITE      7

#define ON_INTENSITY  8
#define OFF_INTENSITY 0

#define ON_BLINK      128
#define OFF_BLINK     0
```

Now that we've defined these equates we need a function to turn these values into the attribute byte. As you continue building the TAB library, compile the C functions and install the object modules in the TAB library before you replace them with the assembly modules. That way you'll be able to get a good feel for how assembly functions alter executable program size and perform-ance. FIGURE 3-24 presents the C source code listing for MKATTR.C. This C function allows you to easily define an attribute byte. Compile this file and check out the file size of MKATTR.OBJ. FIGURE 3-25 presents the assembly

Fig. 3-24. The MKATTR.C (make attribute) function source.

```
/********************
 * Source Code Start
 *
 * File Name:    MKATTR.C
 *
 * Synopsis:     mkAttr(fore,back,intensity,blink)
 *
 * int fore      foreground color
 *
 * int back      background color
 *
 * int intensity iforeground intensity on-off
 *
 * int blink     blink on-off
 *
 * int attr      the properly aligned bits
 *               for a character attribute
 *
 * Description: mkAttr takes the four qualities
 *              of the attribute byte and
 *              brings them together into the
 *              attribute byte's proper bit
 *              arrangement
 *
 * Returns:      attr
 */

/*
 * Include files
 */

#include <tproto.h>

int
mkAttr(fore,back,intensity,blink)
int fore,back,intensity,blink;
{
int attr;

/* backgound equate * 16 */
attr = back*16;

/* OR fore, intensity and blink with back */
return(attr|fore|intensity|blink);
}

/*
 * End of Source
 *************/
```

Fig. 3-25. The assembly source for MKATTR.ASM.

```
;********************
; Source Code Start
;
; File Name:   MKATTR.ASM
;
; Synopsis:    mkAttr(fore,back,intensity,blink)
;
; int fore       foreground color
;
; int back       background color
;
; int intensity  foreground intensity on-off
;
; int blink      blink on-off
;
; int attr       the properly aligned bits
;                for a character attribute
;
; Description: mkAttr takes the four qualities
;                of the attribute byte and
;                brings them together into the
;                attribute byte's proper bit
;                arrangement
;
; Returns:     attr


;
; Small model off defined at 4
; Medium model off defined at 6
;

off        equ     4


;
; parameter 1 is foregrouned
; parameter 2 is background
; parameter 3 is foreground intensity
; parameter 4 is foreground blink
;

fore_c  equ     byte ptr [BP+off+0]
back_c  equ     byte ptr [BP+off+2]
inten_t equ     byte ptr [BP+off+4]
blink_t equ     byte ptr [BP+off+6]


;
; Enable DOS segment-ordering at link time
;

        DOSSEG


;
; Set the memory model for simplified segmentation
; directives
;
```

Fig. 3-25 continued.

```
        .MODEL SMALL

;
; Declare the function as GLOBAL
; so it will be recognized by your
; C functions.  Note the underscore
; preceding the function.  This is
; a standard function naming convention
; for the MICROSOFT and TURBO compilers
;

        PUBLIC _mkAttr
;
; Defines the start of the code segment
;

        .CODE

;
; Set the start of the function
;

_mkAttr PROC NEAR
;
; Save regs
;

        push    BP
        mov     BP,SP

;
; save 1 byte over mov AX,0
;

        xor     AX,AX
;
; background color to AL
;

        mov     AL,back_c   ; back ground color to AL

;
; move background 4 bits left (back*16)
;

        mov     CL,4        ; prep shift 4 left
        shl     AL,CL       ; means AL * 16
;
; OR foreground
;

        or      AL,fore_c   ; or foreground color

;
; OR intensity
;
```

```
        or      AL,inten_t  ; or intensity
;
; OR blink
;
        or      AL,blink_t  ; or blink
;
; attr returned in AL register
;
; Restore regs
;
        pop     BP
;
; Return to caller
;
        ret
;
; End functions
;
_mkAttr ENDP
;
; End assembly source file
;
        END
; End Source Here
;****************
```

Fig. 3-25 ends.

source code listing for MKATTR.ASM. Can you see the relationship between the C source and the assembly source?

One last note for C perfectionists: if you used the bit shift left operator (back << 4) instead of (back * 16) in the C source, would you save any bytes in the MKATTR object module? Try it and see what happens. You may be surprised. Using common logic you'd think that there would be a difference in object module size in favor of the bit shift.

FIGURE 3-26 shows how the mkAttr(...) function is used in your C source code.

Fig. 3-26. MKATTR function use.

```
attr = mkAttr(RED,WHITE,ON_INTENSITY,ON_BLINK);
```

The code presented in FIG. 3-26 sets the attribute byte so that the character's foreground is red, the background white, the red is intense, and the foreground blinks. Great, but what is the character and how do you get it to the screen?

Fortunately, display RAM for CGA, EGA, and VGA are all located at the same physical address B8000h. The HERC display RAM is located at B0000h.

Now that we know the physical address of display RAM, how can we address it in C and assembly? Remembering the earlier discussion on the byzantine SEGMENT:OFFSET addressing arrangement of the 8086, I won't belabor the point further here. This text concentrates primarily on how to program the 8086 and not the whys.

One more concept needs to be introduced before writing directly to the screen. That is the concept of a 'token.' For purposes of your TAB library a token is represented by an INT. The token's LSB (Least Significant Byte) is the character that will be printed to the screen and the token's MSB holds the character's attribute. FIGURE 3-27 presents the token's characteristics.

Fig. 3-27. A TOKEN's characteristics.

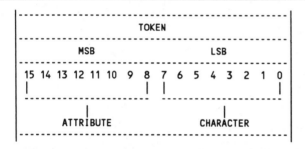

The TAB library has a Video structure to hold the information for the display RAM's address. There is a global variable that holds the display RAM's segment. This value will be used by the assembly video functions. FIGURE 3-28 presents the VIDEO structure.

Fig. 3-28. The VIDEO structure contained in TSTRUCT.H.

```
typedef struct {
    int mode;               /* video mode          */
    int row_width;          /* columns per row     */
    int page;               /* video page          */
    unsigned int far *scrn; /* pointer to video RAM */
} VIDEO;
```

The source code for VIDINIT.C, which initializes the VIDEO structure, is presented in FIG. 3-29. This function calls gtMode to get the video mode and then sets the VIDEO structure with the appropriate values. The source listing for VIDINIT.ASM is presented in FIG. 3-30.

Fig. 3-29. Source code for VIDINIT.C.

```
/********************
 * Source Code Start
 *
 * File Name:   VIDINIT.C
 *
 * Synopsis:   vidInit()
 *
 * Description: Calls gtMode to determine the
 *              video mode and sets the
 *              appropriate global video
 *              addresses to there will
 *              be a direct video write
 *              to display ram.
 *
 *              MONO SEG 0xb000 OFFSET 0x0000
 *              COLR SEG 0xb800 OFFSET 0x0000
 *
 *
 * Returns:    Nothing
 */

/*
 * Include files
 */

#include <stdlib.h>
#include <tproto.h>

/*
 * Declare video structure
 * to hold the current video
 * information
 */

VIDEO *crt;

/*
 * External buffer which holds
 *     a copy of display RAM
 */

extern unsigned int SCRN_MEM[80*25];

/*
 * Global INTs which are read
 * by the direct video routines
 */

int     SCRNSEG;
int     VID_PORT;
int     SPARKLE_FLAG;

/*
 * Define V_SIZE so if there is
 * a change made to the VIDEO structure
 * the call, when re-compiled will
 * automatically adjust
```

```
 */

#define V_SIZE sizeof(VIDEO)

/*
 * vidInit function
 */

void
vidInit()
{
int mode,page,width;

/* allocate memory for the Video structure */
crt = (VIDEO *)calloc(V_SIZE,sizeof(char));

/* get the video mode */
gtMode(&mode,&width,&page);

/* set the members of the crt */
crt->page = page;
crt->mode = mode;
crt->row_width = width;

/* If video is MONO */
if(crt->mode==7)
        {
        /* addr of mono video port */
        VID_PORT =0x03ba;

        /* set far pointer for 'C' direct video routines */
        crt->scrn = (unsigned int far *)0xB0000000L;

        /* set segment for assembly direct video */
        SCRNSEG = 0xb000;
        }
/* If video is COLOR */
else
        {
        /* addr of color video port */
        VID_PORT =0x03da;

        /* set far pointer for 'C' direct video routines */
        crt->scrn = (unsigned int far *)0xB8000000L;

        /* set segment for assembly direct video */
        SCRNSEG = 0xb800;
        }
}

/*
 * End of Source
 ***************/
```

Fig. 3-29 ends.

Now that the code for vidInit( ) has been presented in FIG. 3-30 you're almost ready to replicate TESTCUR.C. All you need to do is print a character to the screen. Once that's done it's ready for a test. After that, you'll learn about the print string function and then you'll be ready to go. The following sequence shows how vidInit(...) fits into your program:

1. Call vidInit at the very beginning of your program. This will set up the video structure for the direct video access.

2. All direct video calls will work now.

Note that all direct video calls go to PAGE 0. For your own upgrade to this library you might want to allow it to work with Page 0,1,2, and 3 in the 80-column video mode. These calls will work only when your video is set up for an 80-column mode. For your own upgrade you might want to have it work in the 40-column mode. The monochrome adapters have only one page.

Fig. 3-30. The assembly code for VIDINIT.ASM.

```
;*******************
; Source Code Start
;
; File Name:    VIDINIT.ASM
;
; Synopsis:     vidInit()
;
; Description: Calls gtMode to determine the
;               video mode and sets the
;               appropriate global video
;               addresses to there will
;               be a direct video write
;               to display ram.
;
;               MONO SEG 0xb000 OFFSET 0x0000
;               COLR SEG 0xb800 OFFSET 0x0000
;
; Returns:      Nothing
;


;
;
; Enable DOS segment-ordering at link time
;

        DOSSEG


;
; Set the memory model for simplified segmentation
; directives
;

        .MODEL SMALL
```

Fig. 3-30 continued.

```
;
; The structure 'v' must match the
; VIDEO structure declared in TSTRUCT.H
;
;   typedef struct {
;       int mode;                   /* video mode          */
;       int row_width;              /* columns per row      */
;       int page;                   /* video page          */
;       unsigned int far *scrn;     /* pointer to video RAM */
;   } VIDEO;
;


;
; structure declaration
;

        v STRUC
;
; int mode;
;

        mode  DW      0
;
; int row_width;
;

        wid   DW      0


;
; int page
;

        pag   DW      0
;
; unsigned int far * scrn
;

        scrn  DW      0,0


;
; End of structure v
;

      v ENDS
;
; Declare the function as GLOBAL
; so it will be recognized by your
; C functions.  Note the underscore
; preceding the function.  This is
; a standard variable naming convention
; for the MICROSOFT, TURBO and WATCOM compilers
;

        PUBLIC  _SCRNSEG,_crt,_VID_PORT,_SPARKLE_FLAG


;
; Defines the start of the DATA segment
```

Fig. 3-30 continued.
```
;
        .DATA

_SPARKLE_FLAG DW 0              ; No sparkle fix default
_VID_PORT DW    0              ; video controller status port
_SCRNSEG DW     0              ; int holds scrn seg
_crt    DW      0,0           ; pointer to VIDEO struct
vid     v       <>            ; structure declaration


;
; Declare the function as GLOBAL
; so it will be recognized by your
; C functions.  Note the underscore
; preceding the function.  This is
; a standard function naming convention
; for the MICROSOFT and TURBO compilers
;

        PUBLIC  _vidInit

;
; Defines the start of the CODE segment
;

        .CODE


;
; Set the start of the function
;

_vidInit PROC NEAR
;
; Save regs
;

        push    BP
        mov     BP,SP


;
; move offset of pointer to video structure to global
;

        mov     _crt,offset vid ; addr of struct -> _crt


;
; get video mode -> int 10h func 15
;

        xor     CX,CX           ; CX -> 0
        mov     AH,15           ; BIOS get mode
        int     10h             ; BIOS int
        mov     CL,AL           ; mode -> vid.mode
        mov     [vid.mode],CX
        mov     CL,AH           ; row wid -> vid.width
        mov     [vid.wid],CX
        mov     CL,BH           ; page -> vid.pag
```

```
        mov     [vid.pag],CX

;
; prep structure for mono or color
;

        cmp     AL,7            ; is mono?
        je      ismono          ; yes ->jump

;
; video adapter is of color type
;

        mov     _VID_PORT,03dah ; stat color controller port
        mov     _SCRNSEG,0b800h ; color scrn seg
        mov     [vid.scrn],00h  ; far * offset
        mov     [vid.scrn+2],0b800h ; far * seg
        jmp     videxit
;
; adapter is of monochrome type
;

ismono:

        mov     _VID_PORT,03bah ; stat mono controller port
        mov     _SCRNSEG,0b000h ; mono scrn seg
        mov     [vid.scrn],00h  ; far * offset
        mov     [vid.scrn+2],0b000h ; far * seg

;
; exit vidinit routine
;

videxit:

;
; Restore regs
;

        pop     BP

;
; Return to calling function
;

        ret
;
; End of procedure
;

_vidInit ENDP

;
; End of assembly source file
;

        END
;**************************
```

Fig. 3-30 ends.

The **vdChar** function writes a token (character and its attribute) to the screen at location row, column. Before you see the code for VDCHAR.C and VDCHAR.ASM it makes sense to give the code for the MKTOKEN.C and MKTOKEN.ASM. The source code listing to MKTOKEN.C is shown in FIG. 3-31 and MKTOKEN.ASM in FIG. 3-32.

Finally, look at the source code for VDCHAR.C, the function that writes the token (character and its attribute) to the screen at location defined by row and column. The source code listing to VDCHAR.C is shown in FIG. 3-33 and VDCHAR.ASM in FIG. 3-34.

Fig. 3-31. The source code for MKTOKEN.C.

```
/*******************
 * Source Code Start
 *
 * File Name:     MKTOKEN.C
 *
 * Synopsis:      token = mkToken(ch,attr)
 *
 * int  ch        character to be printed on the
 *                screen
 *
 * int attr       attribute created using mkAttr
 *
 * int token      LSB holds character to be printed
 *                and the MSB holds the character's
 *                attribute.
 *
 * Description: Received the character to be
 *              printed and its intended
 *              attribute and returns the
 *              token.
 *
 * Returns:       token
 */

/*
 * Include Files
 */

#include <tproto.h>

int
mkToken(ch, attr)
{
int token;
token = attr << 8;
token |= ch;
return(token);
}

/*
 * End of Source
 ***************/
```

Fig. 3-32. The source code for MKTOKEN.ASM.

```
;*******************
; Source Code Start
;
; File Name:     MKTOKEN.ASM
;
; Synopsis:      token = mkToken(ch,attr)
;
; int  ch        character to be printed on the
;                screen
;
; int attr       attribute created using mkAttr
;
; int token      LSB holds character to be printed
;                and the MSB holds the character's
;                attribute.
;
; Description: Received the character to be
;                printed and its intended
;                attribute and returns the
;                token.
;
; Returns:       token
;
;
;
; Small model -> off = 4
; Medium model -> off = 6
; Large model -> off = 6
;

off        equ     4

;
; Define parameters which the C calling
;   function passes
;

chr        equ     BYTE PTR [BP+off]
attr       equ     BYTE PTR [BP+off+2]

;
; Enable DOS segment-ordering at link time
;

        DOSSEG

;
; Set the memory model for simplified segmentation
; directives
;

        .MODEL SMALL

;
; Make function visible to linker
;
```

```
        PUBLIC _mkToken

;
; Defines the start of the code segment
;

        .CODE

;
; Set the start of the function
;

_mkToken PROC NEAR
;
; Save regs

        push    BP
        mov     BP,SP

;
; AX (AL) LSB is the character
; AX (AH) MSB is the attribute
;

        mov     AL,chr
        mov     AH,attr
;
; Restore regs
;

        pop     BP

;
; Return to calling function
;

        ret              ; all done

;
; End of function (ENDP)
;
; and end of assembly source (END)
;

_mkToken ENDP
        END


;*
;* End of Source
;***************
```

Fig. 3-32 ends.

Fig. 3-33. The source code for VDCHAR.C.

```
/********************
 * Source Code Start
 *
 * File Name:    VDCHAR.C
 *
 * Synopsis:     vdChar(row,column,token)
 *
 * int row       row where token will be placed
 *
 * int column    column where the token will be placed
 *
 * int token     LSB holds character to be printed
 *               and the MSB holds the character's
 *               attribute.
 *
 * Description: Sends the token directly
 *              to display RAM at row and
 *              column.  Note that this call
 *              will work only after vidInit()
 *              has been called.  If you
 *              neglect to call vidInit() before
 *              this call is made then unspeakable
 *              and unnatural things will happen
 *              to your computer!
 *
 * Returns:     Nothing
 */

/*
 * Include Files
 */

#include <stdio.h>
#include <tproto.h>

/*
 * External structure declared in
 * VIDINIT.C
 */

extern VIDEO *crt;

/*
 * vdChar function
 */

void
vdChar(row,col,token)
int row,col,token;
{
unsigned int far *scrn;
long offset;

/* set the pointer to the screen address  */
/* - the upper left corner 0,0 -          */
scrn = (unsigned int far *)crt->scrn;
```

```
/* int offset from upper left of screen   */
/* Remember that the screenn is 80 tokens */
/*   accross and twenty five rows high     */
offset = (long)(row*80)+col;

/* now that segment and offset of screen  */
/* address are set we can move the token  */
*(scrn+offset) = token;
}

/*
 * End of Source
 ***************/
```

Fig. 3-33 ends.

Fig. 3-34. The source code for VDCHAR.ASM.

```
;*******************
; Source Code Start
;
; File Name:    VDCHAR.ASM
;
; Synopsis:     vdChar(row,column,token)
;
; int row       row where token will be placed
;
; int column    column where the token will be placed
;
; int token     LSB holds character to be printed
;               and the MSB holds the character's
;               attribute.
;
; Description: Sends the token directly
;              to display RAM at row and
;              column.  Not that this call
;              will work only after vidInit()
;              has been called.  If you
;              neglect to call vidInit() before
;              this call is made then unspeakable
;              and unnatural things will happen
;              to your computer!
;
; Returns:      Nothing
;

;
; Small model -> off = 4
; Medium model -> off = 6
; Large model -> off = 6
;

off     equ     4 ; small model

;
; Define parameters which the C calling
;    function passes
;
```

73

Fig. 3-34 continued.

```
prow     equ     byte ptr [BP+off+0]
pcol     equ     byte ptr [BP+off+2]
ptoken   equ     word ptr [BP+off+4]


;
; Enable DOS segment-ordering at link time
;

        DOSSEG


;
; Set the memory model for simplified segmentation
; directives
;

        .MODEL SMALL


;
; EXTRN in assembly serves the same function as
;  extern in C.  Note that the EXTRN variables'
;  names are followed by a : with their memory
;  size.
;
; WORD is a 'C' INT
; BYTE is a 'C' CHAR
; NEAR is a small memory model function
; FAR  is a medium or large memory
;  model function
;

        EXTRN    _SCRNSEG:WORD


;
; Make function visible to linker
;

        PUBLIC  _vdChar


;
; Defines the start of the code segment
;

        .CODE


;
; Set the start of the function
;

_vdChar PROC NEAR
;
; Save Regs
;

        push    BP
        mov     BP,SP
        push    DI
        push    SI
```

Fig. 3-34 continued.

```
        push    ES

;
; Move screen Segment (gotten during the
;  vidInit() call) to ES
;

        mov     CX,_SCRNSEG
        mov     ES,CX           ; reset extra seg

;
; Save ES on stack
;

        push    ES

;
; Calculate token offset from
;  screen segment
;

        xor     AX,AX           ; 0 -> AX
        mov     AL,prow         ; row -> AL
        mov     BL,160          ; 80 chars wide * 2
        mul     BL              ; row * scrn width  -> AX
        mov     CL,pcol         ; column to CL
        XOR     CH,CH           ; 0 -> CH
        shl     CX,1            ; col * 2
        add     AX,CX           ; column + (row * scrn width)
        mov     DI,AX           ; point DI to scrn

;
; Restore ES from stack
;

        pop     ES

;
; Get token from stack to AX
;

        mov     AX,ptoken

;
; Relocate AX to ES:DI which
;  is screen segment + offset
;

        stosw

;
; Restore registers
;

        pop     ES
        pop     SI
        pop     DI
```

```
        pop     BP

;
; Return to calling function
;
        ret

;
; End of function (ENDP)
;
; and end of assembly source (END)
;

_vdChar ENDP
        END



;*
;* End of Source
;***************
```

Fig. 3-34 ends.

Now that you've got all the ingredients to remake the TESTCUR.EXE program, let's test these direct video functions with a new program called TESTCHAR.C. The source code listing to TESTCHAR.C is shown in FIG. 3-35.

Fig. 3-35. The source code for TESTCHAR.C.

```
/*******************
 * Source Code Start
 *
 * File Name:   TESTCHAR.C
 *
 * Description: Demonstration program for
 *              vdChar, vidInit, mkToken, mkAttr
 */

/*
 * Include files
 */

#include <stdio.h>
#include <tproto.h>

/*
 * global buffer
 */

char test[] = { "TEST VDCHAR MKATTR MKTOKEN" };

void main(void);
```

```
void
main()
{
int attr, token;
int ch, count;
int row, column, len, col;

vidInit();

len = strlen(test);

attr = mkAttr(WHITE,BLACK,OFF_INTENSITY,OFF_BLINK);

for(row=0,column=0; row<22; row++,column++)
        {
        for(col=0; col<len; col++)
                {
                ch = (int)test[col];
                token = mkToken(ch,attr);
                vdChar(row,column+col,token);
                }
        }
}

/*
 * End of source listing
 **********************/
```

Fig. 3-35 ends.

TESRCHAR.C functions in the same fashion as TESTCUR. There are differences, though. By substituting vdChar(...) for printf you can now print characters in all available colors with blink and intensity alterations. Let's look at the size of the TESTCHAR.EXE, the executable file shown in FIG. 3-36.

Fig. 3-36. File comparison.

TESTCUR.EXE	C mvCur	6848	bytes
TESTCUR.EXE	ASM mvCur	6608	bytes
TESRCHAR.EXE	C vdChar	3326	bytes

Without pulling out the calculator, it's clear that our code size has now dropped even further. The test program started a 6848 bytes for the executable file, and now has dropped to 3326 bytes, a whopping 50 percent reduction in code size. However, writing to the screen character by character is not the best we can do. What proves a more efficient method is to devise a function that can write a string to the screen. Such a function is shown in FIG. 3-37. The assembly listing is shown in FIG. 3-38.

Fig. 3-37. The source code for VDWRITE.C.

___

```
/********************
 * Source Code Start
 *
 * File Name:    VDWRITE.C
 *
 * Synopsis:     vdWrite(row,column,length,string,attr)
 *
 * int row       row where string write will start
 *
 * int column    column where string write will start
 *
 * int length    length of the string
 *
 * char *string  pointer to string to be written to
 *               the screen
 *
 * int attr      attribute for characters of string
 *               written to the screen
 *
 * Description:  Sends the string of length
 *               bytes to the screen at
 *               display RAM at row and
 *               column with attr. Note that this call
 *               will work only after vidInit()
 *               has been called.  If you
 *               neglect to call vidInit() before
 *               this call is made then unspeakable
 *               and unnatural things will happen
 *               to your computer!
 *
 * Returns:      Nothing
 */

/*
 * Include files
 */


#include <stdio.h>
#include <tproto.h>

/*
 * External structure declared in
 * VIDINIT.C
 */

extern VIDEO *crt;

/*
 * vdWrite function
 */

void
vdWrite(row,col,length,str,attr)
int row,col,length;
char *str;
```

```
char attr;
{
unsigned char far *scrn;
register        int count;
long offset;

/* Get screen start addr from VIDEO structure */
/* This value was set in vidInit()           */
scrn = (unsigned char far *)crt->scrn;

/* calculate offset from screen start */
offset = (long)(row*160)+(col*2);

/* adjust pointer to screen to proper spot */
scrn = scrn + offset;

/* loop to write string of length bytes */
for(count=0; count<length; count++)
        {
        /* move character byte to display RAM */
        *scrn++ = *str++;

        /* move attr to contiguous attribute byte */
        *scrn++ = (unsigned)attr;
        /* loop until length bytes written */
        }
}

/*
 * End of Source
 ***************/
```

Fig. 3-37 ends.

Fig. 3-38. The source code for VDWRITE.ASM.

```
;******************
; Source Code Start
;
; File Name:    VDWRITE.C
;
; Synopsis:     vdWrite(row,column,length,string,attr)
;
; int row       row where string write will start
;
; int column    column where string write will start
;
; int length    length of the string
;
; char *string  pointer to string to be written to
;               the screen
;
; int attr      attribute for characters of string
;               written to the screen
;
; Description:  Sends the string of length
;               bytes to the screen at
;               display RAM at row and
```

Fig. 3-38 continued.

```
;               column with attr. Note that this call
;               will work only after vidInit()
;               has been called.  If you
;               neglect to call vidInit() before
;               this call is made then unspeakable
;               and unnatural things will happen
;               to your computer!
;
; Returns:      Nothing
;


;
; Small model -> off = 4
; Medium model -> off = 6
; Large model -> off = 6
;

off     equ     4 ; small model


;
; Define parameters which the C calling
;    function passes
;

prow    equ       byte ptr [BP+off+0]
pcol    equ       byte ptr [BP+off+2]
plen    equ       word ptr [BP+off+4]
pptr    equ       word ptr [BP+off+6]
pattr   equ       byte ptr [BP+off+8]


;
; Enable DOS segment-ordering at link time
;

        DOSSEG


;
; Set the memory model for simplified segmentation
; directives
;

        .MODEL SMALL


;
; EXTRN in assembly serves the same function as
;  extern in C.  Note that the EXTRN variables'
;  names are followed by a : with their memory
;  size.
;
; WORD is a 'C' INT
; BYTE is a 'C' CHAR
; NEAR is a small memory model function
; FAR  is a medium or large memory
;  model function
;

        EXTRN    _SCRNSEG:WORD
        EXTRN    _vbwait:NEAR
```

Fig. 3-38 continued.

```
;
; Make function visible to linker
;

        PUBLIC  _vdWrite

;
; Defines the start of the code segment
;

        .CODE

;
; Set the start of the function
;

_vdWrite PROC NEAR
;
; Save Regs
;

        push    BP
        mov     BP,SP
        push    DI
        push    SI
        push    ES


;
; Move screen Segment (gotten during the
;  vidInit() call) to ES
;

        mov     CX,_SCRNSEG
        mov     ES,CX           ; reset extra seg
        mov     SI,pptr         ; pointer to string


;
; Save ES on stack
;

        push    ES              ; save EX


;
; Calculate token offset from
;  screen segment
;

        xor     AX,AX           ; 0 -> AX
        mov     AL,prow         ; row -> AL
        mov     BL,160          ; 160 = (80 chars wide * 2)
        mul     BL              ; row * scrn width  -> AX
        mov     CL,pcol         ; column to CL
        xor     CH,CH           ; 0 -> CH
        shl     CX,1            ; col * 2
        add     AX,CX           ; column + (row * scrn width)
        mov     DI,AX           ; point DI to scrn
```

Fig. 3-38 continued.

```
; Restore ES from stack
;

        pop   ES            ; restore ES


;
; Enable increment using direction flag
; for lodsb and stosw
;

        cld


;
; set loop counter to string length
;

        mov   CX,plen       ; string length -> CX
vdr1:

;
; lodsb  DS:SI -> AL  - string to AL
;

        lodsb               ; get byte from string


;
; attribute to AH
;

        mov   AH,pattr      ; make word token


;
; stosw  AX -> ES:DI  - AX to screen
;

        stosw


;
; loop until CX counts to 0
;

        loop  vdr1


;
; Restore registers
;

        pop   ES
        pop   SI
        pop   DI
        pop   BP


;
; Return to calling function
;

        ret
```

```
;
; End of function (ENDP)
;
; and end of assembly source (END)
;

_vdWrite        ENDP
        END



;*
;* End of Source
;***************
```

Fig. 3-38 ends.

Now we need to test VDWRITE so TARCHAR.C has been updated to TEST-STR.C. The source code listing for TESTSTR.C is presented in FIG. 3-39. Once again, let's check the .EXE files to see what's happening. FIGURE 3-40 compares TESTCHAR.EXE with TESTSTR.EXE. FIGURE 4-40 shows that there is only a 16-byte savings in the executable code. Not impressive.

Fig. 3-39. The source code to TESTSTR.C.

```
/*****************
 * Source Code Start
 *
 * File Name:    TESTSTR.C
 *
 * Description: Demonstration program for
 *              vdWrite, vidInit, mkToken, mkAttr
 */

/*
 * Include files
 */

#include <stdio.h>
#include <tproto.h>

/*
 * global buffer
 */

char test[] = { "TEST VDCHAR MKATTR MKTOKEN" };

void main(void);


void
main()
{
int attr, token;
int ch, count;
int row, column, len, col;
```

```
    vidInit();

    len = strlen(test);

    attr = mkAttr(WHITE,BLACK,OFF_INTENSITY,OFF_BLINK);

    for(row=0,column=0; row<22; row++,column++)
            vdWrite(row,column,len,test,attr);

    }
    /*
     * End of Source
     ***************/
```

Fig. 3-39 ends.

Fig. 3-40. Code size comparison.

TESRCHAR.EXE	C vdChar	3326	bytes
TESTSTR.EXE	C vdWrite	3310	bytes

Now, let's assemble VDWRITE.ASM, VIDINIT.ASM, MKATTR.ASM and exchange the C generated object modules in TAB_T2S.LIB with the assembly generated object modules.

You know how to do this. If you don't remember how to exchange modules then go to the section where MVCUR is discussed. The proper procedure for assembling object modules and replacing old object modules with new ones is explained. Now, recompile and link TESTSTR.C and let's examine the resulting sizes, shown in FIG. 3-41.

Fig. 3-41. The sizes of the files.

TESTCUR.EXE	C mvCur	6848	bytes
TESTCUR.EXE	ASM mvCur	6608	bytes
TESRCHAR.EXE	C vdChar	3326	bytes
TESTSTR.EXE	C vdWrite	3310	bytes
TESTSTR.EXE	All ASM	2678	bytes

We started out with a simple demonstration program showing how to move the cursor in C and assembly. We used a standard C library PRINTF function to display the text. The executable file was 6848 bytes. After a series of program modifications, finally resorting to our small assembly bindings, the executable program size of an equivalent program weighed in at 2678 bytes.

Here we'll get the calculator: a whopping savings of 4170 bytes or a 61 percent savings in code size, with an improvement in program performance. That's one reason why you'll find the TAB library useful in developing top quality programs.

SUMMARY

In this chapter many screen handling functions were added to the TAB library. Each routine was coded in C and in assembly. Our C compiled object modules were installed in TAB_T2S.LIB and our functions tested. Then new object modules were assembled for the new routines and the old C object modules were replaced with the new assembly object modules. The difference in executable code size was rather dramatic: 4170 bytes or 61 percent smaller. That's why it sometimes pays to code in assembly.

4

Keyboard Handling Routines

The BIOS has many useful functions which allow the programmer to read the keyboard. Unfortunately, these functions revolve around reading a keystroke. In real world applications, though, the programmer often needs to read a string of characters into a buffer, or read an integer number, or a decimal number. There are times when the programmer will need to have the program wait for a keypress and other times when the program should not wait for a keypress. When you don't want the program to wait for a keypress, you will need to note when a key has been pressed, evaluate the value of the keypress, and take appropriate action. There are also times when the programmer needs to know if the Shift key, Alt key, Control key, Num lock, or Scroll lock key is pressed; Insert toggled; or any combination of these keys.

In this chapter you are shown three keyboard read routines and how to build three keyboard handlers. The first keyboard handler routine allows you to get a string of predetermined length from the keyboard and return a TRUE when an Enter key or a NUL when an Esc keypress has terminated the handler. The second keyboard handler routine allows you to get a long value of predetermined length from the keyboard and return a TRUE when an Enter key or a NUL when an Esc keypress has terminated the handler. The third keyboard handler routine allows you to get a floating point value of predetermined length from the keyboard and return a TRUE when an Enter key or a NUL when an Esc keypress has terminated the handler. Based on the three keyboard handlers that are presented it is anticipated that you will be armed with enough information to write your own customized keyboard handlers for almost all of your programming applications.

The BIOS keyboard interrupt used as the foundation for the TAB keyboard handlers is Function 0 of Interrupt 0x16. The TAB library function name is **gtKey( )** and the source code for GTKEY.C is presented in FIG. 4-1. FIGURE 4-2 presents the source code listing for GTKEY.ASM.

Fig. 4-1. The source code for GTKEY.C.

```
/********************
 * Source Code Start
 *
 * File Name:  GTKEY.C
 *
 * Synopsis:   key = gtKey()
 *
 * int key      holds scan code in MSB and
 *              char code in LSB
 *
 * Returns:    Value of key press
 */
#include <dos.h>
#include <tproto.h>

/*
 * gtkey function
 */

int
gtKey()
{
union REGS ir, or;

/* AH register gets function 0 */
ir.h.ah = 0;

/* invoke interrupt 0x16 */
int86( 0x16, &ir, &or );

/* char code in AL and scan code in AH */
return( or.x.ax );
}

/*
 * End of Source
 ***************/
```

Fig. 4-2. The assembly source code for GTKEY.ASM.

```
;*******************
; Source Code Start
;
; File Name:   GTKEY.ASM
;
; Synopsis:    key = gtKey()
;
; int key      holds scan code in MSB and
;              char code in LSB
;
; Returns:     Value of key press
;


;
; Enable DOS segment-ordering at link time
;

        DOSSEG


;
; Set the memory model for simplified segmentation
; directives
;

        .MODEL SMALL


;
; Make function visible to linker
;

        PUBLIC  _gtKey


;
; Defines the start of the code segment
;

        .CODE


;
; Set the start of the function
;

_gtKey PROC NEAR
;
; Save Regs
;
        push    BP
        mov     BP,SP


;
; Read Keyboard Function 0
; Interrupt 16h
;

        xor     AX,AX   ; mov AX,0

;
```

```
; Invoke Interrupt 16h
;

        int     16h

;
; AH = Keyboard Scan code
; AL = ASCII character code
;


;
; Restore regs and return to
;  caller

        pop     BP
        ret


;
; End of function (ENDP)
;
; and end of assembly source (END)
;

_gtKey  ENDP
        END


;
; End of Assembly Source
;
; ********************
```

Fig. 4-2 ends.

Now that the code to our basic keyboard read function has been presented, of course, we need to check and see that it works. The program TESTKEY.C, shown in FIG. 4-3, introduces one way to filter keystrokes.

Fig. 4-3. The source code for TESTKEY.C.

```
/*****************
 * Source Code Start
 *
 * File Name:   TESTKEY.C
 *
 * Description: Demonstration program for
 *              gtKey
 */

/*
 * Include files
 */

#include <stdio.h>
#include <tproto.h>
```

```
void main(void);


void
main()
{
int key, exit;

exit = aFALSE;

printf("\nTest of gtKey function\n");
printf("Press F1 to exit program\n");

do
        {
        key = gtKey();
        if(key != F1)
                {
                key &= 0x00ff;
                printf("%c\n",(char)key);
                }
        else
                exit = aTRUE;
        } while(!exit);
}


/*
 * End of Source
 ***************/
```

Fig. 4-3 ends.

There are two simple ways to filter keystrokes using gtKey( ). The first way is described in FIG. 4-4.

The second way is shown in FIG. 4-5, which redoes the if and else code using switch and case.

Using the switch and case method demonstrates that it would be very easy to CASE any keys you wish and print the alphanumeric characters. It is this method that the TAB keyboard handling routines use.

Fig. 4-4. Key value filter using if/else control.

```
if(key != F1)
   {
   key &= 0x00ff;
   printf("%c\n",(char)key);
   }
else
   exit = aTRUE;
```

Fig. 4-5. SWITCH/CASE demonstration.

```
switch(key)
    {
    case F1:
        exit = aTRUE;
        break;
    default:
        key &= 0x00ff;
        printf("%c\n",(char)key);
        break;
    }
```

The first keyboard handling routine, prompt(...), reads a string of keys from the keyboard and returns the string to a buffer whose address has been passed as a prompt(...) parameter. Enter is pressed, prompt(...) returns a TRUE and if Esc is pressed, prompt(...) returns a FALSE. That way the programmer will know what action to take on exit from the prompt(...).

One of the parameters passed also limits the number of character entries that can be made. This is useful if there is a field limit to character entry. Before the source to PROMPT.C is given you need to add three routines to TAB_T2S.LIB. They are needed in order for PROMPT.C to work properly.

The first routine is GTCUR.C and the source code listing is presented in FIG. 4-6. This routine returns the current cursor location.

Fig. 4-6. The source code to GTCUR.C.

```
/******************
 * Start Source File
 *
 * File Name:   GTCUR.C
 *
 * Synopsis:    gtCur(row,column)
 *
 * int *row     put current cursor row
 *              into integer where row
 *              points to
 *
 * int *column  put current cursor column
 *              into integer where column
 *              points to
 *
 * Description: gtCur uses BIOS int 10h,
 *              function 3, to get the
 *              current location of the
 *              cursor
 *
 * Returns:     Nothing
 */

/*
 * get the cursor location
```

```
 */

#include <dos.h>


void
gtCur(row,column)
int *row;
int *column;
{
union REGS ir,or;
ir.h.bh = 0;
ir.h.ah = 3;
int86(0x10,&ir,&or);
*row = or.h.dh;
*column = or.h.dl;
}

/*
 * End of source
 **************/
```

Fig. 4-6 ends.

The next routine needed to complete PROMPT.C is BEEP.C. The **beep( )** function uses the BIOS to beep the console speaker. The source code listing for BEEP.C is presented in FIG. 4-7.

Fig. 4-7. The source code to BEEP.C.

```
/*******************
 * Start Source file
 *
 * File Name:   BEEP.C
 *
 * Synopsis:    beep()
 *
 * Description: beeps the console speaker
 *
 * Returns:     Nothing
 */

/*
 * beep.c
 *
 * console beep
 */

#include <stdio.h>
```

```
#include <ascii.h>

void
beep()
{
putchar(aBEL);
}

/*
 *End of source
 **************/
```

Fig. 4-7 ends.

Finally, the last routine needed to complete PROMPT.C is PUTCHR.C. This routine uses the BIOS to put one character to the screen without moving the cursor's location. The source code for PUTCHR.C is presented in FIG. 4-8 and the source code listing for PUTCHR.ASM is presented in FIG. 4-9.

Fig. 4-8. The source code to PUTCHR.C.

```
/********************
 * Source Code Start
 *
 * File Name:   PUTCHR.C
 *
 * Synopsis:    putChr(ch)
 *
 * char ch      char to be put to screen
 *
 * Description: puts a character to the
 *              screen at the current
 *              cursor location via the
 *              BIOS interrupt 0x10 function
 *              0x0a - the cursor location
 *              is not changed
 *
 * Returns:     Nothing
 */

#include <dos.h>
#include <tproto.h>

void
```

```
putChr(CH)
char ch;
{
union REGS ir,or;
/* AH register gets function 0x0a */
ir.h.ah = 0x0a;

/* BX holds page 0 */
ir.h.bh = 0;

/* CX writes 1 character */
ir.x.cx = 1;

/* AL holds the character */
ir.h.al = ch;

/* invoke interrupt 0x10 */
int86(0x10,&ir,&or);
}

/*
 * End of source
 **************/
```

Fig. 4-8 ends.

Fig. 4-9. The source code for PUTCHR.ASM.

```
;******************
; Source Code Start
;
; File Name:   PUTCHR.ASM
;
; Synopsis:   putChr(chr)
;
; char chr      char to be put to screen
;
; Description: puts a character to the
;               screen at the current
;               cursor locaation via the
;               BIOS interrupt 0x10 funtion
;               0x0a - the cursor location
;               is not changed
;
; Returns:    Nothing
;
;
; Small model off equ 4
;

off      equ     4
```

Fig. 4-9 continued.

```
;
; pointer to passed character
;

chr      equ      BYTE PTR [BP+off]


;
; Enable DOS segment-ordering at link time
;

        DOSSEG


;
; Set the memory model for simplified segmentation
; directives
;

        .MODEL SMALL


;
; Make function visible to linker
;

        PUBLIC  _putChr


;
; Defines the start of the code segment
;

        .CODE


;
; Set the start of the function
;

_putChr PROC NEAR
;
; Save Regs
;
        push    BP
        mov     BP,SP


;
; Put Character function 0ah
; Interrupt 10h
;

        mov     AH,0ah


;
; Character to page 0
;

        mov     BH,0
;
; Put 1 character
;
```

```
        mov     CX,1
;
; Character to print to AL
;

        mov     AL,chr

;
; Invoke Interrupt 10h
;

        int     10h

;
; Restore regs and return to
;  caller

        pop     BP
        ret

;
; End of function (ENDP)
;
; and end of assembly source (END)
;

_putChr ENDP
        END

;
; End of Assembly Source
;************************
```

Fig. 4-9 ends.

Finally, now that the preparatory routines for PROMPT.C are complete, the time is at hand for presenting the source code, shown in FIG. 4-10.

Following the established pattern for library development suggested in the text, a demonstration program for prompt(...) is presented in FIG. 4-11.

There are times when your application will require that the user enter a floating point number. A *floating point number* is a decimal number (ex. 43.12). The **inpflt(...)** function shown in FIG. 4-12, takes care of floating point numbers.

Following our standard procedure, we've written a demonstration program for inpflt(...). Look to FIG. 4-13 for the source.

There are times when your application will require that the user enter a long number. A long number is an integer number (ex. 45005). The function inpnum(...) takes care of that need. The source code listing for INPNUM.C is shown in FIG. 4-14.

Following our standard procedure, we've written a demonstration program for inpnum(...). The source code listing for DONUM.C is presented in FIG. 4-15.

Fig. 4-10. The source code for PROMPT.C.

```
/********************
 * Source Code Start
 *
 * File Name:        PROMPT.C
 *
 * Synopsis:         action = prompt(*response,number)
 *
 * char *response    buffer in which to place the
 *                   character string obtained
 *                   from prompt(...)
 *
 * int number        character entry limit
 *
 * int action        indicates function
 *                   terminating keystroke
 *
 * Description:      Places an ASCII string into the
 *                   buffer which response points to
 *                   and returns indicating the function
 *                   terminating key stroke
 *
 * Returns:          aFALSE on ESCAPE keypress
 *                   aTRUE  on ENTER keypress
 */

/*
 * Include files
 */

#include <string.h>
#include <tproto.h>

/*
 * prompt function
 */

int
prompt(response,length)
char *response;
int length;
{
int key,exit;
int row,column;
int start,stop;
int ret_val;

/* start cur location */
gtCur(&row,&column);

/* set column start and stop and index to response[] */
start = column;

/* set stopper for keyboard entry */
stop = start + length;

/* looping condition */
exit=aFALSE;
```

Fig. 4-10 continued.

```c
do
    {
    /* place cursor at proper location */
    mvCur(row,column);

    /* get scan and char keystroke */
    key = gtKey();

    /* begin key filter */
    switch(key)
        {
        /* ENTER key press -> take action */
        case ENTER:
            ret_val = aTRUE;
            exit = aTRUE;
            break;

        /* ESC press -> abort - no action */
        case ESCAPE:
            ret_val = aFALSE;
            exit = aTRUE;
            break;
        /* print character to screen */
        default:
            /* 0 -> key MSB (scan code) */
            key &=0x00ff;

            /* key is ASCII! */
            if( (key>=0x20)&&(key<=0x7d) )
                {
                /* not time to stop */
                if(column<stop)
                    {
                    /* move cursor */
                    mvCur(row,column);

                    /* print key to screen */
                    putChr(key);

                    /* place key in buffer */
                    *response++ = (char)key;

                    /* increase column counter */
                    column++;
                    }
                else
                    /* stopper reached so beep */
                    beep();
                }
            /* if the key is a backspace */
            if(key==aBS)
                {
                /* if your not a field entry point */
                if(column>start)
                    {
                    /* go back one column */
                    column--;
```

```
                    /* back pointer to buffer */
                    response--;

                    /* back up cursor position */
                    mvCur(row,column);

                    /* erase character on screen */
                    putChr(' ');

                    /* put a null into buffer */
                    *response = (char)aNUL;
                    }
                else
                    /* at beginning of field entry so beep */
                    beep();
                }
            break;
            }
    } while(!exit);
return(ret_val);
}

/*
 * End of Source
 ***************/
```

Fig. 4-10 ends.

Fig. 4-11. The source code for DOPROMPT.C.

```
/********************
 * Source Code Start
 *
 * File Name:    DOPROMPT.C
 *
 * Description: Demonstration program for
 *              prompt(...)
 */

/*
 * Include files
 */

#include <stdio.h>
#include <tproto.h>

void main(void);

/*
 * globals
 */

char buffer[80];
IMAGE box1;
extern VIDEO *crt;
```

```
void
main()
{
printf("\nTest of: if(prompt(buffer,25))\n");
if(prompt(buffer,25))
        {
        printf("\nSize of response is %d\n",strlen(buffer));
        printf("Input response is: %s\n",buffer);
        }
else
        {
        printf("\nESCAPE KEY PRESSED - NO ACTION\n");
        }
}


/*
 * End of Source
 ***************/
```

Fig. 4-11 ends.

Fig. 4-12. The source code for INPFLT.C.

```
/********************
 * Source Code Start
 *
 * File Name:        INPFLT.C
 *
 * Synopsis:         action = inpflt(*val,number)
 *
 * char *val         buffer in which to place the
 *                   float obtained from inpflt
 *
 * int number        character entry limit
 *
 * int action        indicates function
 *                   terminating keystroke
 *
 * Description:      Places an ASCII string into the
 *                   buffer which response points to
 *                   and returns indicating the function
 *                   terminating key stroke
 *
 * Returns:          aFALSE on ESCAPE keypress
 *                   aTRUE  on ENTER keypress
 */

/*
 * Include files
 */


#include <string.h>
#include <ctype.h>
#include <stdlib.h>
#include <tproto.h>
```

Fig. 4-12 continued.

```c
/*
 * inpflt function
 */

int
inpflt(val,length)
float *val;
int length;
{
int key,exit;
int row,column;
int start,stop;
int ret_val;
char response[50];
char *cptr;

/* set cptr to buffer response */
/* and set buffer to 0          */
cptr = (char *)response;
memset(cptr,'\0',50);

/* start cur location */
gtCur(&row,&column);

/* set column start and stop and index to response[] */
start = column;
stop = start + length;

/* looping condition */
exit=aFALSE;
do
    {
    /* adjust cursor location */
    mvCur(row,column);

    /* wait for keypress */
    key = gtKey();          .

    /* filter for key */
    switch(key)
        {
        /* ENTER key pressed means process entry */
        case ENTER:
           /* process entry */
           ret_val = aTRUE;
           /* val points to float */
           /* (a)scii (to) (f)loat */
           *val = atof(response);

           /* yes - exit */
           exit = aTRUE;
           break;

        /* ESC means abort function */
        case ESCAPE:
           /* do not process result */
           ret_val = aFALSE;
```

Fig. 4-12 continued.

```
    /* yes - exit */
    exit = aTRUE;
    break;

/* process key stroke */
default:
    /* 0 -> scan */
    key &=0x00ff;
    if( (key>=0x20)&&(key<=0x7d) )
        {
        if(column<stop)
            {
            /* adjust cursor */
            mvCur(row,column);

            /* if key is digit or minus or dot then ...*/
            if( (isdigit(key)) || (key=='-') || (key=='.') )
                {
                /* print key - no cursor move */
                putChr(key);

                /* put key into buffer */
                *cptr++ = (char)key;

                /* adjust column */
                column++;
                }
            /* invalid key */
            else
                beep();
            }
        else
            beep();
        }
    /* key is back space */
    if(key==aBS)
        {
        /* if not at start */
        if(column>start)
            {
            /* adjust column back one */
            column--;

            /* pointer to buffer back one */
            cptr--;

            /* adjust cursor */
            mvCur(row,column);

            /* erase character */
            putChr(' ');

            /* 0 to buffer */
            *response = (char)aNUL;
            }
        /* beep if at field start */
        else
```

```
            beep();
        }
      break;
    }
  } while(!exit);

/* return process status */
return(ret_val);
}

/*
 * End of Source
 **************/
```

Fig. 4-12 ends.

Fig. 4-13. The source code for DOFLOAT.C.

```
/******************
 * Source Code Start
 *
 * File Name:   DOFLOAT.C
 *
 * Description: Demonstration program for
 *              inpflt(...)
 */

/*
 * Include files
 */

#include <stdio.h>
#include <tproto.h>

void main(void);

void
main()
{
float f;
printf("\n");
printf("Enter a FLOATING POINT NUMBER and press ENTER\n");
if(inpflt(&f,10))
        printf("\nThe number is %f\n",f);
else
        printf("\nESCape has been pressed - no action\n");
}


/*
 * End of Source
 **************/
```

Fig. 4-14. The source code listing for INPNUM.C.

```
/********************
 * Source Code Start
 *
 * File Name:       INPNUM.C
 *
 * Synopsis:        action = inpflt(*val,number)
 *
 * char *val        buffer in which to place the
 *                  long obtained from inpflt
 *
 * int number       character entry limit
 *
 * int action       indicates function
 *                  terminating keystroke
 *
 * Description:     Places an ASCII string into the
 *                  buffer which response points to
 *                  and returns indicating the function
 *                  terminating key stroke
 *
 * Returns:         aFALSE on ESCAPE keypress
 *                  aTRUE  on ENTER keypress
 */


/*
 * include files
 */

#include <string.h>
#include <ctype.h>
#include <stdlib.h>

#include <tproto.h>

int
inpnum(val,length)
long *val;
int length;
{
int key,exit;
int row,column;
int start,stop;
int ret_val;
char response[50];
char *cptr;

/* set cptr to buffer response */
/* and set buffer to 0         */
cptr = (char *)response;
memset(response,'\0',50);

/* start cur location */
gtCur(&row,&column);

/* set column start and stop and index to response[] */
start = column;
```

Fig. 4-14 continued.

```
stop = start + length;

/* looping condition */
exit=aFALSE;
do
   {
   /* adjust cursor location */
   mvCur(row,column);

   /* wait for keypress */
   key = gtKey();

   /* filter for key */
   switch(key)
      {
      /* ENTER key pressed means process entry */
      case ENTER:
         ret_val = aTRUE;

         /* val points to long  */
         /* (a)scii (to) (l)ong */
         *val = atol(response);
         /* yes - exit */
         exit = aTRUE;
         break;

      /* ESC means abort function */
      case ESCAPE:
         /* do not process result */
         ret_val = aFALSE;

         /* yes - exit */
         exit = aTRUE;
         break;

      /* process key stroke */
      default:
         /* 0 -> scan */
         key &=0x00ff;
         if( (key>=0x20)&&(key<=0x7d) )
            {
            if(column<stop)
               {
               /* adjust cursor */
               mvCur(row,column);

               /* if key is digit or minus ...*/
               if( isdigit(key) || key=='-' )
                  {
                  /* print key - no cursor move */
                  putChr(key);

                  /* put key into buffer */
                  *cptr++ = (char)key;

                  /* adjust column */
                  column++;
```

```
                            }
                            /* invalid key */
                            else
                                beep();
                            }
                        else
                            beep();
                        }
                /* key is back space */
                if(key==aBS)
                    {
                    /* if not at start */
                    if(column>start)
                        {
                        /* adjust column back one */
                        column--;

                        /* pointer to buffer back one */
                        cptr--;

                        /* adjust cursor */
                        mvCur(row,column);

                        /* erase character */
                        putChr(' ');

                        /* 0 to buffer */
                        *response = (char)aNUL;
                        }
                    /* beep if at field start */
                    else
                        beep();
                    }
                break;
            }
    } while(!exit);

/* return process status */
return(ret_val);
}

/*
 * End of Source
 ***************/
```

Fig. 4-14 ends.

Fig. 4-15. The source code for DONUM.C.

```
/********************
 * Source Code Start
 *
 * File Name:   DONUM.C
 *
 * Description: Demonstration program for
```

```
*                 inpnum(...)
*/

/*
* Include files
*/

#include <stdio.h>
#include <tproto.h>

void main(void) ;

void
main()
{
long 1;
printf("\nEnter a LONG INTEGER and press ENTER\n");
if(inpnum(&1,10))
      printf("\nThe number is %ld\n",1);
else
      printf("\nESCape has been pressed - no action\n")
}

/*
* End of Source
***************/
```

Fig. 4-15 ends.

Sometimes the programmer needs to tell how the keyboard status flags are set. TABLE 4-1 shows the bit pattern of the BIOS keyboard status flags.

Table 4-1. Bit Pattern for the BIOS Keyboard Status Flags.

7	6	5	4	3	2	1	0	Meaning
0	0	0	0	0	0	0	1	Right Shift Key is Depressed
0	0	0	0	0	0	1	0	Left Shift Key is Depressed
0	0	0	0	0	1	0	0	Ctrl Key is Depressed
0	0	0	0	1	0	0	0	ALT Key is Depressed
0	0	0	1	0	0	0	0	Scroll Lock is Enabled
0	0	1	0	0	0	0	0	Num Lock is Enabled
0	1	0	0	0	0	0	0	Caps Lock is Enabled
1	0	0	0	0	0	0	0	Insert Key has been Toggled

GTBKFLAG.C is the source code that uses BIOS Int 0x16 Function 2 to read the BIOS Keyboard Status Flags. FIGURE 4-16 lists the source code for GTKBFLAG.C and FIG. 4-17 lists the source code for GTKBFLAG.ASM.

FIGURE 4-18 shows the program listing for the gtKBflag( ) demonstration program, DOFLAG.C.

The last keyboard function in this chapter combines the operations of two BIOS functions. The function **gtKBstat( )** returns an INT containing the SCAN and ASCII code on keypress and a 0 on no keypress waiting. The difference between gtKBstat( ) and gtKey is that gtKey *waits* for the keypress and gtKBstat doesn't.

Fig. 4-16. The source code to GTKBFLAG.C.

```
/********************
 * Source Code Start
 *
 * File Name:      GTKBFLAG.C
 *
 * Synopsis:       flag = gtKBflag()
 *
 * int flag        holds Keyboard flag status
 *
 * Description     BIT          Meaning
 *                 --------------------
 *                 00000001     Right Shift depressed
 *                 00000010     Left Shift depressed
 *                 00000100     Control Key depressed
 *                 00001000     ALT Key depressed
 *                 00010000     Scroll Lock Enabled
 *                 00100000     Num Lock Enabled
 *                 01000000     Caps Lock Enabled
 *                 10000000     Insert Key Toggled
 *
 *
 *
 * Returns:    Value of Keybord Flags
 */

#include <dos.h>
#include <tproto.h>

/*
 * gtKey function
 */

int
gtKBflag()
{
union REGS ir, or;
int flag;

/* AH register gets function 0 */
ir.h.ah = 2;
```

109

```
/* invoke interrupt 0x16 */
int86( 0x16, &ir, &or );

/* 0 -> MSB */
flag = 0;

/* flags in AL */
flag = or.h.al;

return( flag );
}

/*
 * End of Source
 ***************/
```

Fig. 4-16 ends.

Fig. 4-17. The assembly code for GTKBFLAG.ASM.

```
;******************
; Source Code Start
;
; File Name:       GTKBFLAG.ASM
;
; Synopsis:        flag = gtKBflag()
;
; int flag         holds Keyboard flag status
;
; Description      BIT           Meaning
;                  --------------------
;                  00000001      Right Shift depressed
;                  00000010      Left Shift depressed
;                  00000100      Control Key depressed
;                  00001000      ALT Key depressed
;                  00010000      Scroll Lock Enabled
;                  00100000      Num Lock Enabled
;                  01000000      Caps Lock Enabled
;                  10000000      Insert Key Toggled
;
;
;
; Returns:       Value of Keybord Flags
;
;
;
; Enable DOS segment-ordering at link time
;
        DOSSEG
;
; Set the memory model for simplified segmentation
; directives
;
```

```
        .MODEL SMALL
;
; Make function visible to linker
;

        PUBLIC  _gtKBflag

;
; Defines the start of the code segment
;

        .CODE

;
; Set the start of the function
;

_gtKBflag PROC NEAR
;
; Save Regs
;
        push    BP
        mov     BP,SP

;
; Read Keyboard Function 0
; Interrupt 16h
;

        mov     AH,02h

;
; Invoke Interrupt 16h
;

        int     16h

;
; AL holds flags
;

;
; End of function (ENDP)
;
; and end of assembly source (END)
;

        pop     BP
        ret
_gtKBflag ENDP
        END

;
; End of Assembly Source
;
;******************
```

Fig. 4-17 ends.

Fig. 4-18. Source code go DOFLAG.C.

```
/*******************
 * Source Code Start
 *
 * File Name:   DOFLAG.C
 *
 * Description: Demonstration program for
 *              gtKBflag(...)
 */

/*
 * Include files
 */

#include <stdio.h>
#include <tproto.h>

void main(void);

/*
 * keyboard messages
 */

char rs[] = "Right Shift";
char ls[] = "Left  Shift";
char ck[] = "Control Key";
char ak[] = "ALT Key";
char sl[] = "Scroll Lock ";
char nl[] = "Num Lock";
char cl[] = "Caps Lock";
char ik[] = "Insert Key";

void
main()
{
int exit,flag,val;
exit=0;

/*
 * Program information
 */

printf("This program prints the BIOS Keyboard Status FLAG Value.\n");
printf("Pressing Shift Keys, Ctrl Key, ALT Key, Num Lock, Scroll Lock\n");
printf("keys put a message on the screen\n\n");
printf("Press RIGHT SHIFT to exit program\n");
printf("Press ANY KEY to start program\n");

/* wait for key press */
gtKey();

do
        {
        /* get keyboard status flags */
        flag = gtKBflag();

        /* bit 0 set (right shift) */
```

Fig. 4-18 continued.

```
val = flag % 2;
if(val)
        /* terminate program looping and return to DOS */
        exit=1;
else
        {
        /* Right shift pressed? */
        val = flag & 1;
        if(val==1)
                /* YES -> print message to screen */
                printf("%s-",rs);

        /* Left shift pressed? */
        val = flag & 2;
        if(val==2)
                /* YES -> print message to screen */
                printf("%s-",ls);

        /* Control key pressed? */
        val = flag & 4;
        if(val==4)
                /* YES -> print message to screen */
                printf("%s-",ck);

        /* ALT key pressed? */
        val = flag & 8;
        if(val==8)
                /* YES -> print message to screen */
                printf("%s-",ak);

        /* Scroll lock pressed? */
        val = flag & 16;
        if(val==16)
                /* YES -> print message to screen */
                printf("%s-",sl);

        /* Num lock pressed? */
        val = flag & 32;
        if(val==32)
                /* YES -> print message to screen */
                printf("%s-",nl);

        /* Caps lock pressed? */
        val = flag & 64;
        if(val==64)
                /* YES -> print message to screen */
                printf("%s-",cl);

        /* Insert key pressed? */
        val = flag & 128;
        if(val==128)
                /* YES -> print message to screen */
                printf("%s-",ik);

        /* print new line */
        printf("\n");
        }
} while(!exit);
```

113

```
/* print message and return to DOS */
printf("Right Shift Key pressed - Program terminated");
}

/*
 * End of Source
 ***************/
```

Fig. 4-18 ends.

Because the Read Keyboard Status function (INT 0x16 Func. 01h) clears the Zero flag on key waiting and sets the Zero flag on no key waiting, I've presented an assembly code version of gtKBstat( ) in FIG. 4-19. FIGURE 4-20 contains the source code for the gtKBstat test and demonstration program.

Fig. 4-19. The assembly source code to GTKBSTAT.ASM.

```
;********************
; Source Code Start
;
; File Name:     GTKBSTAT.ASM
;
; Synopsis:      key = gtKBstat()
;
; int key        On char waiting: holds scan code
;                in MSB and char code in LSB
;
;                On no char: holds 0
;
;
; Returns:       Value of key press on key waiting
;                and 0 on no key waiting
;
;
;
; Enable DOS segment-ordering at link time
;
        DOSSEG

;
; Set the memory model for simplified segmentation
; directives
;
        .MODEL SMALL

;
; Make function visible to linker
;
        PUBLIC  _gtKBstat

;
; Defines the start of the code segment
;
```

Fig. 4-19 continued.

```
        .CODE

;
; Set the start of the function
;

_gtKBstat PROC NEAR
;
; Save Regs
;
        push    BP
        mov     BP,SP


;
; Read Keyboard Status BIOS function
; Return Regs: Zero flag set on NO Key Waiting
;              Zero flag clear on Key Waiting
;

        mov     AH,1    ; kb stat function
        int     16H     ; keybd int


;
; Jump on Zero flag clear - Key Waiting
;

        jnz     yeskey  ; jmp on no key waiting


;
; Key not waiting -> mov AX,0 for return
;

        mov     AX,0
        jmp     keyexit ; exit function

yeskey:


;
; Key Waiting so Read Keyboard Character
;     from the keyboard buffer
;

        mov     AH,0
        int     16H


;
; AH -> Scan Code
; AL -> Character Code
;

keyexit:


;
; Restore regs and return to
;  caller

        pop     BP
```

```
        ret

;
; End of function (ENDP)
;
; and end of assembly source (END)
;

_gtKBstat       ENDP
        END

;
; End of Assembly Source
;
;******************
```

Fig. 4-19 ends.

Fig. 4-20. The source code to TESTSTAT.C.

```
/*******************
 * Source Code Start
 *
 * File Name:   TESTSTAT.C
 *
 * Description: Demonstration program for
 *              gtKBstat
 */

/*
 * Include files
 */

#include <stdio.h>
#include <tproto.h>

void main(void);

void
main()
{
int exit,key;
exit=0;
printf("\nPress F10 to exit\n");
printf("Press ANY other key to get Scan & character code.\n");

do
        {
        key=gtKBstat();
        if(key!=0)
                {
                printf("0x%04X\n",key);
                if(key==F10)
                        exit=1;
                key=0;
                }
        else
```

```
            beep();
    } while(!exit);
}


/*
 * End of Source
 ***************/
```

Fig. 4-20 ends.

SUMMARY

In Chapter 4 you were shown five useful keyboard functions. These functions are summarized here:

Function	Description
gtKey	Wait for keypress returns Scan and ASCII code
gtKBstat	Do not wait for keypress returns 0 – > no keypress returns Scan and ASCII on keypress
gtKBflag	Returns the current status of the keyboard flags
prompt	Allows user to enter string of characters and return that string to a buffer
inpnum	Allows the user to enter a LONG value and returns the value in a long
inpflt	Allows the user to enter a FLOAT value and returns the value in a float

5

More Screen Routines

In this chapter a small demonstration program is developed to show you how to write the currently popular drop down window user interface. There are a variety of approaches that the programmer can use to implement the drop-down window. The method used in this chapter shows how to do so in a simple, but cumbersome fashion. Later in the text the concept of WINDOWS is introduced. Using the WINDOW building routines for each drop-down window, creating a window is simplified dramatically. As all window routines are built using the previously presented screen handling routines along with those routines presented in this chapter, it makes sense to discuss the drop-down windows here. In that way you will be able to see in a 'top down' fashion the logic in building the window routines.

Let's start by adding a few new functions to our TAB library. The first function to be added allows the programmer to easily draw a horizontal line on the screen. The source code for VDHORIZ.C is presented in FIG. 5-1 and the source code listing for VDHORIZ.ASM is presented in FIG. 5-2. Following our standard routine, FIG. 5-3 provides the source code for the program that tests the VDHORIZ function.

Now that the routine to draw a horizontal line has been shown, the companion routine, to draw a vertical line on the screen, is presented in FIG. 5-4 and the source code for VDVERT.ASM is shown in FIG. 5-5. The program to test the VDVERT function is presented in FIG. 5-6.

Now that you have added rudimentary line draw functions to your TAB library, you're ready to start the building of the 'bar' demonstration program. As this program develops throughout Chapter 5 routines are added to the TAB library as their need arises.

Fig. 5-1. The source code for VDHORIZ.C.

```
/*******************
 * Source Code Start
 *
 * File Name:    VDHORIZ.C
 *
 * Synopsis:     vdHoriz(row,column,length,attr)
 *
 * int row       row where string write will start
 *
 * int column    column where string write will start
 *
 * int length    length of the horizontal line
 *
 * int attr      attribute for horizontal line
 *               written to the screen
 *
 * Description: Sends the horizontal line of length
 *              bytes to the screen at
 *              display RAM at row and
 *              column with attr. Note that this call
 *              will work only after vidInit()
 *              has been called.  If you
 *              neglect to call vidInit() before
 *              this call is made then unspeakable
 *              and unnatural things will happen
 *              to your computer!
 *
 * Returns:      Nothing
 */

/*
 * Include files
 */

#include <tproto.h>

/*
 * vdHoriz function
 */

void
vdHoriz(row,column,number,attr)
int row,column,number,attr;
{
int stop,col_start,token;

/* Create token of horizontal line */
/* character and passed attribute  */
token = mkToken(196,attr);

/* set termination for loop */
stop = column+number;

/* print the horizontal line */
for(col_start=column; col_start<stop; col_start++)
        vdChar(row,col_start,token);
```

```
}

/*
 * End of source
 ***************/
```

Fig. 5-1 ends.

Fig. 5-2. The assembly source code for VDHORIZ.ASM.

```
;*******************
; Source Code Start
;
; File Name:    VDHORIZ.ASM
;
; Synopsis:     vdHoriz(row,column,length,attr)
;
; int row       row where string write will start
;
; int column    column where string write will start
;
; int length    length of the horizontal line
;
; int attr      attribute for horizontal line
;                 written to the screen
;
; Description: Sends the horizontal line of length
;                 bytes to the screen at
;                 display RAM at row and
;                 column with attr. Note that this call
;                 will work only after vidInit()
;                 has been called.  If you
;                 neglect to call vidInit() before
;                 this call is made then unspeakable
;                 and unnatural things will happen
;                 to your computer!
;
; Returns:      Nothing
;
;
; EQUATES
;

off      equ    4 ; small model

;
; Define parameters which the C calling
;    function passes
;

prow     equ    byte ptr [BP+off+0]
pcol     equ    byte ptr [BP+off+2]
pnumber  equ    word ptr [BP+off+4]
pattr    equ    byte ptr [BP+off+6]

;
; Enable DOS segment-ordering at link time
;
```

Fig. 5-2 continued.

```
        DOSSEG

;
; Set the memory model for simplified segmentation
; directives
;

        .MODEL SMALL

;
; EXTRN in assembly serves the same function as
;  extern in C.  Note that the EXTRN variables'
;  names are followed by a : with their memory
;  size.
;
; WORD is a 'C' INT
; BYTE is a 'C' CHAR
; NEAR is a small memory model function
; FAR  is a medium or large memory
;  model function
;

        EXTRN   _SCRNSEG:WORD
        EXTRN   _vbwait:NEAR

;
; Make function visible to linker
;

        PUBLIC  _vdHoriz

;
; Defines the start of the code segment
;

        .CODE

;
; Set the start of the function
;

_vdHoriz PROC NEAR

;
; Save Regs
;

        push    BP
        mov     BP,SP

        push    DI
        push    SI
        push    ES

;
; Move screen Segment (gotten during the
;  vidInit() call) to ES
;
```

Fig. 5-2 continued.

```
        mov     CX,_SCRNSEG
        mov     ES,CX           ; reset extra seg

;
; Save ES on stack
;

        push    ES

;
; Calculate token offset from
;   screen segment
;

        xor     AX,AX           ; 0 -> AX
        mov     AL,prow         ; row -> AL
        mov     BL,160          ; 80 chars wide * 2
        mul     BL              ; row * scrn width  -> AX
        mov     CL,pcol         ; column to CL
        XOR     CH,CH           ; 0 -> CH
        shl     CX,1            ; col * 2
        add     AX,CX           ; column + (row * scrn width)
        mov     DI,AX           ; point DI to scrn

;
; Restore ES from stack
;

        pop     ES

;
; Enable increment using direction flag
; for stosw
;

        cld                     ; direction increment

;
; make token of attribute and horizontal line
;

        mov     AL,196          ; horizontal line
        mov     AH,pattr        ; attribute

;
; set loop counter to string length
;

        mov     CX,pnumber      ; row to write
vdv1:
;
; stosw  AX -> ES:DI  - AX to screen
;

        stosw                   ; AX -> screen
;
; loop until CX counts to 0
```

```
;

        loop     vdv1

;
; Restore registers
;

        pop      ES
        pop      SI
        pop      DI
        pop      BP

;
; Return to calling function
;

        ret

;
; End of function (ENDP)
;
; and end of assembly source (END)
;

_vdHoriz        ENDP

        END

;
; End of source listing
;***********************
```

Fig. 5-2 ends.

Fig. 5-3. Source code for TESTHOR.C.

```
/*******************
 * Source Code Start
 *
 * File Name:    TESTHOR.C
 *
 * Description: Demonstration program for
 *              vidInit, mkToken, mkAttr, vdHoriz
 */

/*
 * Include files
 */

#include <stdio.h>
#include <tproto.h>


void main(void);

void
```

```
main()
{
int attr;

/* Initialize video structure */
vidInit();

/* create attribute */
attr = mkAttr(RED,WHITE,ON_INTENSITY,OFF_BLINK);

/* write horizintal line accross screen */
vdHoriz(4,0,80,attr);
}

/*
 * End of source
 **************/
```

Fig. 5-3 ends.

Fig. 5-4. The source code to VDVERT.C.

```
/*******************
 * Source Code Start
 *
 * File Name:   VDVERT.C
 *
 * Synopsis:    vdVert(row,column,length,attr)
 *
 * int row      row where string write will start
 *
 * int column   column where string write will start
 *
 * int length   length of the vertical line
 *
 * int attr     attribute for vertical line
 *              written to the screen
 *
 * Description: Sends the vertical line of length
 *              bytes to the screen at
 *              display RAM at row and
 *              column with attr. Note that this call
 *              will work only after vidInit()
 *              has been called.  If you
 *              neglect to call vidInit() before
 *              this call is made then unspeakable
 *              and unnatural things will happen
 *              to your computer!
 *
 * Returns:     Nothing
 */

/*
 * Include files
 */

#include <tproto.h>
```

125

```
void
vdVert(row,column,number,attr)
int row,column,number,attr;
{
int stop,row_start,token;

/* Create token of vertical line    */
/* character and passed attribute   */
token = mkToken(179,attr);

/* set termination for loop */
stop = row+number;

/* print the horizontal line */
for(row_start=row; row_start<stop; row_start++)
        vdChar(row_start,column,token);
}

/*
 * End of source
 ***************/
```

Fig. 5-4 ends.

Fig. 5-5. The source code to VDVERT.ASM.

```
;*******************
; Source Code Start
;
; File Name:    VDVERT.ASM/
;
; Synopsis:     vdVert(row,column,length,attr)
;
; int row       row where string write will start
;
; int column    column where string write will start
;
; int length    length of the vertical line
;
; int attr      attribute for vertical line
;               written to the screen
;
; Description: Sends the vertical line of length
;              bytes to the screen at
;              display RAM at row and
;              column with attr. Note that this call
;              will work only after vidInit()
;              has been called.  If you
;              neglect to call vidInit() before
;              this call is made then unspeakable
;              and unnatural things will happen
;              to your computer!
;
; Returns:      Nothing

;
; EQUATES
```

Fig. 5-5 continued.

```
;

off      equ     4 ; small model

;
; Define parameters which the C calling
;   function passes
;

prow     equ     byte ptr [BP+off+0]
pcol     equ     byte ptr [BP+off+2]
pnumber  equ     word ptr [BP+off+4]
pattr    equ     byte ptr [BP+off+6]

;
; Enable DOS segment-ordering at link time
;

         DOSSEG

;
; Set the memory model for simplified segmentation
; directives
;

         .MODEL SMALL

;
; EXTRN in assembly serves the same function as
;   extern in C.  Note that the EXTRN variables'
;   names are followed by a : with their memory
;   size.
;
; WORD is a 'C' INT
; BYTE is a 'C' CHAR
; NEAR is a small memory model function
; FAR  is a medium or large memory
;   model function
;

         EXTRN   _SCRNSEG:WORD
         EXTRN   _vbwait:NEAR

;
; Make function visible to linker
;

         PUBLIC  _vdVert

;
; Defines the start of the code segment
;

         .CODE

;
; Set the start of the function
;
```

Fig. 5-5 continued.

```
_vdVert PROC NEAR

;
; Save Regs
;

        push    BP
        mov     BP,SP
        push    DI
        push    SI
        push    ES

;
; Move screen Segment (gotten during the
;  vidInit() call) to ES
;

        mov     CX,_SCRNSEG
        mov     ES,CX           ; reset extra seg

;
; Save ES on stack
;

        push    ES              ; save EX

;
; Calculate token offset from
;   screen segment
;

        xor     AX,AX           ; 0 -> AX
        mov     AL,prow         ; row -> AL
        mov     BL,160          ; 80 chars wide * 2
        mul     BL              ; row * scrn width  -> AX
        mov     CL,pcol         ; column to CL
        XOR     CH,CH           ; 0 -> CH
        shl     CX,1            ; col * 2
        add     AX,CX           ; column + (row * scrn width)
        mov     DI,AX           ; point DI to scrn

;
; Restore ES from stack
;

        pop     ES              ; restore ES

;
; make token of attribute and horizontal line
;

        mov     AL,179          ; vertical line
        mov     AH,pattr        ; attrobute

;
; set loop counter to string length
;
```

```
        mov     CX,pnumber    ; row to write
vdv1:

;
; move token to screen
;
        mov     word ptr ES:[DI],AX

;
; set offset to next row down
;
        add     DI,160        ; next row down

;
; loop until CX counts to 0
;
        loop    vdv1

;
; Restore registers
;
        pop     ES
        pop     SI
        pop     DI
        pop     BP

;
; Return to calling function
;
        ret

;
; End of function (ENDP)
;
; and end of assembly source (END)
;
_vdVert ENDP
        END

;
; End of source listing
;***********************
```

Fig. 5-5 ends.

Fig. 5-6. The source code to TESTVERT.C.

```
/*
 * Source Code Start
 *
 * File Name:   TESTVERT.C
 *
```

```
* Description: Demonstration program for
*              vidInit, mkToken, mkAttr, vdVert
*/

/*
 * Include files
 */

#include <stdio.h>
#include <tproto.h>


void main(void);

void
main()
{
int attr;

/* Initialize video structure */
vidInit();

/* create attribute */
attr = mkAttr(RED,WHITE,ON_INTENSITY,OFF_BLINK);

/* write vertical line */
vdVert(4,39,16,attr);
}

/*
 * End of source
 ***************/
```

Fig. 5-6 ends.

The demonstration program BAR1.C, shown in FIG. 5-7, erases the screen while turning the background white and the foreground black. Once the screen has been rewritten a two-item menu bar is written at the top of the screen and a line is drawn under the menu bar to separate it from the rest of the screen.

Fig. 5-7. The source code to BAR1.C.

```
/*******************
 * Source Code Start
 *
 * File Name:   BAR1.C
 *
 * Description: Demonstration program for
 *              vidInit, mkToken, mkAttr,
 *              vdWrite, vdAttr,
 */

/*
 * Include files
```

Fig. 5-7 continued.

```c
 */

#include <stdio.h>
#include <tproto.h>

/*
 * Global data
 */

char menu[] =
   " Desk    File ";

/*
 * Function prototypes
 */

void main(void);
void menu_bar(void);
void make_white(void);

/*
 * Name:   menu_bar
 *
 * Description: This function
 *         draws a menu bar
 *         on the top line of
 *         the screen
 */

void
menu_bar()
{
int attr;

/* set attribute for menu bar */
attr = mkAttr(BLACK,WHITE,OFF_INTENSITY,OFF_BLINK);

/* write menu bar to screen */
vdWrite(0,0,strlen(menu),menu,attr);

/* draw line below menu */
vdHoriz(1,0,80,attr);
}

/*
 * Name:   make_white
 *
 * Description: This function
 *         erases the existing
 *         screen and turns the
 *         background white
 */

void
make_white()
{
int attr,token,row,column;
```

```
/* set attribute for screen */
attr = mkAttr(BLACK,WHITE,OFF_INTENSITY,OFF_BLINK);

/* create blank token with 'attr' backgroung */
token = mkToken(' ',attr);

/* replace existing screen with blank token */
for(row=0; row<25; row++)
        for(column=0; column<80; column++)
                vdChar(row,column,token);
}

/*
 * Name: main
 */

void
main()
{
/* initialize TAB library video routines */
vidInit();

/* erase screen and make background white */
make_white();

/* draw menu bar */
menu_bar();

/* wait for key press */
gtKey();
}

/*
 * End of Source
 ***************/
```

Fig. 5-7 ends.

Once you compile, link and run BAR1.EXE it becomes very clear that there are still things you need to add to the program, including the ability to:

1. Select and highlight a menu item.
2. Save the old contents of the screen at the start of program execution and restore the contents of the screen before the program returns to DOS.
3. Save the cursor location at the start of program execution and restore the cursor to that location before the program returns to DOS.
4. Drop down a window when a menu bar item is selected. Print drop-down menu items into the window and allow the user to select an item with the keyboard.
5. Turn off the cursor right after the vidInit( ) call and after the program begins.

The list on the previous page gives a clear guideline for the development of new routines. Let's get started with item one on the list, adding a routine that allows you to easily highlight an item on the menu. This routine provides you with a way to change the attribute byte for a group of characters on a row. The source code listing for VDATTR.C is shown in FIG. 5-8 and the source code listing for VDATTR.ASM is shown in FIG. 5-9.

Fig. 5-8. The source code for VDATTR.C.

```
/*******************
 * Source Code Start
 *
 * File Name:   VDATTR.C
 *
 * Synopsis:    vdAttr(row,column,length,attr)
 *
 * int row      row where string write will start
 *
 * int column   column where attribute write will start
 *
 * int length   length of the new attribute
 *
 * int attr     attribute for horizontal line
 *              written to the screen
 *
 * Description: Sends the new attribute of length
 *              bytes to the screen at
 *              display RAM at row and
 *              column with attr. Note that this call
 *              will work only after vidInit()
 *              has been called.  If you
 *              neglect to call vidInit() before
 *              this call is made then unspeakable
 *              and unnatural things will happen
 *              to your computer!
 *
 * Returns:     Nothing
 */

/*
 * Include files
 */

#include <tproto.h>

extern VIDEO *crt;


void
vdAttr(row,col,length,attr)
int row,col,length;
char attr;
{
unsigned char far *scrn;
register      int count;
long offset;
```

```
/* set far pointer to screen address (SEG) */
scrn = (unsigned char far *)crt->scrn;

/* calculate the offset from the screen */
/* segment start                        */
offset = (long)(row*160)+(col*2);

/* far pointer adjusted to exact display */
/* memory start at row,col               */
scrn = scrn + offset;

/* loop for attribute change             */
for(count=0; count<length; count++)
        {
        /* bypass character byte   */
        scrn++;

        /* new attribute to screen */
        *scrn++ = (unsigned)attr;
        }
}

/*
 * End of source
 **************/
```

Fig. 5-8 ends.

Fig. 5-9. The source code for VDATTR.ASM.

```
;******************
; Source Code Start
;
; File Name:    VDATTR.ASM/
;
; Synopsis:     vdAttr(row,column,length,attr)
;
; int row       row where string write will start
;
; int column    column where attribute write will start
;
; int length    length of the new attribute
;
; int attr      attribute for horizontal line
;               written to the screen
;
; Description: Sends the new attribute of length
;              bytes to the screen at
;              display RAM at row and
;              column with attr. Note that this call
;              will work only after vidInit()
;              has been called.  If you
;              neglect to call vidInit() before
;              this call is made then unspeakable
;              and unnatural things will happen
;              to your computer!
;
; Returns:      Nothing
```

Fig. 5-9 continued.

```
;
; EQUATES
;

off      equ      4 ; small model


;
; Define parameters which the C calling
;   function passes
;

prow     equ      byte ptr [BP+off+0]
pcol     equ      byte ptr [BP+off+2]
plen     equ      word ptr [BP+off+4]
pattr    equ      byte ptr [BP+off+6]


;
; Enable DOS segment-ordering at link time
;

        DOSSEG


;
; Set the memory model for simplified segmentation
; directives
;

        .MODEL SMALL


;
; EXTRN in assembly serves the same function as
;   extern in C.  Note that the EXTRN variables'
;   names are followed by a : with their memory
;   size.
;
; WORD is a 'C' INT
; BYTE is a 'C' CHAR
; NEAR is a small memory model function
; FAR  is a medium or large memory
;   model function
;

        EXTRN     _SCRNSEG:WORD
        EXTRN     _vbwait:NEAR


;
; Make function visible to linker
;

        PUBLIC   _vdAttr


;
; Defines the start of the code segment
;

        .CODE

;
```

Fig. 5-9 continued.

```
; Set the start of the function
;

_vdAttr PROC NEAR

;
; Save Regs
;

        push    BP
        mov     BP,SP
        push    DI
        push    SI
        push    ES

;
; Move screen Segment (gotten during the
;  vidInit() call) to ES
;

        mov     CX,_SCRNSEG
        mov     ES,CX           ; reset extra seg

;
; Save ES on stack
;

        push    ES

;
; Calculate token offset from
;  screen segment
;

        xor     AX,AX           ; 0 -> AX
        mov     AL,prow         ; row -> AL
        mov     BL,160          ; 80 chars wide * 2
        mul     BL              ; row * scrn width  -> AX
        mov     CL,pcol         ; column to CL
        xor     CH,CH           ; 0 -> CH
        shl     CX,1            ; col * 2
        add     AX,CX           ; column + (row * scrn width)
        mov     DI,AX           ; point DI to scrn

;
; Restore ES from stack
;

        pop     ES              ; restore ES

;
; Enable increment using direction flag
; for stosw
;

        cld                     ; direction increment
```

```
;
; set loop counter to string length
;
        mov     CX,plen         ; string length parameter
vdr1:
;
; bypass character byte
;
        inc     DI

;
; move attribute to screen
;
        mov     AL,pattr
        stosb

;
; loop until CX counts to 0
;
        loop    vdr1

;
; Restore registers
;
        pop     ES
        pop     SI
        pop     DI
        pop     BP

;
; Return to calling function
;
        ret

;
; End of function (ENDP)
;
; and end of assembly source (END)
;
_vdAttr ENDP

        END

;
; End of source listing
;***********************
```

Fig. 5-9 ends.

Now that you've added to the TAB library the ability to change the attribute byte of a string of characters on a screen row, let's modify BAR1.C to demonstrate this technique. The new demonstration program will be called BAR2.C. This program allows a user to select the 'Desk' menu item by pressing the Alt-D key, or the 'File' menu item by pressing the Alt-F key. Pressing Alt-Q will return the user to DOS. The source code listing for BAR2.C is shown in FIG. 5-10.

Fig. 5-10. The source code for BAR2.C.

```
/********************
 * Source Code Start
 *
 * File Name:   BAR2.C
 *
 * Description: Demonstration program for
 *              vidInit, mkToken, mkAttr,
 *              vdWrite, vdAttr,
 */

/*
 * Include files
 */

#include <stdio.h>
#include <tproto.h>

/*
 * Defines for length of strings
 */

#define DESK_LEN 6
#define FILE_LEN 6
#define QUIT_LEN 6

/*
 * Global data
 */

char menu1[DESK_LEN] = " Desk ";
char menu2[FILE_LEN] = " File ";
char menu3[QUIT_LEN] = " Quit ";

/*
 * Function prototypes
 */

void main(void);
void menu_bar(void);
void make_white(void);

/*
 * Name:  menu_bar
 *
 * Description: This function
```

Fig. 5-10 continued.
```
*          draws a menu bar
*          on the top line of
*          the screen
*/

void
menu_bar()
{
int attr,i_attr;

/* set attribute for menu bar */
attr = mkAttr(BLACK,WHITE,OFF_INTENSITY,OFF_BLINK);

/* write menu bar to screen */
vdWrite(0,0,DESK_LEN,menu1,attr);
vdWrite(0,DESK_LEN,FILE_LEN,menu2,attr);
vdWrite(0,78-strlen(menu3),QUIT_LEN,menu3,attr);

/* draw line below menu */
vdHoriz(1,0,80,attr);
}

/*
 * Name:  make_white
 *
 * Description: This function
 *          erases the existing
 *          screen and turns the
 *          background white
 */

void
make_white()
{
int attr,token,row,column;

/* set attribute for screen */
attr = mkAttr(BLACK,WHITE,OFF_INTENSITY,OFF_BLINK);

/* create blank token with 'attr' backgroung */
token = mkToken(' ',attr);

/* replace existing screen with blank token */
for(row=0; row<25; row++)
        for(column=0; column<80; column++)
                vdChar(row,column,token);
}

/*
 * Name: main
 */

void
main()
{
int i_attr,item,key,quit_flag;
```

Fig. 5-10 continued.

```
/* initialize TAB library video routines */
vidInit();

/* set attribute for item highlight */
i_attr = mkAttr(WHITE,BLUE,ON_INTENSITY,OFF_BLINK);

/* erase screen and make background white */
make_white();

/* draw menu bar */
menu_bar();

/* set item = 0 for no menu item selected */
item = 0;

/* set quit_flag to NO EXIT loop */
quit_flag = aFALSE;

/* main keyboard loop */
do
        {
        /* clear all menu highlights  */
        menu_bar();

        /* Examine item for highlight */
        switch(item)
                {
                /* ALT_D pressed -> highlight 'Desk' */
                case 1:
                        vdAttr(0,0,DESK_LEN,i_attr);
                        break;
                /* ALT_F pressed -> highlight 'File' */
                case 2:
                        vdAttr(0,DESK_LEN,FILE_LEN,i_attr);
                        break;
                }

        /* get key press and evaluate */
        key = gtKey();
        switch(key)
                {
                /* ALT D key press            */
                /* set flag to highlight 'Desk' */
                case ALT_D:
                        item = 1;
                        break;

                /* ALT F key press            */
                /* set flag to highlight 'File' */
                case ALT_F:
                        item = 2;
                        break;

                /* ALT Q key press            */
                /* set flag to highlight 'Desk' */
                case ALT_Q:
                        quit_flag = aTRUE;
```

```
                        break;
                /* Any other key            */
                default:
                        /* clear highlights on menu  */
                        item = 0;

                        /* invalid key press        */
                        beep();
                        break;
                }

        } while(!quit_flag);
}


/*
 * End of Source
 ***************/
```

Fig. 5-10 ends.

By examining the keyboard "read do/while" loop, it becomes clear how the programmer may create a keyboard filter for this budding user interface. Now let's continue building the drop-down window demonstration program by looking at items 3 & 4 on the project development list. Item 3 calls for the creation of a routine to save the current contents of the screen and restore those original contents and the program's termination. Item 4 calls for the saving of the cursor's location and restoring the cursor's location and the program's termination.

Starting with the saving and restoring of the cursor's location, there are three source files. The first two are the C source code. Please note that Turbo C uses a file named ALLOC.H and Watcom C and Microsoft C use an equivalent file name MALLOC.H. The source code listing for saving the cursor's location is shown in FIG. 5-11.

Fig. 5-11. The source code for SCLOC.C.

```
/******************
 * Start Source File
 *
 * File Name:   SCLOC.C
 *
 * Synopsis:    sCloc()
 *
 * Description: saves the current cursor location
 *              to the CUR_LOCATION structure
 *
 * Returns:     Nothing
 */

/*
 * Include files
 */
```

```
#include <dos.h>
#include <alloc.h>
#include <tproto.h>

/*
 * Global pointer to structure
 */

CUR_LOCATION *c_loc;

/*
 * sCloc function
 */

void
sCloc()
{
union REGS ir,or;
/* allocate memory for structure */
c_loc = (CUR_LOCATION *)calloc(sizeof(CUR_LOCATION),sizeof(int));

/* get current cursor location and save to structure */
gtCur(c_loc->row,c_loc->column);
}

/*
 *End of source
 **************/
```

Fig. 5-11 ends.

Now that you've saved the cursor's location, you need to restore it using the **rCloc( )** function. The source code listing for RCLOC.C is shown in FIG. 5-12.

Fig. 5-12. The source code for RCLOC.C.

```
/******************
 * Start Source File
 *
 * File Name:   RCLOC.C
 *
 * Synopsis:    rCloc()
 *
 * Description: restores the previously saved cursor
 *              location from *c_loc
 *
 * Returns:     Nothing
 */

/*
 * Include files
 */
```

```
#include <dos.h>
#include <alloc.h>

#include <tproto.h>

extern CUR_LOCATION *c_loc;

void
rCloc()
{
/* moves the cursor to previously */
/* saved location                 */
mvCur(c_loc->row,c_loc->column);

/* frees up previously allocated memory */
free(c_loc);
}
/*
 * End of source listing
 ***********************/
```

Fig. 5-12 ends.

The assembly binding for **rCloc( )** and **sCloc( )** are placed in the same assembly source listing. Note how two assembly functions are used in the SCLOC.ASM file. The source code listing for SCLOC.ASM is shown in FIG. 5-13.

Fig. 5-13. The source code for SCLOC.ASM.

```
;******************
; Source Code Start
;
; File Name:   SCLOC.ASM
;
; Synopsis:    sCloc()
;
; Description: Uses BIOS to get the
;              current location of the
;              cursor and saves it to
;              the CUR_LOCATION structure
;              (see tstruct.h)
;
;
; Returns:     Nothing
;
;
;
```

143

Fig. 5-13 continued.

```
; Enable DOS segment-ordering at link time
;

    DOSSEG

;
; Set the memory model for simplified segmentation
; directives
;

    .MODEL SMALL

;
; The structure 'v' must match the
; VIDEO structure declared in TSTRUCT.H
;
; typedef struct {
;    int row;                       /* cursor row      */
;    int column;                    /* cursor column   */
; } CUR_LOCATION;


;
; structure declaration
;

    c_loc STRUC

;
; int to byte row;
;

       row    DB     0

;
; int to byte column;
;

       column DB     0

;
; End of structure c_loc
;
```

Fig. 5-13 continued.

```
      c_loc ENDS

;
; Defines the start of the DATA segment
;

      .DATA

c     c_loc        <>                  ; structure declaration

;
; Declare the function as GLOBAL
; so it will be recognized by your
; C functions.  Note the underscore
; preceding the function.  This is
; a standard function naming convention
; for the MICROSOFT and TURBO compilers
;

      PUBLIC    _sCloc,_rCloc

;
; Defines the start of the CODE segment
;

      .CODE
;
; Set the start of the function
;

_sCloc PROC NEAR

;
;Save regs
;

   push BP
   mov  BP,SP

;
; get cur location -> int 10h func 3
;
```

Fig. 5-13 continued.

```
        xor   CX,CX           ; CX -> 0
        mov   AH,3            ; BIOS cur location
        int   10h            ; BIOS int
        mov   [c.row],DH     ; move row
        mov   [c.column],DL  ; move column


;
; Restore regs
;

        pop  BP


;
; Return to calling function
;

        ret


;
; End of procedure
;

_sCLoc ENDP

;
; Synopsis:    rCloc()
;
; Description: Uses previously saved
;              cursor location as
;              setting for new cursor
;              location
;
; Returns:     Nothing
;

;
; Set the start of the function
;

_rCloc PROC NEAR
        push BP
        mov  BP,SP
```

```
        mov  DH,[c.row]
        mov  DL,[c.column]
        mov  BH,0 ; 0 -> BH

;
; Move Cursor BIOS function
;

        mov  AH,2

;
; Invoke BIOS int 10h
;

        int  10h  ; BIOS video int
        pop  BP
        ret

_rCloc ENDP

        END

;
; End of assembly listing
;*************************
```

Fig. 5-13 ends.

Now that you've created a way to save and restore the cursor location, it's time to present the routines to save and restore the screen. Because you're going to save screen tokens you need a way to read the token from the video display. The direct video function that accomplishes this is **vrdChar(...)**. The source code listing for VRDCHAR.C is shown in FIG. 5-14 and the source code listing for VRDCHAR.ASM is shown in FIG. 5-15.

Now let's present the C routine that saves the screen and restores the screen image. Note that as in the save and restore, the cursor location and the assembly bindings are in the same assembly source listing. The source code listing for SAVESCRN.C is shown in FIG. 5-16 and the source code listing for RESTSCRN.C is shown in FIG. 5-17. The source code for assembly version of **saveScrn( )** and **restScrn( )** is shown in FIG. 5-18.

Fig. 5-14. The source code to VRDCHAR.C.

```
/*******************
 * Source Code Start
 *
 * File Name:    VRDCHAR.C
 *
 * Synopsis:     token = vrdChar(row,column)
 *
 * int row       row where token will be read
 *
 * int column    column where the token will be read
 *
 * int token     LSB holds screen character
 *               and the MSB holds the character's
 *               attribute.
 *
 * Description:  Reads the screen token directly
 *               from display RAM at row and
 *               column.  Note that this call
 *               will work only after vidInit()
 *               has been called.  If you
 *               neglect to call vidInit() before
 *               this call is made then unspeakable
 *               and unnatural things will happen
 *               to your computer!
 *
 * Returns:      Nothing
 */

/*
 * Include files
 */

#include <stdio.h>
#include <tproto.h>

extern VIDEO *crt;

int
vrdChar(row,col)
int row,col;
{
long offset;
unsigned int far *scrn;

/* set the pointer to screen start */
scrn = (unsigned int far *)crt->scrn;

/* set the offset from video display RAM start */
offset = (long)(row*80)+col;

/* return the token */
return(*(scrn+offset));
}

/*
 * End of source listing
 **********************/
```

Fig. 5-15. The assembly listing for VRDCHAR.ASM.

```
;*******************
; Source Code Start
;
; File Name:    VRDCHAR.ASM
;
; Synopsis:     token = vrdChar(row,column)
;
; int row       row where token will be read
;
; int column    column where the token will be read
;
; int token     LSB holds screen character
;               and the MSB holds the character's
;               attribute.
;
; Description:  Reads the screen token directly
;               from display RAM at row and
;               column.  Note that this call
;               will work only after vidInit()
;               has been called.  If you
;               neglect to call vidInit() before
;               this call is made then unspeakable
;               and unnatural things will happen
;               to your computer!
;
; Returns:      Nothing
;
;
; Small model -> off = 4
; Medium model -> off = 6
; Large model -> off = 6
;
off        equ    4 ; small model
;
; Define parameters which the C calling
;   function passes
;
prow       equ     byte ptr [BP+off+0]
pcol       equ     byte ptr [BP+off+2]
;
; Enable DOS segment-ordering at link time
;
           DOSSEG
;
; Set the memory model for simplified segmentation
; directives
;
           .MODEL SMALL
```

Fig. 5-15 continued.

```
;
; EXTRN in assembly serves the same function as
;  extern in C.  Note that the EXTRN variables'
;  names are followed by a : with their memory
;  size.
;
; WORD is a 'C' INT
; BYTE is a 'C' CHAR
; NEAR is a small memory model function
; FAR  is a medium or large memory
;  model function
;

        EXTRN    _SCRNSEG:WORD

;
; Make function visible to linker
;

        PUBLIC   _vrdChar

;
; Defines the start of the code segment
;

        .CODE

;
; Set the start of the function
;

_vrdChar PROC NEAR
;
; Save Regs
;

        push    BP
        mov     BP,SP
        push    DI
        push    SI
        push    ES

;
; Move screen Segment (gotten during the
;  vidInit() call) to ES
;

        mov     CX,_SCRNSEG
        mov     ES,CX           ; reset extra seg

;
; Save ES on stack
;

        push    ES

;
```

```
; Calculate token offset from
;  screen segment
;

        xor     AX,AX           ; 0 -> AX
        mov     AL,prow         ; row -> AL
        mov     BL,160          ; 80 chars wide * 2
        mul     BL              ; row * scrn width  -> AX
        mov     CL,pcol         ; column to CL
        XOR     CH,CH           ; 0 -> CH
        shl     CX,1            ; col * 2
        add     AX,CX           ; column + (row * scrn width)
        mov     DI,AX           ; point DI to scrn

;
; Restore ES from stack
;

        pop     ES

;
; Get token from screen
;
; Note that WORD value is
; returned in the AX register

        mov     AX,WORD PTR ES:[DI]

;
; Restore registers
;

        pop     ES
        pop     SI
        pop     DI
        pop     BP

;
; Return to calling function
;

        ret

;
; End of function (ENDP)
;
; and end of assembly source (END)
;

_vrdChar        ENDP
        END

;
; End of assembly listing
;************************
```

Fig. 5-15 ends.

Fig. 5-16. The source code to SAVESCRN.C.

```
/*******************
 * Start Source File
 *
 * File Name:    SAVESCRN.C
 *
 * Synopsis:    saveScrn()
 *
 * Description: saves the screen to memory
 *
 * Returns:     Nothing
 */

/*
 * Include files
 */

#include <dos.h>
#include <tproto.h>

/*
 * Save text screen to unsigned int SCRN_MEM[80*25]
 *
 * WARNING - vidInit MUST be called before this
 *           routine!
 */

/* Note: int array for tokens */
extern unsigned int SCRN_MEM[80*25];

/*
 * saveScrn function
 */

void
saveScrn()
{
unsigned int *iptr;
register int row;
register int column;

/* set integer pointer to int buffer   */
/* where current screen tokens will go */
iptr = SCRN_MEM;

/* go row by row */
for(row=0; row<25; row++)

        /* one column after another */
        for(column=0; column<80; column++)

                /* and finally get the token */
                *iptr++ = vrdChar(row,column);
}

/*
 * End of source listing
 **********************/
```

Fig. 5-17. The source code to RESTSCRN.C.

```
/*******************
 * Start Source File
 *
 * File Name:    RESTSCRN.C
 *
 * Synopsis:     restScrn()
 *
 * Description: restores the previously saved
 * screen from memory to the video display
 *
 * Returns:      Nothing
 */

/*
 * Save text screen to unsigned int SCRN_MEM[80*25]
 *
 * WARNING - vidInit MUST be called before this
 *           routine!
 */

/*
 * Include files
 */

#include <tproto.h>

/* int to hold tokens */
unsigned int SCRN_MEM[80*25];

/*
 * restScrn function
 */

void
restScrn()
{
unsigned int *iptr;
register int row;
register int column;

/* set pointer to token buffer */
iptr = SCRN_MEM;

/* go row by row */
for(row=0; row<25; row++)

        /* one column after another */
        for(column=0; column<80; column++)

                /* write token by token to video display */
                vdChar(row,column,*iptr++);
}

/*
 * End of source listing
 ***********************/
```

Fig. 5-18. The source named SAVESCRN.ASM.

```
;******************
; Source Code Start
;
; File Name:    SAVESCRN.ASM
;
; Synopsis:     saveScrn.asm()
;
; Description: Saves screen to 2000 WORDS
;              allocated in code segment
;
; Returns:      Nothing
;


;
;
; Enable DOS segment-ordering at link time
;

        DOSSEG


;
; Set the memory model for simplified segmentation
; directives
;

        .MODEL SMALL


;
; Declare the function as GLOBAL
; so it will be recognized by your
; C functions.  Note the underscore
; preceding the function.  This is
; a standard function naming convention
; for the MICROSOFT and TURBO compilers
;

        PUBLIC  _saveScrn,_restScrn

;
; Defines the start of the CODE segment
;

        .CODE

;
; Set the start of the function
;

_saveScrn PROC NEAR
;
; bypass memory allocated in code segment
;
        jmp     bss1
_SCRN   DW      2000 DUP(0)
bss1:
;
```

Fig. 5-18 continued.

```
; save regs
;

        push    BP
        mov     BP,SP
        push    ES
        push    SI
        push    DI


;
; get video mode and set ES segment reg
;

        mov     AH,15   ; get mode
        int     10H     ; bios
        cmp     AL,7    ; is mono?
        je      setm    ; yes => jump
        mov     CX,0b800H ; color addr
        jmp     bs1     ; jump on
setm:
        mov     CX,0b000H ; mono addr
bs1:
        mov     ES,CX   ; save scrn seg
        mov     DI,0    ; offset to 0
        mov     SI,OFFSET _SCRN ; set screen counter
        mov     CX,4000 ; move 4000 bytes
lp1:
        mov     AX,ES:[DI] ; get scrn byte
        mov     CS:[SI],AX ; to buffer
        inc     DI      ; next byte
        inc     SI
        loop    lp1     ; loop until 4000 bytes moved
;
        pop     DI
        pop     SI
        pop     ES
        mov     SP,BP
        pop     BP
        ret
_saveScrn ENDP


;
; Synopsis:    restScrn.asm()
;
; Description: restores screen from 2000 WORDS
;              allocated in code segment
;
; Returns:     Nothing
;

_restScrn PROC NEAR
;
; Save regs
;

        push    BP
        mov     BP,SP
```

```
        push    ES
        push    SI
        push    DI

;
; get video mode and set ES segment reg
;

        mov     AH,15    ; get mode
        int     10H      ; bios
        cmp     AL,7     ; is mono?
        je      setm1    ; yes => jump
        mov     CX,0b800H ; color addr
        jmp     bs11     ; jump on
setm1:
        mov     CX,0b000H ; mono addr
bs11:
        mov     ES,CX
        mov     DI,0      ; offset to 0
        mov     SI,OFFSET _SCRN ; set screen counter
        mov     CX,4000 ; move 4000 bytes
lp11:
        mov     AX,CS:[SI] ; buffer byte
        mov     ES:[DI],AX ; to display RAM
        inc     DI       ; next byte
        inc     SI
        loop    lp11     ; loop until 4000 bytes moved
;
; Restore regs
;
        pop     DI
        pop     SI
        pop     ES
        mov     SP,BP
        pop     BP
        ret
_restScrn ENDP
        END

;
; End of assembly source listing
;*******************************
```

Fig. 5-18 ends.

Last, but not least, you need to turn the cursor off and on. Stated simply, the TAB library method of disabling and enabling the cursor involves the following steps:

1. Use BIOS Function 3 INT 10h to get the current cursor shape (held in an int).

2. *To Enable*: Turn off BIT 5 of int's MSB which holds the current shape.

3. *To Disable*: Turn on BIT 5 of int's MSB which holds the current shape.

4. Use BIOS Function 1 INT 10h to reset cursor shape.

Table 5-1. Values Useful in Enabling or Disabling the Cursor.

VALUE	BIT PATTERN
0x20	0 0 1 0 0 0 0 0
~0x20	1 1 0 1 1 1 1 1
0xdf	1 1 0 1 1 1 1 1

The C source code to enable the cursor uses the ~ (ones' complement) Bitwise Negation unary operator. The ones' complement operator simply flips the bits of a variable. The MSB of the cursor is held in the 8-bit CH register. Because enabling and disabling the cursor involves turning bit 5 on and off, TABLE 5-1 describes the values that are useful in accomplishing that bit "twiddling."

Note that ORing the value 0x20 with an 8-bit number will turn bit 5 on. That action will disable the cursor. Because 0xdf and ~0x20 are equivalent, ANDing either of those values with an 8-bit number will turn bit 5 off. That action will enable the cursor. The ONCUR.C file uses the ~0x20 values and the ONCUR.ASM file uses the 0xdf value. The source code listing for ONCUR.C is shown in FIG. 5-19 and the source code listing for ONCUR.ASM is shown in FIG. 5-20.

Fig. 5-19. The source for ONCUR.C.

```
/******************
 * Start Source File
 *
 * File Name:    ONCUR.C
 *
 * Synopsis:     onCur()
 *
 * Description: enables the cursor by
 *               getting the current
 *               cursor shape and flipping
 *               bit 5 of the MSB off and
 *               re-setting cursor shape
 *
 * Returns:      Nothing
 */

/*
 * Include files
 */

#include <dos.h>

/*
 * Define for on mask
 *
 *  Hex          BIT          ACTION
 *  -----     ---------------  ------
```

157

```
*   0x20    0 0 1 0 0 0 0 0      OFF
*  ~0x20    1 1 0 1 1 1 1 1      ON
*/

#define CH_MASK ~0x20 /* ON */

/*
 * Function onCur
 */

void
onCur()
{
union REGS ir,or;

/* Function 3 is:                  */
/* Get Current Cursor Shape into CX */
ir.h.ah = 3;

/* Invoke int 10h */
int86(0x10,&ir,&or);

/* Reset CH so bit 5 off */
ir.h.ch = or.h.ch & CH_MASK;
ir.h.cl = or.h.cl;

/* Function 1 is:                  */
/* Set Cursor Shape                */
ir.h.ah = 1;

/* Invoke int 10h */
int86(0x10,&ir,&or);
}

/*
 * End of source
 ***************/
```

Fig. 5-19 ends.

Fig. 5-20. The source for ONCUR.ASM.

```
;*******************
; Start Source File
;
; File Name      ONCUR.ASM
;
; Synopsis:      onCur()
;
; Description    enables the cursor by
;                turning bit 5 of CH on
;                after current shape is
;                obtained.  The modified
;                current shape is then
;                used to set the cursor
;
;
; Small model off defined at 4
```

```
; Medium model off defined at 6
;
off       equ     4    ; Small Model offset
;
          DOSSEG
;
          .MODEL SMALL
;
          PUBLIC _onCur
;
          .CODE
;
; Set the start of the function
;
_onCur PROC NEAR
;
; Save regs
;
          push    BP
          mov     BP,SP
;
; Get cursor shape function 3
;
          mov     AH,3
;
; Invoke BIOS int 10h
;
          int     10H    ; BIOS video int
;
; Turn BIT 5 of CH off
;
          and     CH,0dfh
;
; Set cursor shape function 1
;
          mov     AH,1
;
; Invoke BIOS int 10h
;
          int     10H    ; BIOS video int
;
; Restore BP and return to caller
;
          pop     BP

          ret
;
; End of procedure
;
_onCur ENDP

          END

; End Source Here
;****************
```

Fig. 5-20 ends.

The source code listing for OFFCUR.C is shown in FIG. 5-21 and the source code listing for OFFCUR.ASM is shown in FIG. 5-22.

The updated version of the evolving 'bar' program saves the existing screen, the cursor location and disables the cursor before beginning its own screen rewrites to restore the pre-program screen and cursor before returning to DOS. The source code listing for BAR3.C is shown in FIG. 5-23.

Fig. 5-21. The source code for OFFCUR.C.

```
/*******************
 * Start Source File
 *
 * File Name:   OFFCUR.C
 *
 * Synopsis:    offCur()
 *
 * Description: disables the cursor by
 *              getting the current
 *              cursor shape and flipping
 *              bit 5 of the MSB on and
 *              re-setting cursor shape
 *
 * Returns:     Nothing
 */

/*
 * Include files
 */

#include <dos.h>

/*
 * Define for on mask
 *
 * Hex          BIT         Action
 * -----    ---------------  ------
 * 0x20     0 0 1 0 0 0 0 0   OFF
 * ~0x20    1 1 0 1 1 1 1 1   ON
 */

#define CH_MASK 0x20 /* OFF */

/*
 * Function offCur
 */

void
offCur()
{
union REGS ir,or;

/* Function 3 is:       */
/* Get Current Cursor Shape into CX */
ir.h.ah = 3;

/* Invoke int 10h       */
```

```
int86(0x10,&ir,&or);

/* Reset CH so bit 5 on */
ir.h.ch = or.h.ch | CH_MASK;
ir.h.cl = or.h.cl;

/* Function 1 is:        */
/* Set Cursor Shape      */
ir.h.ah = 1;

/* Invoke int 10h        */
int86(0x10,&ir,&or);
}

/*
 * End of source
 ***************/
```

Fig. 5-21 ends.

Fig. 5-22. The source code for OFFCUR.ASM.

```
;*******************
; Start Source File
;
; File Name      OFFCUR.ASM
;
; Synopsis:      offCur()
;
; Description    enables the cursor by
;                turning bit 5 of CH on
;                after current shape is
;                obtained.  The modified
;                current shape is then
;                used to set the cursor
;
;
;
; Small model off defined at 4
; Medium model off defined at 6
;
off      equ     4   ; Small Model offset
;
; Enable DOS segment-ordering at link time
;
        DOSSEG
;
        .MODEL SMALL
;
        PUBLIC _offCur
;
        .CODE
;
; Set the start of the function
;
_offCur PROC NEAR
;
; Save regs
```

```
;
        push    BP
        mov     BP,SP
;
; Get cursor shape function 3
;
        mov     AH,3
;
; Invoke BIOS int 10h
;
        int     10H
;
; Turn BIT 5 of CH on
;
        or      CH,020h
;
; Set cursor shape function 1
;
        mov     AH,1
;
; Invoke BIOS int 10h
;
        int     10H
;
; Restore BP and return to caller
;
        pop     BP

        ret
;
; End of procedure
;

_offCur ENDP

        END

; End Source Here
;****************
```

Fig. 5-22 ends.

Fig. 5-23. The source code for BAR3.C.

```
/*******************
 * Source Code Start
 *
 * File Name:   BAR3.C
 *
 * Description: Demonstration program for
 *              vidInit, mkToken, mkAttr,
 *              vdWrite, vdAttr,sCloc,
 *              rCloc
 */

/*
```

162

Fig. 5-23 continued.

```
 * Include files
 */

#include <stdio.h>
#include <tproto.h>

/*
 * Defines for length of strings
 */

#define DESK_LEN 6
#define FILE_LEN 6
#define QUIT_LEN 6

/*
 * Global data
 */

char menu1[DESK_LEN] = " Desk ";
char menu2[FILE_LEN] = " File ";
char menu3[QUIT_LEN] = " Quit ";

/*
 * Function prototypes
 */

void main(void);
void menu_bar(void);
void make_white(void);

/*
 * Name:  menu_bar
 *
 * Description: This function
 *         draws a menu bar
 *         on the top line of
 *         the screen
 */

void
menu_bar()
{
int attr,i_attr;

/* set attribute for menu bar */
attr = mkAttr(BLACK,WHITE,OFF_INTENSITY,OFF_BLINK);

/* write menu bar to screen */
vdWrite(0,0,DESK_LEN,menu1,attr);
vdWrite(0,DESK_LEN,FILE_LEN,menu2,attr);
vdWrite(0,78-strlen(menu3),QUIT_LEN,menu3,attr);

/* draw line below menu */
vdHoriz(1,0,80,attr);
}

/*
```

Fig. 5-23 continued.

```
 * Name:  make_white
 *
 * Description: This function
 *        erases the existing
 *        screen and turns the
 *        background white
 */

void
make_white()
{
int attr,token,row,column;

/* set attribute for screen */
attr = mkAttr(BLACK,WHITE,OFF_INTENSITY,OFF_BLINK);

/* create blank token with 'attr' backgroung */
token = mkToken(' ',attr);

/* replace existing screen with blank token */
for(row=0; row<25; row++)
        for(column=0; column<80; column++)
                vdChar(row,column,token);
}

/*
 * Name: main
 */

void
main()
{
int i_attr,item,key,quit_flag;

/* initialize TAB library video routines */
vidInit();

/* save current cursor location */
sCloc();

/* save the current screen */
saveScrn();

/* Turn cursor off */
offCur();

/* set attribute for item highlight */
i_attr = mkAttr(WHITE,BLUE,ON_INTENSITY,OFF_BLINK);

/* erase screen and make background white */
make_white();

/* draw menu bar */
menu_bar();

/* set item = 0 for no menu item selected */
item = 0;
```

Fig. 5-23 continued.

```
/* set quit_flag to NO EXIT loop */
quit_flag = aFALSE;

/* main keyboard loop */
do
        {
        /* clear all menu highlights  */
        menu_bar();

        /* Examine item for highlight */
        switch(item)
                {
                /* ALT_D pressed -> highlight 'Desk' */
                case 1:
                        vdAttr(0,0,DESK_LEN,i_attr);
                        break;
                /* ALT_F pressed -> highlight 'File' */
                case 2:
                        vdAttr(0,DESK_LEN,FILE_LEN,i_attr);
                        break;
                }

        /* get key press and evaluate */
        key = gtKey();
        switch(key)
                {
                /* ALT D key press              */
                /* set flag to highlight 'Desk' */
                case ALT_D:
                        item = 1;
                        break;

                /* ALT F key press              */
                /* set flag to highlight 'File' */
                case ALT_F:
                        item = 2;
                        break;

                /* ALT Q key press              */
                /* set flag to highlight 'Desk' */
                case ALT_Q:
                        quit_flag = aTRUE;
                        break;

                /* Any other key                */
                default:
                        /* clear highlights on menu  */
                        item = 0;

                        /* invalid key press         */
                        beep();
                        break;
                }

        } while(!quit_flag);
```

```
/* restore the previously save screen */
restScrn();

/* restore previously save cursor location */
rCloc();

/* Turn cursor on */
onCur();
}

/*
 * End of Source
 ****************/
```

Fig. 5-23 ends.

SUMMARY

In Chapter 5 you began to develop a demonstration program, step by step, of a menu bar highlight routine. Routines were added to save the screen, restore the screen, save the current cursor location, restore the cursor location, disable the cursor, enable the cursor, read a token from the screen, draw a horizontal line and draw a vertical line on the screen.

In the next chapter the concept of rectangles is introduced. Rectangles are used in the completion of the bar demonstration series programs.

6

Rectangles

Rectangular areas of screen text provide very sensible ways of organizing information on the screen. Rectangular screen areas surrounded by a border of graphics characters has been dubbed a *window*. For purposes of this text, the major difference between a rectangle and a window is where the origin starts. For the rectangle, the origin (row 0, column 0) will always start at the upper left of the screen. For the window, the origin will always start at the upper left corner of the window border. More on windows in the next chapter.

The TAB library has a structure to describe the upper left corner and lower right corner of the window. There will also be a pointer to an allocated area of memory that will be available to hold the screen image data. The RECT structure is shown in FIG. 6-1.

Now that the structure is defined you need a way to fill the structure with data. FIGURE 6-2 presents the TAB call setRect(...).

The program listed in FIG. 6-3 demonstrates how setRect(...) is used. TESTRECT.C in the name of this test program.

Now that the RECT structure has been defined and a routine to fill the structure with data, let's look at TABLE 6-1, which describes the TAB rectangle routines.

Before the source code for this list of rectangular functions is discussed, it is important to describe one preparatory routine. This routine will clear the screen and move the cursor to the upper left corner of the screen. The source code for SCRNCLR.C is shown in FIG. 6-4.

The screen clear in assembly uses a different approach. The assembly routine uses the BIOS scroll function to erase the screen. For page 0, though, the results are the same. SCRNCLR.ASM is shown in FIG. 6-5.

Fig. 6-1. The RECT structure in TSTRUCT.H.

```
typedef struct {
  int ul_row;                /* upper left row        */
  int ul_col;                /* upper left column     */
  int lr_row;                /* lower right row        */
  int lr_col;                /* lower right column     */
  unsigned int *image;       /* pointer to scrn image */
} RECT;
```

Fig. 6-2. The source code listing for SETRECT.C.

```
/********************
 * Source Code Start
 *
 * File Name:    SETRECT.C
 *
 * Synopsis:     R = setRect(R,ul_row,ul_col,lr_row,lr_col)
 *
 * RECT *R       pointer to RECT structure
 *
 * int ul_row    upper left row
 *
 * int ul_col    upper left column
 *
 * int lr_row    lower right row
 *
 * int lr_col    lower right column
 *
 * Description: Allocates memory which
 *              is pointed to by RECT *
 *              for the data in the
 *              structure.  Memory is also
 *              allocated for the screen
 *              image data
 *
 * Returns:     The RECT *
 */

/*
 * Include files
 */

#include <alloc.h>
#include <string.h>
#include <tproto.h>

/*
 * function setRect
 */

RECT
*setRect(R,ur,uc,lr,lc)
RECT *R;
int ur,uc,lr,lc;
```

```
{
int height, width, image_mem;

/* alloocate memory for the structure */
/* data and return pointer to that    */
/* allocated memory                   */
R = (RECT *)malloc(sizeof(RECT));

/* load the structure with corner     */
/* coordinates                        */
R->ul_row = ur;
R->ul_col = uc;
R->lr_row = lr;
R->lr_col = lc;

/* calculate memory requirements for  */
/* screen image size of rectangle     */
height = lr-ur+1;
width = lc-uc+1;
image_mem = height * width;

/* allocate memory for screen image   */
R->image = (unsigned int *)calloc(image_mem,sizeof(int));

/* return the pointer to structure    */
return(R);
}

/*
 * End of source
 ***************/
```

Fig. 6-2 ends.

Fig. 6-3. The source to TESTRECT.C.

```
/********************
 * Source Code Start
 *
 * File Name:   TESTRECT.C
 *
 * Description: Demonstration program for
 *              setRect
 */

/*
 * Include files
 */

#include <stdio.h>
#include <tproto.h>

/*
 * Global pointer to structure
 */

RECT *R;
```

```
void main(void);

void
main()
{
/* Allocate memory for RECT structure */
/* and load with appropriate data      */
R = setRect(R,10,20,15,30);

/* Print values in structure           */
printf("\nTest:   R = setRect(R,10,20,15,30);\n\n");
printf("R->ul_row = %d\n",R->ul_row);
printf("R->ul_col = %d\n",R->ul_col);
printf("R->lr_row = %d\n",R->lr_row);
printf("R->lr_col = %d\n",R->lr_col);
printf("R points to: 0x%04X\n",R->image);
}

/*
 * End of source
 ***************/
```

Fig. 6-3 ends.

PUTTING A BORDER ON A RECTANGLE

All PCs have a built-in character set. This character set is composed of ASCII characters and a host of special purpose characters. Some of these special purpose characters allow the programmer to create solid line borders around rectangles. The character-generated line draw features permit the generation of single line and double line borders.

Table 6-1. The Rectangle Routines.

Routine	*Description*
saveRect	Saves rectangular screen region to dynamically allocated memory
restRect	Restores rectangular screen region that had been previously saved to screen using saveRect
clrRect	Clears a rectangular region of the screen
fillRect	Fills a rectangular region of the screen with any character and attribute
boxRect	Outlines a rectangular region of the screen with the PC's box characters

Fig. 6-4. The source code to clear the screen and move the cursor to row 0, column 0.

```
/********************
 * Source Code Start
 *
 * File Name:   SCRNLR.C
 *
 * Synopsis:    scrnClr()
 *
 * Description: Clears the screen with
 *              a white foreground and
 *              black background.  The
 *              cursor is moved to row
 *              0 and column 0.
 *
 * Returns:     Nothing
 */

/*
 * Include files
 */

#include <tproto.h>

/*
 * function scrnClr
 */

void
scrnClr()
{
int row, column;
int token;
int attr, ch;

/* character to fill screen */
ch = aSPC;

/* attribute to fill screen */
attr = mkAttr(WHITE,BLACK,OFF_INTENSITY,OFF_BLINK);

/* create erase token       */
token = mkToken(ch,attr);

/* erase by row             */
for(row=0; row<25; row++ )

        /* erase by column       */
        for(column=0; column<80; column++)

                /* erase character    */
                vdChar(row,column,token);

/* move cursor to row = 0 & */
/* column = 0               */
mvCur(0,0);
}
```

```
/*
 * End of source
 ***************/
```

Fig. 6-4 ends.

Fig. 6-5. The source code to SCRNCLR.ASM.

```
;******************
; Source Code Start
;
; File Name:   SCRNCLR.ASM
;
; Synopsis:    scrnClr()
;
; Description: Clears the screen with
;              a white foreground and
;              black background.  The
;              cursor is moved to row
;              0 and column 0.
;
; Returns:     Nothing
;
;
; Enable DOS segment-ordering at link time
;

        DOSSEG

;
; Set the memory model for simplified segmentation
; directives
;

        .MODEL SMALL

;
; Make function visible to linker
;

        PUBLIC  _scrnClr

;
; Defines the start of the code segment
;

        .CODE

;
; Set the start of the function
;

_scrnClr PROC NEAR
;
; Save Regs
;

        push    BP
```

Fig. 6-5 continued.

```
        mov     BP,SP

;
; lines to scroll 0
;

        xor     AL,AL

;
; Upper left row to start scroll
;

        mov     CH,AL

;
; Upper left column to start scroll
;

        mov     CL,AL

;
; Lower right row to scroll
;

        mov     DH,24

;
; Lower right column to scroll
;

        mov     DL,79

;
; Foreground white and background black
;

        mov     BH,7

;
; BIOS scroll video UP function
;

        mov     AH,6

;
; Use BIOS int 10h to erase screen
;

        int     10H

;
; Put active display page number in BH
; via BIOS int 10h function 0fh
;

        mov     AH,0fh
        int     10H
```

```
;
; Move cursor to row 0 column 0
; via BIOS int 10h function 02h
;

        mov     DX,0    ; row & col to 0
        mov     AH,2    ; reset cursor position
        int     10H


;
; Restore registers and return to calling function
;

        pop     BP

        ret


;
; End of function (ENDP)
;
; and end of assembly source (END)
;

_scrnClr ENDP
        END


;
; End of source
;***************
```

Fig. 6-5 ends.

The TAB routine that draws a rectangular border is called boxRect(...). This routine has been designed to permit the rectangular borders described in TABLE 6-2.

The assembly version of boxRect(...) explains how to call a C function from assembly. The presentation is sufficiently clear to permit a call to any C routine from an assembly coded function. In order to call a C function from assembly, you must mimic the parameter passing convention of your compiler with your assembly code. Go slowly when examining BOXRECT.ASM if this is

Table 6-2. TAB Rectangle Borders.

Name	Border	Type
S_S_S_S	Top & Bottom	Single Line
	Left & Right	Single Line
S_S_D_D	Top & Bottom	Single Line
	Left & Right	Double Line
D_D_S_S	Top & Bottom	Double Line
	Left & Right	Single Line
D_D_D_D	Top & Bottom	Double Line
	Left & Right	Double Line

a new topic to you. FIGURE 6-6 presents the C version of boxRect(...) and FIG. 6-7 presents the source code listing to BOXRECT.ASM.

The TESTBOX1 program makes sure that scrnClr( ) and boxRect(...) are working properly. The program simply clears the screen and then draws four rectangles with each of the predesignated border patterns. TESTBOX1.C is modified later in this chapter to test the other rectangle functions. The source code for TESTBOX1.C is shown in FIG. 6-8.

Fig. 6-6. The source code to BOXRECT.C.

```
/********************
 * Source Code Start
 *
 * File Name:    BOXRECT.C
 *
 * Synopsis:     boxRect(R,box,attr)
 *
 * RECT *R       pointer to RECT structure
 *
 * int box       box type defined in TSTRUCT.H
 *
 *               T => top of box
 *               B => bottom of box
 *               L => left side of box
 *               R => right side of box
 *
 *               S => sigle line
 *               D => double line
 *
 *               T B L R  #
 *               ----------
 *               S_S_S_S  0
 *               S_S_D_D  1
 *               D_D_S_S  2
 *               D_D_D_D  3
 *
 *
 *
 * Description: Places a box around a rectangle
 *              described by the structure
 *              which the RECT * is pointing
 *              to.  The box's line attributes
 *              are defined by 'box' parameter
 *              and attribute is defined by
 *              'attr' parameter.
 *
 *              Note that vidInit() must be
 *              called along with setRect(...)
 *              before this function will work.
 *
 * Returns:     Nothing.
 */

/*
 * Include files
 */
```

Fig. 6-6 continued.

```c
#include <tproto.h>

/*
 * function boxRect
 */

void
boxRect(R,box,attr)
RECT *R;
int box,attr;
{
register int row,column;
int top_bot,left_right,ul,ur,ll,lr; /* box choices */

/* examine 'box' to determine */
/* the single-double line     */
/* configuration              */
switch(box)
        {
        case S_S_D_D:
                /* top and bottom single line */
                top_bot = 196;

                /* left and right sides have  */
                /* a double line              */
                left_right = 186;

                /* matching upper left corner */
                /* BIOS box character         */
                ul = 214;

                /* matching upper right       */
                /* corner BIOS box character  */
                ur = 183;

                /* matching lower left corner */
                /* BIOS box character         */
                ll = 211;

                /* matching lower right       */
                /* corner BIOS box character  */
                lr = 189;
                break;
        case 2:
                /* top and bottom double line */
                top_bot = 205;

                /* left and right sides have  */
                /* a single line              */
                left_right = 179;

                /* matching upper left corner */
                /* BIOS box character         */
                ul = 213;

                /* matching upper right       */
                /* corner BIOS box character  */
```

Fig. 6-6 continued.

```
            ur = 184;

            /* matching lower left corner */
            /* BIOS box character         */
            ll = 212;

            /* matching lower right       */
            /* corner BIOS box character  */
            lr = 190;
            break;
case 3:
            /* top and bottom double line */
            top_bot = 205;

            /* left and right sides have  */
            /* a double line              */
            left_right = 186;

            /* matching upper left corner */
            /* BIOS box character         */
            ul = 201;

            /* matching upper right       */
            /* corner BIOS box character  */
            ur = 187;

            /* matching lower left corner */
            /* BIOS box character         */
            ll = 200;

            /* matching lower right       */
            /* corner BIOS box character  */
            lr = 188;
            break;
default:
            /* top and bottom single line */
            top_bot = 196;

            /* left and right sides have  */
            /* a single line              */
            left_right = 179;

            /* matching upper left corner */
            /* BIOS box character         */
            ul = 218;

            /* matching upper right       */
            /* corner BIOS box character  */
            ur = 191;

            /* matching lower left corner */
            /* BIOS box character         */
            ll = 192;

            /* matching lower right       */
            /* corner BIOS box character  */
```

```
                lr = 217;
                break;
        }

/* draw top and bottom rows of box  */
for(column=R->ul_col; column<R->lr_col; ++column)
        {
        /* draw top row of box            */
        vdChar(R->ul_row,column,mkToken(top_bot,attr));

        /* draw bottom roe of box         */
        vdChar(R->lr_row-1,column,mkToken(top_bot,attr));
        }

/* draw left and rt. borders of box */
for(row=R->ul_row; row<R->lr_row; ++row)
        {
        /* draw left border of box        */
        vdChar(row,R->ul_col,mkToken(left_right,attr));

        /* draw right border of box       */
        vdChar(row,R->lr_col-1,mkToken(left_right,attr));
        }

/* the upper left corner of box       */
vdChar(R->ul_row,R->ul_col,mkToken(ul,attr));

/* the upper right corner of box      */
vdChar(R->ul_row,R->lr_col-1,mkToken(ur,attr));

/* the lower left corner of box       */
vdChar(R->lr_row-1,R->ul_col,mkToken(ll,attr));

/* the upper right corner of box      */
vdChar(R->lr_row-1,R->lr_col-1,mkToken(lr,attr));
}

/*
 * End of source
 ***************/
```

Fig. 6-6 ends.

Fig. 6-7. The source code to BOXRECT.ASM.

```
;******************
; Source Code Start
;
; File Name:    BOXRECT.ASM
;
; Synopsis:     boxRect(R,box,attr)
;
; RECT *R       pointer to RECT structure
;
; int box       box type defined in TSTRUCT.H
;
;               T => top of box
;               B => bottom of box
```

Fig. 6-7 continued.

```
;               L => left side of box
;               R => right side of box
;
;               S => sigle line
;               D => double line
;
;               T B L R  #
;               ----------
;               S_S_S_S  0
;               S_S_D_D  1
;               D_D_S_S  2
;               D_D_D_D  3
;
;
;
; Description: Places a box around a rectangle
;               described by the structure
;               which the RECT * is pointing
;               to.  The box's line attributes
;               are defined by 'box' parameter
;               and attribute is defined by
;               'attr' parameter.
;
;               Note that vidInit() must be
;               called along with setRect(...)
;               before this function will work.
;
; Returns:      Nothing.
;
;
; Small model -> off = 4
; Medium model -> off = 6
; Large model -> off = 6
;

off       equ     4


;
; Define parameters which the C calling
;    function passes
;

prect    equ      WORD PTR [BP+off]
pbox     equ      WORD PTR [BP+off+2]
pattr    equ      BYTE PTR [BP+off+4]


;
; Enable DOS segment-ordering at link time
;

        DOSSEG


;
; Set the memory model for simplified segmentation
; directives
;

        .MODEL SMALL
```

179

Fig. 6-7 continued.

```
;
; EXTRN in assembly serves the same function as
;  extern in C.  Note that the EXTRN variables'
;  names are followed by a : with their memory
;  size.
;
; WORD is a 'C' INT
; BYTE is a 'C' CHAR

; NEAR is a small memory model function
; FAR  is a medium or large memory
;        model function
;

        EXTRN    _vdChar:NEAR


;
; The structure 'v' must match the
; VIDEO structure declared in TSTRUCT.H
;
; typedef struct {
;       int ul_row;            /* upper left row       */
;       int ul_col;            /* upper left column    */
;       int lr_row;            /* lower right row       */
;       int lr_col;            /* lower right column   */
;       unsigned int *image;   /* pointer to scrn image */
; } RECT;
;

        rect STRUC

;       int ul_row;            /* upper left row       */

          ulrow DW      0

;       int ul_col;            /* upper left column    */

          ulcol DW      0

;       int lr_row;            /* lower right row       */

          lrrow DW      0

;       int lr_col;            /* lower right column   */

          lrcol DW      0
        rect ENDS



;
; Defines the start of the DATA segment
;

        .DATA

r       rect    <>

ul      DB      0 ; upper left corner
```

Fig. 6-7 continued.

```
ur       DB      0 ; upper right corner
ll       DB      0 ; lower left corner
lr       DB      0 ; lower right corner
token    DW      0 ; token for vdChar
topbot   DB      0 ; top & bot char
lftrite  DB      0 ; left & rt char
saveCX   DW      0 ; save CX register
saveBX   DW      0 ; save BX register


;
; Declare the function as GLOBAL
; so it will be recognized by your
; C functions.  Note the underscore
; preceding the function.  This is
; a standard variable naming convention
; for MICROSOFT, TURBO and WATCOM EXPRESS
;

        PUBLIC  _boxRect


;
; Defines the start of the CODE segment
;

        .CODE


;
; Set the start of the function
;

_boxRect         PROC NEAR
;
; Save regs
;

        push    BP
        mov     BP,SP
        push    SI
        push    DI
;
; Copy structure pointed to by
; RECT * into structure declared
; in BOXRECT.ASM .DATA
;


;
; RECT * => SI
;

        mov     AX,prect    ; RECT * -> SI
        mov     SI,AX


;
; load string element pointed to by SI
; to AX register. SI inc by 2 after
; lodsw instruction
;
```

Fig. 6-7 continued.

```
        lodsw

;
; move AX to structure
;

        mov     [r.ulrow],AX

;
; get next element in structure
;

        lodsw

;
; move AX to structure
;

        mov     [r.ulcol],AX

;
; get next element in structure
;

        lodsw

;
; move AX to structure
;

        mov     [r.lrrow],AX

;
; get next element in structure
;

        lodsw

;
; move AX to structure
;

        mov     [r.lrcol],AX

;       inc     SI
;       inc     SI

;
; adjust right and bottom box values
; to conform to BOXRECT.C
;
        dec     [r.lrrow]
        dec     [r.lrcol]

;
; switch & case type decision routine
;
```

Fig. 6-7 continued.

```
;
; switch(box)
;
        mov     AX,pbox

;
; case S_S_D_D:
;
        cmp     AX,1
        je      box1

;
; case D_D_S_S:
;
        cmp     AX,2
        je      box2

;
; case D_D_D_D:
;
        cmp     AX,3
        je      box3

;
; default: /* S_S_S_S */
;

; top and bottom rows single side
        mov     topbot,196

; left and right columns single side
        mov     lftrite,179

; upper left corner
        mov     ul,218

; upper right corner
        mov     ur,191

; lower left corner
        mov     ll,192

; lower right corner
        mov     lr,217

; all done
        jmp     corner_set
```

Fig. 6-7 continued.
box1:

```
; top and bottom rows single line
        mov     topbot,196
; left and right columns double line
        mov     lftrite,186
; upper left corner
        mov     ul,214
; upper right corner
        mov     ur,183
; lower left corner
        mov     ll,211
; lower right corner
        mov     lr,189
; all done
        jmp     corner_set
box2:
; top and bottom rows double line
        mov     topbot,205
; left and right columns single line
        mov     lftrite,179
; upper left corner
        mov     ul,213
; upper right corner
        mov     ur,184
; lower left corner
        mov     ll,212
; lower right corner
        mov     lr,190
; all done
```

Fig. 6-7 continued.

```
          jmp       corner_set
box3:

; top and bottom rows double line

          mov       topbot,205

; left and right columns double line

          mov       lftrite,186

; upper left corner

          mov       ul,201

; upper right corner

          mov       ur,187

; lower left corner

          mov       ll,200

; lower right corner

          mov       lr,188

corner_set:

;
; prepare the token for top and bottom rows
;

          mov       AL,topbot
          mov       AH,pattr
          mov       token,AX
;
; set column counter
;
          mov       CX,[r.lrcol]
          sub       CX,[r.ulcol]

;
; set start column
;

          mov       BX,[r.ulcol]

tb1:
;
; save regs as they are used in _vdChar
;
          mov       saveCX,CX
          mov       saveBX,BX

;
```

Fig. 6-7 continued.

```
; Write top and bottom rows of box using
; _vdChar.  _vdChar must be called using
; standard C parameter passing conventions.
;
; vdChar(row,column,token)
;
        push    token           ; token
        push    BX              ; column
        push    [r.ulrow]       ; row
        call    _vdChar         ; call C function
        add     SP,6            ; adjust stack pointer

        mov     BX,saveBX       ; upper left col -> BX
        push    token           ; push token on stack
        push    BX              ; push column on stack
        push    [r.lrrow]       ; push row on stack
        call    _vdChar         ; call C function
        add     SP,6            ; adjust stack

        mov     CX,saveCX       ; counter -> CX
        mov     BX,saveBX       ; column BX
        inc     BX              ; column++
        loop    tb1             ; loop until CX is 0


;
; Write the left and right sides of
; the box
;


;
; token = mkAttr(lftrite,attr)
;
        mov     AL,lftrite
        mov     AH,pattr
        mov     token,AX


;
; set column counter
;
        mov     CX,[r.lrrow]
        sub     CX,[r.ulrow]


;
; set column start
;
        mov     BX,[r.ulrow]

tb2:
;
; save CX and BX as they are used in _vdChar
;
        mov     saveCX,CX
        mov     saveBX,BX


;
; write left side of box
; vdChar(row,column,token)
;
```

Fig. 6-7 continued.

```
            push    token           ; token -> stack
            push    [r.ulcol]       ; left side col -> stack
            push    BX              ; row -> stack
            call    _vdChar         ; call C function
            add     SP,6            ; adjust stack

;
; restore column
;

            mov     BX,saveBX

;
; write left side of box
; vdChar(row,column,token)
;

            push    token           ; token -> stack
            push    [r.lrcol]       ; right side col -> stack
            push    BX              ; row -> stack
            call    _vdChar         ; call C function
            add     SP,6            ; adjust stack

            mov     CX,saveCX
            mov     BX,saveBX
            inc     BX
            loop    tb2

;
; write upper left corner
;

            mov     AX,token        ; attr -> AH
            mov     AL,ul           ; up left char -> AL
            push    AX              ; token -> stack
            push    [r.ulcol]       ; upper left col
            push    [r.ulrow]       ; upper left row
            call    _vdChar         ; call C function
            add     SP,6            ; adjuct stack

;
; write lower left corner
;

            mov     AX,token        ; attr -> AH
            mov     AL,ll           ; lower left char -> AL
            push    AX              ; token -> stack
            push    [r.ulcol]       ; lower left col
            push    [r.lrrow]       ; lower left row
            call    _vdChar         ; call C function
            add     SP,6            ; adjust stack

;
; write upper right corner
;

            mov     AX,token        ; attr -> AL
```

```
        mov     AL,ur       ; upper right char -> AL
        push    AX          ; token -> stack
        push    [r.lrcol]   ; upper right col
        push    [r.ulrow]   ; upper right row
        call    _vdChar     ; call C function
        add     SP,6        ; adjust stack

;
; write lower right corner
;

        mov     AX,token    ; attr -> AH
        mov     AL,lr       ; lower right char -> AL
        push    AX          ; token -> stack
        push    [r.lrcol]   ; lower right col
        push    [r.lrrow]   ; lower right row
        call    _vdChar     ; call C function
        add     SP,6        ; adjust stack

;
; restore regs
;

        pop     DI
        pop     SI
        pop     BP

;
; return to caller
;

        ret

;
; end of function
;

_boxRect        ENDP

;
; end of assembly
;

        END

;
; end of source
;**************
```

Fig. 6-7 ends.

Fig. 6-8. The source code to TESTBOX1.C.

```
/*******************
 * Source Code Start
 *
 * File Name:   TESTBOX1.C
 *
```

```
 * Description: Demonstration program for
 *              boxRect,setRect,scrnClr
 */

/*
 * Include files
 */

#include <stdio.h>
#include <tproto.h>

/*
 * global buffer
 */

RECT *R1, *R2, *R3, *R4;

void main(void);

void
main()
{
int attr1, attr2, attr3, attr4;

/* Initialize TAB video structure */
vidInit();

/* Clear the screen and move    */
/* cursor to row 0 column 0     */
scrnClr();

/* Set attributes for all 4 boxes */
attr1 = mkAttr(WHITE,RED,OFF_INTENSITY,OFF_BLINK);
attr2 = mkAttr(WHITE,BLUE,OFF_INTENSITY,OFF_BLINK);
attr3 = mkAttr(WHITE,GREEN,OFF_INTENSITY,OFF_BLINK);
attr4 = mkAttr(WHITE,MAGENTA,OFF_INTENSITY,OFF_BLINK);

/* Prep rectangle structures &  */
/* pointers                     */
R1 = setRect(R1,0,0,10,40);
R2 = setRect(R2,0,41,10,79);
R3 = setRect(R3,11,0,20,40);
R4 = setRect(R4,11,41,20,79);

/* Draw 4 rectangular boxes using */
/* all four border style types    */
boxRect(R1,S_S_S_S,attr1);
boxRect(R2,S_S_D_D,attr2);
boxRect(R3,D_D_S_S,attr3);
boxRect(R4,D_D_D_D,attr4);

}

/*
 * End of source
 *****************/
```

Fig. 6-8 ends.

TESTBOX1 provides a fine starting point for testing rectangle functions. The next function added to the TAB library is clrRect(...). This function clears the rectangle described by the structure pointed to by RECT *. Note that all rectangle functions receive a pointer to a RECT structure. This permits you to operate on various rectangular screen segments with ease. FIGURE 6-9 shows the source code to CLRRECT.C.

Now let's test clrRect(...) with TESTBOX2. Note that the structure of TESTBOX2 has changed in order to prepare for the testing of other rectangle functions. This will become clearer in TESTBOX3.C. FIGURE 6-10 presents the source code to TESTBOX2.C.

Fig. 6-9. The source code to CLRRECT.C.

```
/********************
 * Source Code Start
 *
 * File Name:    CLRRECT.C
 *
 * Synopsis:     clrRect(R)
 *
 * RECT *R       pointer to RECT structure
 *
 * Description: Clears the rectangle
 *              described by the structure
 *              which the RECT * is pointing
 *              to.  The foreground is white
 *              and the background is black.
 *
 *              Note that vidInit() must be
 *              called along with setRect(...)
 *              before this function will work.
 *
 * Returns:      Nothing.
 */

/*
 * Include files
 */

#include <tproto.h>

/*
 * function clrRect
 */

void
clrRect(R)
RECT *R;
{
register int row;
register int column;
int row_stop, col_stop;
int ch, token, attr;

/* Space needed for clear            */
```

```
ch = aSPC;

/* set attribute to WHITE foreground */
/* and BLACK background - Intensity */
/* off and blink off              */
attr = mkAttr(WHITE,BLACK,OFF_INTENSITY,OFF_BLINK);

/* Make a token of ch and attr    */
token = mkToken(ch,attr);

/* Set loop conditions using  passed */
/* RECT *                      */
row_stop = R->lr_row;
col_stop = R->lr_col;

/* Go row by row                  */
for(row=R->ul_row; row<row_stop; row++)

        /* and column by column          */
        for(column=R->ul_col; column<col_stop; column++)

                /* put token to screen         */
                vdChar(row,column,token);

}

/*
 * End of source
 ***************/
```

Fig. 6-9 ends.

Fig. 6-10. The source code to TESTBOX2.C.

```
/*******************
 * Source Code Start
 *
 * File Name:    TESTBOX2.C
 *
 * Description: Demonstration program for
 *              boxRect,setRect,clrRect
 */

/*
 * Include files
 */

#include <stdio.h>
#include <tproto.h>


/*
 * global buffer
 */

RECT *R1, *R2, *R3, *R4;
/*
```

Fig. 6-10 continued.

```
 * Function prototypes
 */

void main(void);
void dot_screen(void);
void do_box(RECT *,int,int);

/*
 * Name:         dot_screen
 *
 * Description:  Fill the screen with dots
 *
 */

void
dot_screen()
{
int row, column, token, attr;

/* create '.' attribute */
attr = mkAttr(WHITE,BLACK,OFF_INTENSITY,OFF_BLINK);

/* create ('.',attr) token */
token = mkToken('.',attr);

/*
/* fill row                 */
for(row=0; row<25; row++)

        /* Fill column          */
        for(column=0; column<80; column++)

                /* write ','            */
                vdChar(row,column,token);
}

/*
 * Function:    do_box
 *
 * Description: clear screen rectangle
 *             and draw box over
 *             rectangular screen segment
 */

void
do_box(R,box,attr)
RECT *R;
int box;
int attr;
{
/* clear the retangle described */
/* by structure pointed to by R */
clrRect(R);

/* Draw box around rectangle     */
/* descrivec by structure        */
/* pointed to by R               */
```

Fig. 6-10 continued.

```
boxRect(R,box,attr);
}

/*
 * Name:      main
 *
 */

void
main()
{
int attr1, attr2, attr3, attr4;
int row, column;

/* Initialize TAB video structure */
vidInit();

/* save current cursor location */
sCloc();

/* save the current screen */
saveScrn();

/* Turn cursor off */
offCur();

/* Fill the screen with '.' */
dot_screen();

/* Set attributes for all 4 boxes */
attr1 = mkAttr(WHITE,RED,OFF_INTENSITY,OFF_BLINK);
attr2 = mkAttr(WHITE,BLUE,OFF_INTENSITY,OFF_BLINK);
attr3 = mkAttr(WHITE,GREEN,OFF_INTENSITY,OFF_BLINK);
attr4 = mkAttr(WHITE,MAGENTA,OFF_INTENSITY,OFF_BLINK);

/* Prep rectangle structures &    */
/* pointers                       */
R1 = setRect(R1,0,0,10,40);
R2 = setRect(R2,0,41,10,79);
R3 = setRect(R3,11,0,20,40);
R4 = setRect(R4,11,41,20,79);

/* Erase screen rectangle and     */
/* Draw 4 rectangular boxes using */
do_box(R1,S_S_S_S,attr1);
do_box(R2,S_S_D_D,attr2);
do_box(R3,D_D_S_S,attr3);
do_box(R4,D_D_D_D,attr4);

/* wait for key stroke            */
gtKey();

/* restore the previously save screen */
restScrn();

/* restore previously save cursor location */
rCloc();
```

```
/* Turn cursor on */
onCur();
}

/*
 * End of source
 ****************/
```

Fig. 6-10 ends.

OVERLAPPING RECTANGLES

The functions saveRect(...) and restRect(...) permit you to have overlapping rectangles on the screen. TESTBOX3.C has been modified once again. The program now demonstrated how to pop up four rectangles in an overlapping function. FIGURE 6-11 presents the source code to SAVERECT.C, FIG. 6-12 presents the source code to RESTRECT.C, and FIG. 6-13 presents the source code to FILLRECT.C.

Fig. 6-11. The source code to SAVERECT.C.

```
/********************
 * Source Code Start
 *
 * File Name:    SAVERECT.C
 *
 * Synopsis:     saveRect(R)
 *
 * RECT *R       pointer to RECT structure
 *
 * Description: Saves the rectangle
 *              described by the structure
 *              which the RECT * is pointing
 *              to. The display RAM holding
 *              the rectangular image is
 *              saved to memory.
 *
 *              Note that vidInit() must be
 *              called along with setRect(...)
 *              before this function will work.
 *
 * Returns:      Nothing.
 */

/*
 * Include files
 */

#include <tproto.h>

/*
 * Function saveRect
 *
 */
```

```
void
saveRect(R)
RECT *R;
{
unsigned int *iptr;
register int row;
register int column;

/* Set pointer to previously opened */
/* malloc which is large enough to  */
/* to hold screen image of rect.    */
/* The malloc was opened in setRect */
iptr = (unsigned int *)R->image;

/* Save tokens by row               */
for(row=R->ul_row; row<=R->lr_row; row++)

        /* Save tokens by column        */
        for(column=R->ul_col; column<=R->lr_col; column++)

                /* Save token by row, column */
                *iptr++ = vrdChar(row,column);
}

/*
 * End of source
 **************/
```

Fig. 6-11 ends.

Fig. 6-12. The source code to RESTRECT.C.

```
/********************
 * Source Code Start
 *
 * File Name:    RESTRECT.C
 *
 * Synopsis:     restRect(R)
 *
 * RECT *R       pointer to RECT structure
 *
 * Description: Restores the rectangle
 *              described by the structure
 *              which the RECT * is pointing
 *              to.  saveRect(...) MUST have
 *              been called before restRect(...)
 *
 *              Note that vidInit() must be
 *              called along with setRect(...)
 *              before this function will work.
 *
 * Returns:      Nothing.
 */

/*
 * Include files
 */
```

```
#include <tproto.h>

/*
 * Function restRect
 *
 */

void
restRect(R)
RECT *R;
{
unsigned int *iptr;
register int row;
register int column;


/* Set pointer to previously opened */
/* malloc which is large enough to   */
/* to hold screen image of rect.     */
/* The malloc was opened in setRect  */
iptr =(unsigned int *) R->image;

/* Save tokens by row               */
for(row=R->ul_row; row<=R->lr_row; row++)

        /* Save tokens by column        */
        for(column=R->ul_col; column<=R->lr_col; column++)

                /* Save token by row, column  */
                vdChar(row,column,*iptr++);
}

/*
 * End of source
 **************/
```

Fig. 6-12 ends.

Fig. 6-13. The source code to FILLRECT.C.

```
/********************
 * Source Code Start
 *
 * File Name:    FILLRECT.C
 *
 * Synopsis:     fillRect(R, token)
 *
 * RECT *R       pointer to RECT structure
 *
 * int token     token holds fill character
 *               and attribute
 *
 * Description: Fills the rectangle
 *               described by the structure
 *               which the RECT * is pointing
 *               to.  The rectangle is filled
 *               with token.
```

```
*
*               Note that vidInit() must be
*               called along with setRect(...)
*               before this function will work.
*
* Returns:      Nothing.
*/

/*
 * Include files
 */

#include <tproto.h>


void
fillRect(R,token)
RECT *R;
int token;
{
register int row;
register int column;
int row_stop, col_stop;

/* Set loop conditions using  passed */
/* RECT *                            */
row_stop = R->lr_row;
col_stop = R->lr_col;

/* Go row by row                      */
for(row=R->ul_row; row<row_stop; row++)

        /* and column by column       */
        for(column=R->ul_col; column<col_stop; column++

                /* put token to screen         */
                vdChar(row,column,token);

}

/*
 * End of source
 ***************/
```

Fig. 6-13 ends.

Please note that when you wish to have rectangles overlap they must be handled as a *stack*. By that I mean, the last rectangle drawn to the screen will be the first rectangle removed from the screen. TESTBOX3 uses four rectangles. They are drawn to the screen with R1 first, R2 second, R3 third, and R4 fourth. After the rectangles are drawn, each keystroke will remove a rectangle. The first keystroke will remove R4, then R3, followed by R2 and, last but not least, R1.

The function fillRect(...) has also been added so the background of the rectangle will be the same as the background of the border. Once TESTBOX3 is completed, let's go back to the BAR demonstration program to finally put the drop-down window interface together. The source code to TESTBOX3.C is presented in FIG. 6-14.

Fig. 6-14. The source code to TESTBOX3.C.

```
/********************
 * Source Code Start
 *
 * File Name:    TESTBOX3.C
 *
 * Description: Demonstration program for
 *              boxRect,setRect,fillRect
 *              restRect,saveRect
 */

/*
 * Include files
 */

#include <stdio.h>
#include <tproto.h>


/*
 * global buffer
 */

RECT *R1, *R2, *R3, *R4;

/*
 * Function prototypes
 */

void main(void);
void dot_screen(void);
void do_box(RECT *,int,int);

/*
 * Name:        dot_screen
 *
 * Description: Fill the screen with dots
 *
 */

void
dot_screen()
{
int row, column, token, attr;

/* create '.' attribute */
attr = mkAttr(WHITE,BLACK,OFF_INTENSITY,OFF_BLINK);

/* create ('.',attr) token */
token = mkToken('.',attr);
```

Fig. 6-14 continued.

```
/*
/* fill row                    */
for(row=0; row<25; row++)

        /* Fill column              */
        for(column=0; column<80; column++)

                /* write ','               */
                vdChar(row,column,token);
}

/*
 * Function:    do_box
 *
 * Description: clear screen rectangle
 *              and draw box over
 *              rectangular screen segment
 */

void
do_box(R,box,attr)
RECT *R;
int box;
int attr;
{
int token;

/* save rectangle screen image */
/* to memory                   */
saveRect(R);
/* make (' ',attr) token        */
token = mkToken(aSPC,attr);

/* Fill the retangle described  */
/* by structure pointed to by R */
/* with token                   */
fillRect(R,token);

/* Draw box around rectangle    */
/* descrivec by structure       */
/* pointed to by R              */
boxRect(R,box,attr);
}

/*
 * Name:    main
 *
 */

void
main()
{
int attr1, attr2, attr3, attr4;
int row, column;

/* Initialize TAB video structure */
vidInit();
```

Fig. 6-14 continued.

```
/* save current cursor location */
sCloc();

/* save the current screen */
saveScrn();

/* Turn cursor off */
offCur();

/* Fill the screen with '.' */
dot_screen();

/* Set attributes for all 4 boxes */
attr1 = mkAttr(WHITE,RED,OFF_INTENSITY,OFF_BLINK);
attr2 = mkAttr(WHITE,BLUE,OFF_INTENSITY,OFF_BLINK);
attr3 = mkAttr(WHITE,GREEN,OFF_INTENSITY,OFF_BLINK);
attr4 = mkAttr(WHITE,MAGENTA,OFF_INTENSITY,OFF_BLINK);

/* Prep rectangle structures &    */
/* pointers                       */
R1 = setRect(R1,0,0,10,40);
R2 = setRect(R2,4,12,14,52);
R3 = setRect(R3,8,24,18,64);
R4 = setRect(R4,12,36,22,76);

/* Erase screen rectangle and     */
/* Draw 4 rectangular boxes using */
do_box(R1,S_S_S_S,attr1);
do_box(R2,S_S_D_D,attr2);
do_box(R3,D_D_S_S,attr3);
do_box(R4,D_D_D_D,attr4);

/* wait for key stroke            */
gtKey();

/* restore screen image of box 4  */
restRect(R4);

/* wait for key stroke            */
gtKey();

/* restore screen image of box 3  */
restRect(R3);

/* wait for key stroke            */
gtKey();

/* restore screen image of box 2  */
restRect(R2);

/* wait for key stroke            */
gtKey();

/* restore screen image of box 1  */
restRect(R1);

/* wait for key stroke            */
```

```
gtKey();

/* restore the previously save screen */
restScrn();

/* restore previously save cursor location */
rCloc();

/* Turn cursor on */
onCur();
}

/*
 * End of source
 *****************/
```

Fig. 6-14 ends.

GETTING A LIBRARY LISTING OF TAB_T2S.LIB

Our TAB library has been growing at leaps and bounds. If you are maintaining more than one library, it is important to keep track of all the functions in all your libraries. From experience, it is very easy to forget to update all the libraries you are maintaining. To get a listing of TAB_T2S.LIB simply enter the \ tc \ lib directory and type:

tlib tab_t2s,tab_t2s.1st

and then press Enter.

The file TAB_T2S.LST is now in your \ tc \ lib subdirectory. FIGURE 6-15 presents the current TAB_T2S library listing.

Fig. 6-15. The TAB_T2S.LIB library file listing.

```
Publics by module

BEEP      size = 36
  _beep

BOXRECT   size = 428
  _boxRect

CLRRECT   size = 111
  _clrRect

FILLRECT  size = 70
  _fillRect

GTCUR     size = 56
  _gtCur

GTKBFLAG  size = 47
  _gtKBflag
```

Fig. 6-15 continued.

```
GTKBSTAT    size = 21
  _gtKBstat

GTKEY       size = 37
  _gtKey

GTMODE      size = 62
  _gtMode

INPFLT      size = 275
  _inpflt

INPNUM      size = 271
  _inpnum

MKATTR      size = 23
  _mkAttr

MKTOKEN     size = 21
  _mkToken

MVCUR       size = 17
  _mvCur

OFFCUR      size = 68
  _offCur

ONCUR       size = 16
  _onCur

PROMPT      size = 215
  _prompt

PUTCHR      size = 17
  _putChr

RESTRECT    size = 77
  _restRect

SAVERECT    size = 76
  _saveRect

SAVESCRN    size = 4105
  _restScrn                        _saveScrn

SCLOC       size = 40
  _rCloc                           _sCloc

SCRNCLR     size = 97
  _scrnClr

SETRECT     size = 94
  _setRect

VDATTR      size = 50
  _vdAttr
```

```
VDCHAR      size = 66
  _vdChar

VDHORIZ     size = 58
  _vdHoriz

VDVERT      size = 56
  _vdVert

VDWRITE     size = 105
  _vdWrite

VIDINIT     size = 110
  _SCRNSEG                        _SPARKLE_FLAG
  _VID_PORT                       _crt
  _vidInit

VRDCHAR     size = 42
  _vrdChar
```

Fig. 6-15 ends.

There are currently 31 functions in your TAB library. If you have a macro assembler you can increase the speed of your programs while reducing the size by making sure that the assembly generated object modules are in your TAB library wherever possible.

Now that you've taken stock of TAB's library growth, it's time to return to the final section of Chapter 6. Here you will use the rectangle functions to create drop-down windows in the BAR demonstration programs. Note though, that Chapter 7 introduces the concept of windows, which will make window generation significantly easier.

DROP-DOWN WINDOWS USING RECTANGLES

FIGURE 6-16 presents the source code to a souped up BAR4 program. It has come a long way from BAR1.C. BAR4.C demonstrates how to:

- Highlight a menu item on Alt-D, Alt-F or Alt-Q.
- Save screen image under rectangle.
- Drop down rectangle below menu bar item.
- Fill drop-down rectangle with drop-down items.
- Keypress returns restores screen and menu bar.
- Alt-Q (Quit to DOS option) demonstrates how to pop up a window, read the keyboard and return a value to the calling function.

All in all there are many instructive routines in BAR4.C. I strongly suggest that you get a firm handle on what's happening in BAR4.C and then go on to

Chapter 7. Chapter 7 deals with window creation and there are a variety of window styles and user input methods discussed. Understanding Windows will prove easier if you understand BAR4.C.

Fig. 6-16. The source code to BAR4.C.

```
/*******************
 * Source Code Start
 *
 * File Name:    BAR4.C
 *
 * Description: Demonstration program for
 *              drop down windows called
 *              by ALT D, F, or Q key press
 *
 */

/*
 * Include files
 */

#include <stdio.h>
#include <tproto.h>

/*
 * Defines for length of strings
 */

#define DESK_LEN 6
#define FILE_LEN 6
#define QUIT_LEN 6
#define DESK     1
#define FILE     2


/*
 *  Character messages for menu bar
 */

char menu1[DESK_LEN] = " Desk ";
char menu2[FILE_LEN] = " File ";
char menu3[QUIT_LEN] = " Quit ";

/*
 * RECT * pointers to drop
 * down windows
 */

RECT *DESK_R;
RECT *FILE_R;
RECT *QUIT_R;


/*
 * Function prototypes
 */
```

Fig. 6-16 continued.

```c
void main(void);
void menu_bar(void);
void make_white(void);
void do_box(RECT *,int,int);
int pop_QUIT(int);
void drop_RECT(RECT *,int,int);
void item_DESK(int);
void item_FILE(int);

/*
 * Function:    pop_QUIT
 *
 * Description: Quit window
 * returns aTRUE on QUIT
 *         aFALSE on no QUIT
 */

int
pop_QUIT(attr)
int attr;
{
int key;

/* save screen area under drop down window */
saveRect(QUIT_R);

/* drop down window */
do_box(QUIT_R,S_S_S_S,attr);
/* Print quit messages */
vdWrite(QUIT_R->ul_row+1,QUIT_R->ul_col+2,15," QUIT WINDOW ",attr);
vdWrite(QUIT_R->ul_row+3,QUIT_R->ul_col+2,15,"Press Y to QUIT",attr);
vdWrite(QUIT_R->ul_row+4,QUIT_R->ul_col+2,15,"   to DOS    ",attr);
vdWrite(QUIT_R->ul_row+5,QUIT_R->ul_col+2,15,"Any Key to prog",attr);

/* get key press */
key = gtKey();

/* erase quit rectangle */
restRect(QUIT_R);

/* to ascii */
key &= 0x00ff;

if( (key=='y') || (key=='Y') )
        return(aTRUE);
else
        return(aFALSE);
}

/*
 * Function:    item_DESK
 *
 * Description: print items in
 * drop down DESK window
 */

void
```

Fig. 6-16 continued.

```
item_DESK(attr)
int attr;
{
vdWrite(2,DESK_R->ul_col+2,11,"Time of Day",attr);
vdWrite(3,DESK_R->ul_col+2,11,"Calendar    ",attr);
vdWrite(4,DESK_R->ul_col+2,11,"Memo Pad    ",attr);
vdWrite(5,DESK_R->ul_col+2,11,"Telephone   ",attr);
}


/*
 * Function:    item_FILE
 *
 * Description: print items in
 * drop down DESK window
 */

void
item_FILE(attr)
int attr;
{
vdWrite(2,FILE_R->ul_col+2,11,"Open File  ",attr);
vdWrite(3,FILE_R->ul_col+2,11,"Create File",attr);
vdWrite(4,FILE_R->ul_col+2,11,"Delete File",attr);
vdWrite(5,FILE_R->ul_col+2,11,"Rename File",attr);
vdWrite(6,FILE_R->ul_col+2,11,"File Attrib",attr);
vdWrite(7,FILE_R->ul_col+2,11,"File Stats ",attr);
}


/*
 * Function:    drop_DESK
 *
 * Description: drop down DESK window
 */

void
drop_RECT(R,attr,drop)
RECT *R;
int attr;
int drop;
{
/* save screen area under drop down window */
saveRect(R);

/* drop down window */
do_box(R,S_S_S_S,attr);

/* which window ? */
switch(drop)
        {
        /* DESK drop */
        case DESK:
                /* print desk item messages */
                item_DESK(attr);

                /* wait for key press */
                gtKey();
                break;
```

Fig. 6-16 continued.

```
        /* FILE drop */
        case FILE:
                /* print desk file messages */
                item_FILE(attr);

                /* wait for key press */
                gtKey();
                break;
        }

/* restore screen under dropped window */
restRect(R);
}


/*
 * Function:    do_box
 *
 * Description: clear screen rectangle
 *              and draw box over
 *              rectangular screen segment
 */

void
do_box(R,box,attr)
RECT *R;
int box;
int attr;
{
int token;

/* save rectangle screen image  */
/* to memory                     */
saveRect(R);

/* make (' ',attr) token         */
token = mkToken(aSPC,attr);

/* Fill the retangle described   */
/* by structure pointed to by R  */
/* with token                    */
fillRect(R,token);

/* Draw box around rectangle     */
/* descrivec by structure        */
/* pointed to by R               */
boxRect(R,box,attr);
}

/*
 * Name:  menu_bar
 *
 * Description: This function
 *        draws a menu bar
 *        on the top line of
 *        the screen
 */
```

Fig. 6-16 continued.

```
void
menu_bar()
{
int attr,i_attr;

/* set attribute for menu bar */
attr = mkAttr(BLACK,WHITE,OFF_INTENSITY,OFF_BLINK);

/* write menu bar to screen */
vdWrite(0,0,DESK_LEN,menu1,attr);
vdWrite(0,DESK_LEN,FILE_LEN,menu2,attr);
vdWrite(0,70,QUIT_LEN,menu3,attr);

/* draw line below menu */
vdHoriz(1,0,80,attr);
}

/*
 * Name:  make_white
 *
 * Description: This function
 *          erases the existing
 *          screen and turns the
 *          background white
 */

void
make_white()
{
int attr,token,row,column;

/* set attribute for screen */
attr = mkAttr(BLACK,WHITE,OFF_INTENSITY,OFF_BLINK);

/* create blank token with 'attr' backgroung */
token = mkToken(' ',attr);

/* replace existing screen with blank token */
for(row=0; row<25; row++)
        for(column=0; column<80; column++)
                vdChar(row,column,token);
}

/*
 * Name: main
 */

void
main()
{
int i_attr,item,key,quit_flag;

/* initialize TAB library video routines */
vidInit();

/* save current cursor location */
sCloc();
```

Fig. 6-16 continued.

```
/* save the current screen */
saveScrn();

/* Turn cursor off */
offCur();

/* set attribute for item highlight */
i_attr = mkAttr(WHITE,BLUE,ON_INTENSITY,OFF_BLINK);

/* prep structure for DESK drop down window */
DESK_R = setRect(DESK_R,1,0,7,0+15);

/* prep structure for DESK drop down window */
FILE_R = setRect(FILE_R,1,DESK_LEN,9,DESK_LEN+15);

/* prep structure for QUIT drop down window */
QUIT_R = setRect(QUIT_R,10,30,17,49);


/* erase screen and make background white */
make_white();

/* draw menu bar */
menu_bar();

/* set item = 0 for no menu item selected */
item = 0;

/* set quit_flag to NO EXIT loop */
quit_flag = aFALSE;

/* main keyboard loop */
do
        {
        /* clear all menu highlights  */
        menu_bar();
/* Examine item for highlight */
switch(item)
        {
        /* ALT_D pressed -> highlight 'Desk' */
        case 1:
                vdAttr(0,0,DESK_LEN,i_attr);
                break;
        /* ALT_F pressed -> highlight 'File' */
        case 2:
                vdAttr(0,DESK_LEN,FILE_LEN,i_attr);
                break;
        }

/* open drop down window */
switch(item)
        {
        /* ALT_D pressed -> highlight 'Desk' */
        case 1:
                drop_RECT(DESK_R,i_attr,DESK);
                menu_bar();
```

```
                                break;
                /* ALT_F pressed -> highlight 'File' */
                case 2:
                        drop_RECT(FILE_R,i_attr,FILE);
                        menu_bar();
                        break;
                }

        /* get key press and evaluate */
        key = gtKey();
        switch(key)
                {
                /* ALT D key press              */
                /* set flag to highlight 'Desk' */
                case ALT_D:
                        item = 1;
                        break;

                /* ALT F key press              */
                /* set flag to highlight 'File' */
                case ALT_F:
                        item = 2;
                        break;

                /* ALT Q key press              */
                /* pop up QUIT WINDOW           */
                case ALT_Q:
                        quit_flag = pop_QUIT(i_attr);
                        break;

                /* Any other key                */
                default:
                        /* clear highlights on menu  */
                        item = 0;

                        /* invalid key press         */
                        beep();
                        break;
                }

        } while(!quit_flag);

/* restore the previously save screen */
restScrn();

/* restore previously save cursor location */
rCloc();

/* Turn cursor on */
onCur();
}

/*
 * End of Source
 ***************/
```

Fig. 6-16 ends.

SUMMARY

Chapter 6 introduced the concept of rectangles along with a variety of routines. Rectangles may be drawn with borders and be filled with characters. The process of drawing a rectangle to the screen is summarized here:

1. Declare pointer to RECT structure.
2. Use setRect(...) to fill structure with Data.
3. Use saveRect(...) to save screen image to memory in defined rectangle.
4. Fill rectangle using fillRect(...).
5. Put border around rectangle using boxRect(...).
6. Operate on rectangular screen area.
7. Restore original screen image from memory when your work is done.

On to Chapter 7 and windows.

7

Windows

For purposes of this text, a Window is defined as a rectangular region of the screen, surrounded by a border and capable of being operated on with screen handling functions that use a local coordinate system. There, now that the definition for a Window has been presented, let's take this definition and explore it in depth.

By this time you should be thoroughly familiar with the ins and outs of screen rectangles. The TAB library functions permit you to save a rectangular screen region to memory, restore that previously saved screen region from memory to the screen, color a rectangular screen image, and draw a border around the screen rectangle. To the end user a screen rectangle surrounded by a line border *is* a Window. To the programmer, though, a Window has a very special property. This special property allows the rectangular screen region to be written to using a set of screen handling functions that use a local coordinate system.

For purposes of this text, two coordinate systems are needed. They are the global coordinate system and local coordinate system. You are already familiar with the global coordinate system, although it has not been named such prior in the text. The *global coordinate system* refers to the standard PC screen text row and text column format. Row 0, column 0, refers to a screen character location in the upper left hand of the screen. The lower right hand of the screen would be described using a row of 24 and a column of 79. The standard 80-column text screen uses 80-column and 25 rows with the row and column numbering system starting at 0. You are no doubt familiar with this system.

A *local coordinate system* means that row 0, column 0 is no longer at the upper left hand section of the screen. For purposes of this text, the local coordinate system refers to a specified Window. The local coordinate system of a Window dictates that row 0, column 0 refers to the upper left hand corner character of the Window border.

There are many advantages in the use of a local coordinate system. First, you can consider the Window a mini-screen. This means that it is much easier to visualize the row and column coordinates of a screen write to a window than to a rectangle. For example, if you wanted to write a string to the row below the top border and the column to the right of the left border you might address the string write as described in FIG. 7-1.

Fig. 7-1. Writing to a rectangle.

```
.
RECT *R;
.
vdWrite(R->ul_row+1,R->ul_col+1,12,"Hello World!",...);
.
.
.
```

Parameter 1 of the vdWrite in FIG. 7-1 is $R \rightarrow ul\_row + 1$. This is a somewhat cumbersome way to address the upper left corner of the nonborder section of the window. However, what if you defined a Window structure and then created a call similar to vdWrite(...), except that the new call would permit you to pass a pointer to a window structure? Then you could address the nonborder upper left section of the window as row 1, column 1. This new call is briefly described in FIG. 7-2.

Fig. 7-2. A description of wvdWrite(...).

```
/* (W)indow (v)ideo (d)direct (W)rite              */
/* wvdWrite(WIND *,row, col, length, string, attribute */
.
.
WIND *W;
.
.
wvdWrite(W,1,1,12,"Hello World!",...);
.
.
```

As you might have guessed by now, the window screen write works in a Window in the same fashion as the screen writes do on a screen. The only difference is that the screen writes, such as vdWrite(...), use the global coordinate system of the screen and the window writes use the local coordinate system of the Window. For convenience, the Window screen write functions' names are identical to the regular screen handling routines with the exception that the

Window call begins with 'w'. For example the string screen write TAB library function is named vdWrite(...) and the Window string write is called wvdWrite(...).

The parameters for the screen string write and the Window string write are identical with the exception of the first parameter for the wvdWrite(WIND *,...) being a pointer to a window structure.

Following this presentation one step further, it now becomes clear it is very easy to put quite a few windows on the screen at once and write to those windows with ease. The wvdWrite(...) call may be directed to a new window by simply changing the WIND * to the appropriate window. And the Window routines are plenty fast.

Before the source listings to the Window routines are shown, it makes sense to look at the Window creation sequence shown in TABLE 7-1.

Table 7-1. The Window Creation Sequence.

Step	Description	Code
1	Declare pointer to Window structure	WIND *W_name
2	Allocate memory for Window structure and memory	setWind(...)
3	Select Window attribute	setAttr(...)
4	Select Window border	setBord(...)
5	Select Window title	setTitle(...)
6	Display Window for first time	strWind(...)
7	Write text to displayed Window	wvdWrite(...)
8	Program tasks come here	
9	Remove Window from screen	remvWind(...)
10	Additional program tasks come here	
11	Pop-up previously created Window	dispWind(...)
12	Program tasks come here	

Now that the Window creation sequence has been outlined let's go step-by-step and discuss each item on the list. The source code for the functions will be presented when appropriate and a final test and demonstration program will put all the elements of a simple Window program together.

The first item on the Window creation sequence list dictates that the programmer should declare a pointer to a WIND structure in the program. The WIND structure is located in TSTRUCT.H, and is shown in FIG. 7-3.

The first few elements of the WIND structure presented in FIG. 7-3 are very similar to the RECT structure. The upper left and lower right corners of the Window location are held in ul_row, ul_col, lr_row, and lr_col. The size of the Window image is held in INT img_size and pointers to memory containing the Window image and the screen image under the Window follow.

The INT box_type holds an integer value that is one of the four defined choices in the program. TABLE 7-2 is a reminder of the four predefined Window border types.

Fig. 7-3. The WIND structure.

```
typedef struct {
        int ul_row;                     /* upper left row      */
        int ul_col:                     /* upper left column   */
        int lr_row;                     /* lower right row      */
        int lr_col;                     /* lower right column   */
        unsigned int img_size;          /* window img size      */
        unsigned int far *img_ptr;      /* pointer scrn image  */
        unsigned int far *wind_ptr;     /* pointer scrn image  */
        int box_type;                   /* border selection    */
        int attr;                       /* window attribute    */
        int visible;                    /* window on           */
        int top_offset;                 /* col offset title    */
        int top_length;                 /* length title str    */
        int show_top;                   /* display title       */
        int bot_offset;                 /* col offset title    */
        int bot_length;                 /* length title str    */
        int show_bot;                   /* display title       */
        char *t_title;                  /* ptr to t title str */
        char *b_title;                  /* ptr to b title str */
} WIND;
```

Table 7-2. Predefined Window Border Types.

	Borders			
Top	Bottom	Left	Right	Number
S	S	S	S	0
S	S	D	D	1
D	D	S	S	2
D	D	D	D	3

*S means single line
*D means double line

The INT attr holds the default attribute for the Window text and border. Windows with multiple attributes can be managed with ease, though. This will be demonstrated in the program MENU.C which is presented at the end of Chapter 7.

The INT visible is a flag that tells certain Window functions whether the window is visible or not. This is an important feature as it prevents accidentally saving the existing window image into the allocated memory, which should hold the original screen image under the Window.

The int top_offset and bot_offset hold the number of columns from the left of the Window to have the Window title centered. Not that there are no routines in the TAB library to display a title at the bottom of the Window. Once

216

you've gotten your feet wet with the TAB library, figuring out how to add a bottom title to the Window border is a good assignment to do.

The character pointer t_title points to memory where the character string for the Window title is held.

The first condition of the window creation sequence has been satisfied. The WIND structure has been presented and explained. FIGURE 7-4 takes care of the second step in the Window creation sequence by presenting the source code listing to SETWIND.C.

Fig. 7-4. The source code listing for SETWIND.C.

```
/*******************
 * Source Code Start
 *
 * File Name:    SETWIND.C
 *
 * Synopsis:     setWind(W,ul_row,ul_col,lr_row,lr_col)
 *
 * WIND *W       Pointer to window structure
 *
 * int ul_row    window upper left row
 *
 * int ul_col    window upper left column
 *
 * int lr_row    window lower right row
 *
 * int lr_col    window lower right col
 *
 * Description: Sets the window upper
 *              left and lower right
 *              boundaries. Memory is
 *              allocated to hold screen
 *              image for window and
 *              screen image under window.
 *
 *
 * Returns:      Nothing
 */

/*
 * Include Files
 */

#include <alloc.h>
#include <tproto.h>

#define W_SIZE sizeof(WIND)


WIND
*setWind(R,ul_row,ul_col,lr_row,lr_col)
int ul_row,ul_col;
int lr_row,lr_col;
WIND *R;
{
```

217

```
/* allocate memory for window structure */
R = (WIND *)calloc(W_SIZE,sizeof(char));

/* set upper left row in structure */
R->ul_row = ul_row;

/* set upper left col in structure */
R->ul_col = ul_col;

/* set lower rt. row in structure  */
R->lr_row = lr_row;

/* set lower rt. col in structure  */
R->lr_col = lr_col;

/* calculate the memory required    */
/* to hold screen image             */
R->img_size = sizeImg(R);

/* allocate memory for scrn image   */
R->img_ptr = (unsigned int *)calloc(R->img_size,sizeof(int));

/* allocate mem. for window image   */
R->wind_ptr = (unsigned int *)calloc(R->img_size,sizeof(int));

/* window not visible               */
R->visible=aFALSE;

/* default border type -> single    */
/* line                             */
R->box_type=0;

/* set defaut attribute to WHITE    */
/* foreground and black background */
R->attr=NORMAL;

/* NULL pointers for title          */
R->t_title=0;
R->b_title=0;

/* window top name and bottom name */
/* set for no display               */
R->show_top=aFALSE;
R->show_bot=aFALSE;

/* return pointer to window         */
return(R);
}

/*
 * End of source code
 ********************/
```

Fig. 7-4 ends.

Note that SETWIND.C calls function sizeImg(...) which returns the size of the Window image. FIGURE 7-5 presents the source listing to SIZEIMG.C.

Fig. 7-5. The source code listing to SIZEIMG.C.

```
/********************
 * Source Code Start
 *
 * File Name:    SIZEIMG.C
 *
 * Synopsis:     size = sizeImg(W)
 *
 * WIND *W       Pointer to window structure
 *
 * unsigned int size      number of tokens
 *                        required to hold
 *                        screen image
 *
 * Description: Calculates the number of
 *              memory tokens required to
 *              hold the window image and
 *              the screen image under the
 *              window
 *
 * Returns:     Nothing
 */

/*
 * Include Files
 */

#include <alloc.h>
#include <tproto.h>

/*
 * Function sizeImg
 */

unsigned int
sizeImg(R)
WIND *R;
{
int height,width,size;

/* calculate height of window */
height = R->lr_row - R->ul_row;

/* calculate width of window  */
width = R->lr_col-R->ul_col;

/* add 1 for ultra safety     */
++height;
++width;

/* rows * columns = size      */
size = height * width;
```

```
/* return the size of window  */
/* image                      */
return( size );
}

/*
 * End of source code
 *********************/
```

Fig. 7-5 ends.

The third step in the TAB Window creation sequence calls for the pro-grammer to set the value of the Window attribute, as shown in FIG. 7-6.

Fig. 7-6. The source code listing for SETATTR.C.

```
/********************
 * Source Code Start
 *
 * File Name:   SETATTR.C
 *
 * Synopsis:    setAttr(W,attr)
 *
 * WIND *W      Pointer to window structure
 *
 * int attr     window attribute
 *
 * Description: Sets the window attribute
 *              for the WIND structure
 *
 * Returns:     Nothing
 */

/*
 * Include Files
 */

#include <tstruct.h>

/*
 * Function setAttr
 */

void
setAttr(R,attr)
WIND *R;
int attr;
{
/* set WIND attribute */
/* structure element  */
R->attr = attr;
}

/*
 * End of source code
 *********************/
```

The next step is to set the Window border type. This is done by using set-Bord(...). The listing to SETBORD.C is shown in FIG. 7-7.

Fig. 7-7. The source code listing to SETBORD.C.

```
/********************
 * Source Code Start
 *
 * File Name:    SETBORD.C
 *
 * Synopsis:     setBord(W,box)
 *
 * int box       sets one of 4
 *               predefined border
 *               types
 *
 *               S -> single line
 *               D -> double line
 *               T -> top line
 *               B -> bottom line
 *               L -> left line
 *               R -> right line
 *
 *               #   T B L R
 *               -   - - - -
 *               0 = S_S_S_S
 *               1 = S_S_D_D
 *               2 = D_D_S_S
 *               3 = D_D_D_D
 *
 * Description: Sets window border
 *              according to the four
 *              predefined patterns
 *
 * Returns:      Nothing
 */

/*
 * Include Files
 */

#include <tproto.h>

/*
 * Function setBord
 */

void
setBord(R,type)
WIND *R;
int type;
{
/* set border value in */
/* WIND structure      */
R->box_type = type;
}
```

```
/*
 * End of source code
 ********************/
```

Fig. 7-7 ends.

Once the Window border has been set, the top Window title must be prepared. This is accomplished with setTitle(...). The listing for SETTITLE.C is shown in FIG. 7-8.

Fig. 7-8. The source code listing to SETTITLE.C.

```
/********************
 * Source Code Start
 *
 * File Name:    SETTITLE.C
 *
 * Synopsis:    setTitle(W,name)
 *
 * WIND *W      Pointer to window structure
 *
 * char *name   Points to character string
 *              of widow name
 *
 * Description: Sets the window name.
 *              This name is centered
 *              on the TOP BORDER line.
 *
 * Returns:     Nothing
 */

/*
 * Include Files
 */

#include <string.h>
#include <stdlib.h>
#include <tproto.h>
#include <mem.h>

void
setTitle(R,top)
WIND *R;
char *top;
{
/* length of window name string */
/* placed in WIND structure      */
R->top_length = strlen(top);

/* Offset from left side of      */
/* window to center name         */
R->top_offset = ( (R->lr_col-R->ul_col) - R->top_length )/2;
R->top_offset += 1;

/* Allocate memory and set       */
/* pointer to memory             */
R->t_title = (char *)malloc(R->top_length+1);
```

```
/* NULL allocated memory      */
memset(R->t_title,'\0',R->top_length+1);

/* Copy name string to newly   */
/* allocated memory            */
strcpy(R->t_title,top);

/* tell structure that window  */
/* name exists                 */
R->show_top=aTRUE;
}

/*
 * End of source code
 ********************/
```

Fig. 7-8 ends.

Before the source code to strtWind(...), remvWind(...) and dispWind(...) is discussed, it makes sense to present the source code of four TAB library internal routines that are required by the previously mentioned Window routines. These routines are **rdImg(...)**, **rdWind(...)**, **wrImg(...)**, **wrWind(...)**, and **wrBox(...)**. The source code listings for these functions are presented in FIGS. 7-9 through 7-13, respectively.

Fig. 7-9. The source code listing to RDIMG.C.

```
/********************
 * Source Code Start
 *
 * File Name:    RDIMG.C
 *
 * Synopsis:     rdImg(W)
 *
 * WIND *W       Pointer to window structure
 *
 * Description: Transfers a rectangular
 *              region of the screen which
 *              currently shows where the
 *              window will be displayed to
 *              a buffer and blanks the
 *              screen rectangle where the
 *              window will be displayed.
 *              window and restores
 *              previously saved window
 *              image.
 *
 * Returns:      Nothing
 */
```

```
/*
 * Include Files
 */

#include <stdio.h>
#include <dos.h>
#include <tproto.h>

/*
 * Function rdImg
 */

void
rdImg(R)
WIND *R;
{
register int row,column;
unsigned int *buf_ptr;

/* set pointer to memory which had */
/* previously been allocated       */
/* during setWind(...)             */
buf_ptr = (unsigned int *)R->img_ptr;

/* save screen image by row        */
for(row=R->ul_row; row<=R->lr_row; row++)

    /* save token by column        */
    for( column=R->ul_col; column<=R->lr_col; column++)

        /* screen token to buffer  */
        *buf_ptr++ = vrdChar(row,column);
}

/*
 * End of source
 ***************/
```

Fig. 7-9 ends.

Fig. 7-10. The source code listing to RDWIND.C.

```
/********************
 * Source Code Start
 *
 * File Name:    RDWIND.C
 *
 * Synopsis:     rdWind(W)
 *
 * WIND *W       Pointer to window structure
 *
 * Description: Transfers window image to
 *              memory.
 *
 * Returns:      Nothing
 */
```

```c
/*
 * Include Files
 */

#include <stdio.h>
#include <dos.h>
#include <tproto.h>

void
rdWind(R)
WIND *R;
{
register int row,column;
unsigned int *buf_ptr;

/* set pointer to allocated memory */
buf_ptr = (unsigned int *)R->wind_ptr;

/* get window image by row        */
for(row=R->ul_row; row<=R->lr_row; row++)

    /* get window token by column   */
    for( column=R->ul_col; column<=R->lr_col; column++)

       /* screen token to buffer     */
       *buf_ptr++ = vrdChar(row,column);
}

/*
 * End of source
 ***************/
```

Fig. 7-10 ends.

Fig. 7-11. The source code listing to WRIMG.C.

```c
/********************
 * Source Code Start
 *
 * File Name:   WRIMG.C
 *
 * Synopsis:    wrImg(W)
 *
 * WIND *W      Pointer to window structure
 *
 * Description: Transfers previously saved
 *              window from memory to the
 *              appropriate portion of the
 *              screen.
 *
 * Returns:     Nothing
 */

/*
 * Include Files
 */

#include <stdio.h>
```

```
#include <dos.h>
#include <tproto.h>

/*
 * Funciton wrImg
 */

void
wrImg(R)
WIND *R;
{
register int row,column;
unsigned int *img_ptr;

/* set pointer to memory which had */
/* previously been allocated       */
/* during setWind(...)             */
img_ptr = (unsigned int *)R->img_ptr;

/* restore window image by row     */
for(row=R->ul_row; row<=R->lr_row; row++)

    /* restore token by column     */
    for( column=R->ul_col; column<=R->lr_col; column++
        {
        /* write token to screen    */
        vdChar(row,column,*img_ptr);

        /* pointer to next token    */
        img_ptr++;
        }
}

/*
 * End of source
 **************/
```

Fig. 7-11 ends.

Fig. 7-12. The source code listing to WRWIND.C.

```
/********************
 * Source Code Start
 *
 * File Name:   WRWIND.C
 *
 * Synopsis:    wrWind(W)
 *
 * WIND *W      Pointer to window structure
 *
 * Description: Transfers window image from
 *              memory to screen.
 *
 * Returns:     Nothing
 */

/*
 * Include Files
```

226

```
                    */

#include <stdio.h>
#include <dos.h>
#include <tproto.h>

/*
 * Function wrWind
 */

void
wrWind(R)
WIND *R;
{
register int row,column;
unsigned int *img_ptr;

/* set pointer to window image in memory */
img_ptr = (unsigned int *)R->wind_ptr;

/* write window image row by row        */
for(row=R->ul_row; row<=R->lr_row; row++)

        /* write token column by column       */
        for( column=R->ul_col; column<=R->lr_col; column++)
                {
                /* write token to screen            */
                vdChar(row,column,*img_ptr);

                /* point to next token              */
                img_ptr++;
                }
}


/*
 * End of source
 ***************/
```

Fig. 7-12 ends.

Fig. 7-13. The source code listing to WRBOX.C.

```
/********************
 * Source Code Start
 *
 * File Name:   WRBOX.C
 *
 * Synopsis:    wrBox(W)
 *
 * WIND *W      Pointer to window structure
 *
 * Description: Draws a BOX described in
 *              WIND structure
 *
 * Returns:     Nothing
 */
```

Fig. 7-13 continued.

```
/*
 * Include Files
 */

#include <stdio.h>
#include <tproto.h>
#include <mem.h>

char wb_blank[80];

/*
 * Function wrBox
 */

void
wrBox(W)
WIND *W;
{
register int row,column;
int top_bot,left_right,ul,ur,ll,lr; /* box choices */

/* initialize wb_blank              */
memset(wb_blank,'\0',80);

/* determine border type for window */
switch(W->box_type)
    {
    case S_S_D_D:
        top_bot = 196;
        left_right = 186;
        ul = 214;
        ur = 183;
        ll = 211;
        lr = 189;
        break;
    case D_D_S_S:
        top_bot = 205;
        left_right = 179;
        ul = 213;
        ur = 184;
        ll = 212;
        lr = 190;
        break;
    case D_D_D_D:
        top_bot = 205;
        left_right = 186;
        ul = 201;
        ur = 187;
        ll = 200;
        lr = 188;
        break;
    /* S_S_S_S */
    default:
        top_bot = 196;
        left_right = 179;
        ul = 218;
        ur = 191;
```

```
            ll = 192;
            lr = 217;
            break;
        }

    /* row by row                              */
    for(row=W->ul_row; row<W->lr_row; row++)

    /* blank row  under window          */
    vdWrite(row,W->ul_col,W->lr_col - W->ul_col,wb_blank,W->attr);

/* column by column */
for(column=W->ul_col; column<W->lr_col; ++column)
    {
    /* draw top row                          */
    vdChar(W->ul_row,column,mkToken(top_bot,W->attr));

    /* draw bottom row                            */
    vdChar(W->lr_row,column,mkToken(top_bot,W->attr));
    }

/* row by row                               */
for(row=W->ul_row; row<W->lr_row; ++row)
    {
    /* draw left side                        */
    vdChar(row,W->ul_col,mkToken(left_right,W->attr));

    /* draw right side                    */
    vdChar(row,W->lr_col,mkToken(left_right,W->attr));
    }

/* upper left corner                         */
vdChar(W->ul_row,W->ul_col,mkToken(ul,W->attr));

/* upper right corner                     */
vdChar(W->ul_row,W->lr_col,mkToken(ur,W->attr));

/* lower left corner                       */
vdChar(W->lr_row,W->ul_col,mkToken(ll,W->attr));

/* lower right corner                       */
vdChar(W->lr_row,W->lr_col,mkToken(lr,W->attr));
}

/*
 * End of source
 ***************/
```

_____

Fig. 7-13 ends.

Now that the preparatory routines have been presented in FIGS. 7-9 through 7-13, the source code listings for **strtWind(...)**, **dispWind(...)**, and **remvWind(...)** are presented in FIGS. 7-14 through 7-16, respectively.

Fig. 7-14. The source code listing to STRTWIND.C.

```
/*******************
 * Source Code Start
 *
 * File Name:    STRTWIND.C
 *
 * Synopsis:     strtWind(W)
 *
 * WIND *W       Pointer to window structure
 *
 * Description: Saves screen image under window
 *              and writes the border with TOP
 *              centered title.
 *
 * Returns:      Nothing
 */

/*
 * Include Files
 */

#include <alloc.h>
#include <tproto.h>

/*
 * Function strtWind
 */

void
strtWind(R)
WIND *R;
{
char *tptr;

/* pointer to top window border title */
tptr = R->t_title;

/* save screen image under window      */
rdImg(R);

/* draw window border              */
wrBox(R);

/* set window to visible           */
R->visible = 1;

/* show window title               */
if(R->show_top)
    wvdWrite(R,0,R->top_offset,R->top_length,tptr,R->attr);
}
```

```
/*
 * End of source
 ***************/
```

Fig. 7-14 ends.

Fig. 7-15. The source code listing to DISPWIND.C.

```
/*******************
 * Source Code Start
 *
 * File Name:    DISPWIND.C
 *
 * Synopsis:     dispWind(W)
 *
 * WIND *W       Pointer to window structure
 *
 * Description: Saves the image under the
 *              window and restores
 *              previously saved window
 *              image.
 *
 * Returns:      Nothing
 */

/*
 * Include Files
 */

#include <tproto.h>

/*
 * Function dispWind
 */

void
dispWind(R)
WIND *R;
{
/* if window is not visible */
if(!R->visible)
   {
   /* read screen image to memory */
   rdImg(R);

   /* write presiously saved       */
   /* window image                 */
   wrWind(R);

   /* declare window visible       */
   R->visible = 1;
   }
}

/*
 * End of source
 ***************/
```

Fig. 7-16. The source code listing to REMVWIND.C.

```
/*******************
 * Source Code Start
 *
 * File Name:    REMVWIND.C
 *
 * Synopsis:     remvWind(W)
 *
 * WIND *W       Pointer to window structure
 *
 * Description: Saves the window image
 *              and restores previously
 *              saved screen image.
 *
 * Returns:      Nothing
 */

/*
 * Include Files
 */

#include <tproto.h>

/*
 * Function remvWind
 */

void
remvWind(R)
WIND *R;
{
/* if window is visible */
if(R->visible)
    {
    /* read window image to memory */
    rdWind(R);

    /* write presiously saved    */
    /* screen image              */
    wrImg(R);

    /* window not visible        */
    R->visible = 0;
    }
}

/*
 * End of source
 ***************/
```

YOUR FIRST WINDOW PROGRAM

FIGURE 7-17 is a listing of the source code for WIND1.C. This is the first window demonstration program. It is instructive for a few reasons. The first reason is that all the previously presented window routines are put together to demonstrate how to pop up a window on the screen and remove it from the screen. This is done by pressing the F1 key during the execution of WIND1.EXE. Also, note that the Window code and direct screen code may be used together to get interesting and useful displays. This technique will be further demonstrated in Chapter 9, where the source code to a DOS shell will be presented.

Fig. 7-17. The source code listing to WIND1.C.

```
/********************
 * Source Code Start
 *
 * File Name:    WIND1.C
 *
 * Description: Demonstration program for
 *              setWind,setAttr,setBord,setTitle,
 *              strtWind,remvWind,dispWind
 */

/*
 * Include files
 */

#include <stdio.h>
#include <tproto.h>

/*
 * Function prototypes
 */

void main(void);
void on_wind(WIND *);
void off_wind(WIND *);
WIND *open_W1(WIND *);

/*
 * Name:  on_wind
 *
 * Description: This function
 *        displays a previously
 *        opened Window
 */

/* window display toggle   */
/* 0 => window never       */
/*      displayed          */
/* 1 => window previously  */
/*      displayed          */
int W1_first = 0;
```

Fig. 7-17 continued.

```
void
on_wind(W)
WIND *W;
{
if(!W1_first)
   {
   /* initialize window   */
   /* structure & display */
   /* window              */
   strtWind(W);

   /* set W1_first to      */
   /* window previously    */
   /* displayed            */
   W1_first = 1;
   }

else
   /* Display previously   */
   /* displayed window.    */
   /* The previously       */
   /* displayed window     */
   /* must have been       */
   /* opened with:         */
   /* strtWind(...).       */
   dispWind(W);
}

/*
 * Name:  off_wind
 *
 * Description: This function
 *         removes a displayed
 *         Window
 */

void
off_wind(W)
WIND *W;
{
/* Remove displayed window from screen. */
remvWind(W);
}

/*
 * Name:  open_W1
 *
 * Description: This function
 *         prepared the WIND
 *         structure and displays
 *         the window
 */

WIND
*open_W1(W)
WIND *W;
{
```

Fig. 7-17 continued.

```
int attr;

/* prep window structure    */
/* up left row is 10         */
/* up left col is 5          */
/* lower right row is 15     */
/* lower right col is 45     */
W = setWind(W,10,5,15,45);

/* set attribute for window */
attr = mkAttr(BLACK,WHITE,OFF_INTENSITY,OFF_BLINK);
setAttr(W,attr);

/* set Window border for    */
/* single sides             */
setBord(W,S_S_S_S);

/* set title for:           */
/* 'Window 1'               */
setTitle(W," Window 1 ");

/* return pointer to WIND   */
/* structure                */
return(W);
}

/*
 * Function: main
 */

void
main()
{
WIND *W1;
int cnt, attr, key, lock;
char mess1[] = { "F1  -> Window ON/Off " };
char mess2[] = { "F10 -> Exit to DOS    " };

/* initialize TAB library video routines */
vidInit();

/* print instructions on    */
/* screen's bottom row       */
attr = mkAttr(WHITE,RED,ON_INTENSITY,OFF_BLINK);
vdWrite(22,0,strlen(mess1),mess1,attr);
vdWrite(23,0,strlen(mess2),mess2,attr);

/* prepare window 1          */
/* structure                 */
W1 = open_W1(W);

/* display window 1          */
on_wind(W1);

/* set lock to hold          */
/* keyboard loop             */
lock = aTRUE;
```

```
/* keyboard loop          */
do
   {
   /* get keypress         */
   key = gtKey();

   /* evaluate key value   */
   switch(key)
      {
      /* toggle window on   */
      /* and off            */
      case F1:
         if(!W1->visible)
            on_wind(W1);
         else
            off_wind(W1);
         break;

      /* Exit to DOS        */
      case F10:
         lock = aFALSE;
         break;
      }
   } while(lock);
}


/*
 * End of Source
 ***************/
```

Fig. 7-17 ends.

MORE WINDOW ROUTINES

Now it's time to add routines to write 1) characters 2) strings of characters 3) vertical bars 4) horizontal bars and 5) change the attributes of a row all within a Window. These routines are presented in FIGS. 7-18 through 7-22 respectively.

FIGURE 7-23 presents the source code to WIND2.C. This second demonstration program writes two windows with text to the screen, permits the turning on and off of the windows with F1 or F2 keypresses, and once again exits to DOS with F10.

Fig. 7-18. The source code to WVDATTR.C.

```
/********************
 * Source Code Start
 *
 * File Name:    WVDCHAR.C
 *
 * Synopsis:     wvdChar(W,row,column,token)
 *
 * WIND *W       pointer to window structure
```

Fig. 7-18 continued.

```
 *
 * int row      row in window where token
 *              will be placed
 *
 * int column   column in window where
 *              the token will be placed
 *
 * int token    LSB holds character to be printed
 *              and the MSB holds the character's
 *              attribute.
 *
 * Description: Sends the token directly to
 *              display RAM at window row and
 *              column.  Note that this call
 *              will work only after vidInit()
 *              has been called.  If you
 *              neglect to call vidInit() before
 *              this call is made then unspeakable
 *              and unnatural things will happen
 *              to your computer!
 *
 * Returns:     Nothing
 */

/*
 * Include Files
 */

#include <stdio.h>
#include <tproto.h>

/*
 * EXTERNS
 */

extern VIDEO *crt;

/*
 * Function wvdChar
 */

void
wvdChar(W,row,col,token)
WIND *W;
int row,col,token;
{
unsigned int far *scrn;
long offset;

/* convert window row location to */
/* screen location              */
row += W->ul_row;

/* convert window column location */
/* to screen location            */
col += W->ul_col;

/* set the pointer to the screen address  */
```

```
/* - the upper left corner 0,0 -          */
scrn = (unsigned int far *)crt->scrn;

/* int offset from upper left of screen    */
/* Remember that the screenn is 80 tokens */
/*   accross and twenty five rows high     */
offset = (long)(row*80)+col;

/* now that segment and offset of screen  */
/* address are set we can move the token  */
*(scrn+offset) = token;
}

/*
 * End of Source
 ***************/
```

Fig. 7-18 ends.

Fig. 7-19. The source code to WVDWRITE.C.

```
/*********************
 * Source Code Start
 *
 * File Name:    WVDWRITE.C
 *
 * Synopsis:     wvdWrite(W,row,column,length,string,attr)
 *
 * WIND *W       pointer to window structure
 *
 * int row       row in window where string
 *               write will start
 *
 * int column    column in window where string
 *               write will start
 *
 * int length    length of the string
 *
 * char *string  pointer to string to be written to
 *               the screen
 *
 * int attr      attribute for characters of string
 *               written to the screen
 *
 * Description: Sends the string of length
 *               bytes to the window at
 *               display RAM at row and
 *               column with attr. Note that this call
 *               will work only after vidInit()
 *               has been called.  If you
 *               neglect to call vidInit() before
 *               this call is made then unspeakable
 *               and unnatural things will happen
 *               to your computer!
 *
 * Returns:      Nothing
 */
```

WINDOWS

Fig. 7-19 continued.

```c
/*
 * Include files
 */


#include <stdio.h>
#include <tproto.h>

/*
 * EXTERNS
 */

extern VIDEO *crt;

/*
 * Function wvdWrite
 */

void
wvdWrite(W,row,col,length,str,attr)
WIND *W;
int row,col,length;
char *str;
char attr;
{
unsigned char far *scrn;
register   int count;
long offset;

/* convert window row location to */
/* screen location               */
row += W->ul_row;

/* convert window column location */
/* to screen location            */
col += W->ul_col;

/* Get screen start addr from VIDEO structure */
/* This value was set in vidInit()            */
scrn = (unsigned char far *)crt->scrn;

/* calculate offset from screen start */
offset = (long)(row*160)+(col*2);

/* adjust pointer to screen to proper spot */
scrn = scrn + offset;

/* loop to write string of length bytes */
for(count=0; count<length; count++)
   {
   /* move character byte to display RAM */
   *scrn++ = *str++;

   /* move attr to contiguous attribute byte */
   *scrn++ = (unsigned)attr;

   /* loop until length bytes written */
```

239

```
    }
}

/*
 * End of Source
 ***************/
```

Fig. 7-19 ends.

Fig. 7-20. The source code listing to WVDVERT.C.

```
/*******************
 * Source Code Start
 *
 * File Name:    WVDVERT.C
 *
 * Synopsis:     wvdVert(W,row,column,length,attr)
 *
 * WIND *W       pointer to window structure
 *
 * int row       row in window where line
 *               write will start
 *
 * int column    column in window where line
 *               write will start
 *
 * int length    length of the vertical line
 *
 * int attr      attribute for vertical line
 *               written to the screen
 *
 * Description: Sends the vertical line of length
 *               bytes to the window at
 *               display RAM at row and
 *               column with attr. Note that this call
 *               will work only after vidInit()
 *               has been called.  If you
 *               neglect to call vidInit() before
 *               this call is made then unspeakable
 *               and unnatural things will happen
 *               to your computer!
 *
 * Returns:      Nothing
 */

/*
 * Include files
 */

#include <tproto.h>

/*
 * Function wvdVert
 */

void
wvdVert(W,row,column,number,attr)
```

```
WIND *W;
int row,column,number,attr;
{
int stop,row_start,token;

/* convert window row location to */
/* screen location               */
row += W->ul_row;

/* convert window column location */
/* to screen location             */
column += W->ul_col;

/* Create token of horizontal line */
/* character and passed attribute  */
token = mkToken(179,attr);

/* set termination for loop        */
stop = row+number;

/* print the vertical line         */
for(row_start=row; row_start<stop; row_start++)
   vdChar(row_start,column,token);
}

/*
 * End of source
 **************/
```

Fig. 7-20 ends.

Fig. 7-21. The source code listing to WVDHORIZ.C.

```
/********************
 * Source Code Start
 *
 * File Name:     WVDHORIZ.C
 *
 * Synopsis:      wvdHoriz(W,row,column,length,attr)
 *
 * WIND *W        pointer to window structure
 *
 * int row        row in window where line
 *                write will start
 *
 * int column     column in window where line
 *                write will start
 *
 * int length     length of the horizontal line
 *
 * int attr       attribute for horizontal line
 *                written to the screen
 *
 * Description: Sends the horizontal line of length
 *              bytes to the window at
 *              display RAM at row and
 *              column with attr. Note that this call
```

```
*               will work only after vidInit()
*               has been called.  If you
*               neglect to call vidInit() before
*               this call is made then unspeakable
*               and unnatural things will happen
*               to your computer!
*
* Returns:      Nothing
*/

/*
 * Include files
 */

#include <tproto.h>

/*
 * Function wvdHoriz
 */

void
wvdHoriz(W,row,column,number,attr)
WIND *W;
int row,column,number,attr;
{
int stop,col_start,token;

/* convert window row location to */
/* screen location               */
row += W->ul_row;

/* convert window column location */
/* to screen location            */
column += W->ul_col;

/* Create token of horizontal line */
/* character and passed attribute  */
token = mkToken(196,attr);

/* set termination for loop       */
stop = column+number;

/* print the horizontal line      */
for(col_start=column; col_start<stop; col_start++)
   vdChar(row,col_start,token);
}

/*
 * End of source
 ***************/
```

Fig. 7-21 ends.

242

Fig. 7-22. The source code to WVDCHAR.C.

```
/*******************
 * Source Code Start
 *
 * File Name:    WVDATTR.C
 *
 * Synopsis:     wvdAttr(W,row,column,length,attr)
 *
 * WIND *W       pointer wo window structure
 *
 * int row       row in window where string
 *               write will start
 *
 * int column    column in window where attribute
 *               write will start
 *
 * int length    length of the new attribute
 *
 * int attr      attribute for horizontal line
 *               written to the screen
 *
 * Description: Sends the new attribute of length
 *              bytes to the window at
 *              display RAM at row and
 *              column with attr. Note that this call
 *              will work only after vidInit()
 *              has been called.  If you
 *              neglect to call vidInit() before
 *              this call is made then unspeakable
 *              and unnatural things will happen
 *              to your computer!
 *
 * Returns:      Nothing
 */

/*
 * Include files
 */


#include <stdio.h>
#include <tproto.h>

/*
 * externs
 */
extern VIDEO *crt;

/*
 * Function wvdAttr
 */

void
wvdAttr(R,row,col,length,attr)
WIND *R;
int row,col,length;
char attr;
```

```
{
unsigned char far *scrn;
register    int count;
long offset;

/* set far pointer to screen address (SEG) */
scrn = (unsigned char far *)crt->scrn;

/* row + window offset                      */
row += R->ul_row;

/* column + window offset                   */
col += R->ul_col;

/* calculate the offset from the screen */
/* segment start                        */
offset = (long)(row*160)+(col*2);

/* far pointer adjusted to exact display */
/* memory start at row,col                */
scrn = scrn + offset;

/* loop for attribute change              */
for(count=0; count<length; count++)
    {
    /* bypass character byte   */
    scrn++;

    /* new attribute to screen */
    *scrn++ = (unsigned)attr;
    }
}

/*
 * End of source
 ***************/
```

Fig. 7-22 ends.

Fig. 7-23. The source code listing to WIND2.C.

```
/*******************
 * Source Code Start
 *
 * File Name:   WIND2.C
 *
 * Description: Demonstration program for
 *              setWind,setAttr,setBord,setTitle,
 *              strtWind,remvWind,dispWind,wvdWrite,
 *              wvdHoriz, wvdVert, wvdAttr
 */

/*
 * Include files
 */

#include <stdio.h>
```

Fig. 7-23 continued.

```c
#include <tproto.h>

/*
 * Function prototypes
 */

void main(void);
void on_wind1(WIND *);
void on_wind2(WIND *);
void off_wind(WIND *);
WIND *open_W1(WIND *);

/*
 * Global pointers to WIND structures
 */

WIND *W1, *W2;

/*
 * Name:  on_wind1
 *
 * Description: This function
 *          displays a previously
 *          opened Window
 */

/* window display toggle    */
/* 0 => window never        */
/*      displayed           */
/* 1 => window previously   */
/*      displayed           */
int W1_first = 0;

void
on_wind1(W)
WIND *W;
{
if(!W1_first)
   {
   /* initialize window     */
   /* structure & display   */
   /* window                */
   strtWind(W);

   /* set W1_first to       */
   /* window previously     */
   /* displayed             */
   W1_first = 1;
   }

else
   /* Display previously    */
   /* displayed window.     */
   /* The previously        */
   /* displayed window      */
   /* must have been        */
   /* opened with:          */
```

245

Fig. 7-23 continued.

```
    /* strtWind(...).        */
    dispWind(W);
}


/*
 * Name:   on_wind2
 *
 * Description: This function
 *         displays a previously
 *         opened Window
 */

/* window display toggle   */
/* 0 => window never       */
/*      displayed          */
/* 1 => window previously  */
/*      displayed          */
int W2_first = 0;

void
on_wind2(W)
WIND *W;
{
if(!W2_first)
    {
    /* initialize window   */
    /* structure & display */
    /* window              */
    strtWind(W);

    /* set W1_first to     */
    /* window previously   */
    /* displayed           */
    W2_first = 1;
    }

else
    /* Display previously  */
    /* displayed window.   */
    /* The previously      */
    /* displayed window    */
    /* must have been      */
    /* opened with:        */
    /* strtWind(...).      */
    dispWind(W);
}


/*
 * Name:  off_wind
 *
 * Description: This function
 *         removes a displayed
 *         Window
 */

void
off_wind(W)
```

Fig. 7-23 continued.

```
WIND *W;
{
/* Remove displayed window from screen. */
remvWind(W);
}

/*
 * Name:  open_W1
 *
 * Description: This function
 *         prepared the WIND
 *         structure and displays
 *         the window
 */

WIND
*open_W1(W)
WIND *W;
{
int attr;

/* prep window structure    */
/* up left row is 10         */
/* up left col is 5          */
/* lower right row is 15     */
/* lower right col is 45     */
W = setWind(W,10,5,15,45);

/* set attribute for window */
attr = mkAttr(BLACK,WHITE,OFF_INTENSITY,OFF_BLINK);
setAttr(W,attr);

/* set Window border for     */
/* single sides              */
setBord(W,S_S_S_S);

/* set title for:            */
/* 'Window 1'                */
setTitle(W," Window 1 ");

/* return pointer to WIND    */
/* structure                 */
return(W);
}

/*
 * Name:  open_W2
 *
 * Description: This function
 *         prepared the WIND
 *         structure and displays
 *         the window
 */

WIND
*open_W2(W)
WIND *W;
```

Fig. 7-23 continued.

```
{
int attr;

/* prep window structure   */
/* up left row is 10        */
/* up left col is 5         */
/* lower right row is 55    */
/* lower right col is 75    */
W = setWind(W,10,55,15,75);

/* set attribute for window */
attr = mkAttr(WHITE,RED,OFF_INTENSITY,OFF_BLINK);
setAttr(W,attr);

/* set Window border for    */
/* double sides             */
setBord(W,D_D_D_D);

/* set title for:           */
/* 'Window 2'               */
setTitle(W," Window 2 ");

/* return pointer to WIND   */
/* structure                */
return(W);
}

/*
 * Function: main
 */

void
main()
{
int cnt, attr, key, g_attr, lock;
char mess1[] = { "F1  -> Window 1 ON/Off " };
char mess2[] = { "F2  -> Window 2 On/Off " };
char mess3[] = { "F10 -> Exit to DOS      " };
char w11text[] = { " WINDOW 1 NAME " };
char w21text[] = { " WINDOW 2 NAME " };

/* initialize TAB library video routines */
vidInit();

/* print instructions on    */
/* screen's bottom row       */
attr = mkAttr(WHITE,RED,ON_INTENSITY,OFF_BLINK);
vdWrite(21,0,strlen(mess1),mess1,attr);
vdWrite(22,0,strlen(mess2),mess2,attr);
vdWrite(23,0,strlen(mess3),mess3,attr);

/* prepare window 1          */
/* structure                 */
W1 = open_W1(W1);

/* display window 1          */
on_wind1(W1);
```

Fig. 7-23 continued.

```
/* display text in Window  */
/* 1                       */
wvdWrite(W1,1,1,strlen(w11text),w11text,W1->attr);
wvdHoriz(W1,2,1,W1->lr_col-W1->ul_col-1,W1->attr);
wvdAttr(W1,1,1,W1->lr_col-W1->ul_col-1,
        mkAttr(WHITE,MAGENTA,ON_INTENSITY,OFF_BLINK));

/* prepare window 2        */
/* structure              */
W2 = open_W2(W2);

/* display window 2        */
on_wind2(W2);

/* display text in Window  */
/* 2                       */
g_attr = mkAttr(WHITE,GREEN,ON_INTENSITY,OFF_BLINK);
wvdWrite(W2,1,1,strlen(w21text),w21text,W2->attr);
wvdHoriz(W2,2,1,W2->lr_col-W2->ul_col-1,W2->attr);
wvdAttr(W2,1,1,W2->lr_col-W2->ul_col-1,g_attr);
wvdVert(W2,3,8,2,W2->attr);

/* set lock to hold        */
/* keyboard loop          */
lock = aTRUE;

/* keyboard loop           */
do
   {
   /* get keypress         */
   key = gtKey();

   /* evaluate key value   */
   switch(key)
      {
      /* toggle window 1    */
      /* on and off         */
      case F1:
         if(!W1->visible)
            on_wind1(W1);
         else
            off_wind(W1);
         break;

      /* toggle window 2    */
      /* on and off         */
      case F2:
         if(!W2->visible)
            on_wind2(W2);
         else
            off_wind(W2);
         break;

      /* Exit to DOS         */
      case F10:
         lock = aFALSE;
         break;
```

```
        }
    } while(lock);
}


/*
 * End of Source
 ***************/
```

Fig. 7-23 ends.

PUTTING IT ALL TOGETHER

FIGURE 7-24 shows the largest program up to this point in the text. The MENU.EXE demonstration program gives precise instructions on how to use the TAB library to write LOTUS style, GRID style, SIMPLE style, and VERTI-CAL COLUMN highlight bar user interface windows. Each menu item may be selected by pressing a key which represents the first letter of the menu item, or you may move the highlight bar by pressing an arrow key and making your selection by pressing the Enter key.

Because each style of window is coded in a separate and clearly labeled function you may pull segments of the source and plop them directly in your program.

There's a lot of juicy meat in MENU.C. If you're not an intermediate or advanced C programmer, studying the source to MENU.C can prove highly instructive.

Fig. 7-24. The source code listing to MENU.C.

```
/********************
 * Source Code Start
 *
 * File Name:    MENU.C
 *
 * Description: Demonstration program for
 *              LOTUS style, GRID style, INFO style
 *              VERTICAL HIGHLIGHT BAR style
 *              windows
 */


/*****************/
/* Include Files */
/*****************/

#include <stdio.h>

/*************************/
/* C function prototypes */
/* TAB Lib Routines      */
/*************************/

#include <tproto.h>
```

Fig. 7-24 continued.

```
/*******************************/
/* C function prototypes       */
/* Routines used by this demo */
/*******************************/

int tgrid(void);        /* display grid type window        */
void info1(void);       /* simple pop-up information window */
int tlotus(void);       /* display lotue style window      */
int main(int, char *[]); /* program main                    */

/********************************************/
/* Make variables which must retain their  */
/* value after the function exits, global   */
/********************************************/

int lotus_flag=0;
int lotus_item=0;
int grid_item=0;
int grid_flag=0;

/**************************/
/* Structute Declatations */
/**************************/

/* Pointers to Window Structures */
WIND *FIRST;
WIND *GRID;
WIND *INFORM;
WIND *LOTUS;

/********************/
/* Window Messages */
/********************/

/* Messages for FIRST Window */
char title[29]   = "      C-erious Toolkit #1      ";
unsigned char i_bar[31]
    = { 195,196,196,196,196,196,196,196,196,
        196,196,196,196,196,196,196,196,196,
        196,196,196,196,196,196,196,196,196,
        196,196,196,180 };
char item1[29]   = " Lotus Style Menu            ";
char item2[29]   = " Grid Style Menu             ";
char item3[29]   = " Some Historical Information ";
char item5[29]   = " Quit C-erious Demo          ";

/* Messages for LOTUS Window */
char menu1[47] =
  " Mean  Mode  Median  Range  Standard Deviation ";
char mess1[47] =
  " Mean is the Average score of the distribution ";
char mess2[47] =
  " Mode is the most frequent score               ";
char mess3[47] =
  " Median is the middle score of sample          ";
char mess4[47] =
  " Range is the distance from highest to lowest  ";
```

251

Fig. 7-24 continued.

```c
char mess5[47] =
  " Standard dev. is avg. distance from mean       ";

/* lot_map holds mess column offset & length */
int lot_map[5][2] = {
   1,6,
   7,6,
   13,8,
   21,7,
   28,20 };

/* messages for GRID window - holds row & column */
char gmenu[21]   = "   SELECT A NUMBER   ";
char grid1[21]   = "      1  2  3        ";
char grid2[21]   = "      4  5  6        ";
char grid3[21]   = "      7  8  9        ";
char grid4[21] = " Press ENTER to Exit ";

/* grid_map row,column for start of inverse item */
int grid_map[9][2] = {
   3,7,
   3,10,
   3,13,
   4,7,
   4,10,
   4,13,
   5,7,
   5,10,
   5,13 };

/* info1 window data */
char speed1[28]  = "   TSR 'C'ERIOUS  History  ";
unsigned char speed2[30] =
  { 199,196,196,196,196,196,196,196,196,
    196,196,196,196,196,196,196,196,196,
    196,196,196,196,196,196,196,196,196,
    196,196,182 };
char speed3[28]  = "    TSR  SYSTEMS LIMITED    ";
char speed4[28]  = " ----------------------- ";
char speed5[28]  = "  'C'erious by Len Dorfman ";
char speed6[28]  = "    & Chuckie and Frisky   ";
char speed7[28]  = " ----------------------- ";
char speed8[28]  = "   Press ANY KEY to exit.  ";

/********************/
/* global variables */
/********************/

int inverse;           /* attribute for inverse       */
int hl_tense;          /* highlight bar intensity      */

extern int SPARKLE_FLAG;

/*********************************/
/*                               */
/* Lotus Style Window            */
/*                               */
```

Fig. 7-24 continued.

```
/* Receives: nothing              */
/* Returns: item selection number */
/*                                */
/* Displays Lotus style window    */
/* with attendant cursor, high-   */
/* light and item description     */
/* routines.                      */
/*                                */
/**********************************/

int
tlotus()
{
int key;   /* scan and char value  */
int exit;  /* val for loop cond chk */
int exp_a; /* item explanation attr */

/*************************************************************/
/* Initialize lotus menu window structure and display window */
/*************************************************************/
/* Set lotus explanation Attr - Fore,Back,Intensity,Blink */
exp_a = mkAttr(MAGENTA,BLUE,ON_INTENSITY,OFF_BLINK);

/* call window initialization routines only once */
if(!lotus_flag)
   {
   /* ensure window startup bypassed nexe window call */
   lotus_flag=1;

   /* Allocate memory and return pointer to structure */
   LOTUS = setWind(LOTUS,6,20,9,68);

   /* Set Window Attr - Fore,Back,Intensity,Blink */
   setAttr(LOTUS,mkAttr(WHITE,BLUE,ON_INTENSITY,OFF_BLINK));

   /* Set Window Border - top, bot, left, right */
   setBord(LOTUS,S_S_S_S);

   /* Set the top and bottom title - 0 set no bottom title */
   setTitle(LOTUS," Lotus Style Window ");

   /* Display window */
   strtWind(LOTUS);
   }
else
   dispWind(LOTUS);

/* set loop condition */
exit=aFALSE;

do
   {
   /* Write title bar - erasing old inverse  */
   wvdWrite(LOTUS,1,1,47,menu1,LOTUS->attr);
   /* Inverse proper menu item using lot_map[][] */
   wvdAttr(LOTUS,1,
           lot_map[lotus_item][0],
```

253

Fig. 7-24 continued.

```
            lot_map[lotus_item][1],
            hl_tense);
   switch(lotus_item)      /* print item explanation */
      {
      case 0:
         wvdWrite(LOTUS,2,1,47,mess1,exp_a);
         break;
      case 1:
         wvdWrite(LOTUS,2,1,47,mess2,exp_a);
         break;
      case 2:
         wvdWrite(LOTUS,2,1,47,mess3,exp_a);
         break;
      case 3:
         wvdWrite(LOTUS,2,1,47,mess4,exp_a);
         break;
      case 4:
         wvdWrite(LOTUS,2,1,47,mess5,exp_a);
         break;
      }
   key = gtKey();
   switch(key)
      {
      case RIGHT_ARROW:    /* At right item?   */
         if(lotus_item==4) /* Yes?             */
            lotus_item=0;  /*  set left item   */
         else              /* Else             */
            lotus_item++;  /* move rt 1 item   */
         break;
      case LEFT_ARROW:     /* At left item?    */
         if(lotus_item==0) /* Yes?             */
            lotus_item=4;  /*  set right item  */
         else              /* Else             */
            lotus_item--;  /*  move lft 1 item */
         break;
      case ENTER:
         exit=aTRUE;
         break;
      }
   } while(!exit);

/* Remove Lotus Window */
remvWind(LOTUS);

/* return selected item number */
return(lotus_item);
}


/*********************************/
/*                               */
/* Grid Style Window             */
/*                               */
/* Receives: nothing             */
/* Returns: item selection number */
/*                               */
/* Displays Grid style window    */
/* with attendant cursor & high- */
/* light description routines.   */
```

Fig. 7-24 continued.

```
/*                                    */
/********************************/

/*******************************************/
/* Make variables which must retain their */
/* value after the function exits global  */
/*******************************************/

int
tgrid()
{
int key;   /* scan and char value   */
int exit;  /* val for loop cond chk */

/**************************************************************/
/* Initialize grid menu window structure and display window */
/**************************************************************/

if(!grid_flag)
   {
   /* ensure window initialization bypass */
   grid_flag=1;

   /* Allocate memory and return pointer to structure */
   GRID = setWind(GRID,10,10,18,32);

   /* Set Window Attr - Fore,Back,Intensity,Blink */
   setAttr(GRID,mkAttr(WHITE,
           RED,OFF_INTENSITY,OFF_BLINK));

   /* Set Window Border */
   setBord(GRID,D_D_D_D);

   /* Set the top and bottom title - 0 set no bottom title */
   setTitle(GRID," Grid Style Window ");

   /* Display window */
   strtWind(GRID);
   }
else
   dispWind(GRID);

/* Write name and exit messages */
wvdWrite(GRID,1,1,21,gmenu,inverse);
wvdWrite(GRID,7,1,21,grid4,GRID->attr);
wvdWrite(GRID,7,8,5,"ENTER",
        mkAttr(WHITE,RED,OFF_INTENSITY,ON_BLINK));

/* set loop condition */
exit=aFALSE;

do
   {
   /* Write grid entries bar  */
   wvdWrite(GRID,3,1,21,grid1,GRID->attr);
   wvdWrite(GRID,4,1,21,grid2,GRID->attr);
   wvdWrite(GRID,5,1,21,grid3,GRID->attr);
```

Fig. 7-24 continued.

```
/* Inverse proper menu item using grid_map[][] */
wvdAttr(GRID,grid_map[grid_item][0],
        grid_map[grid_item][1],3,inverse);

key = gtKey();

switch(key)
  {
  case RIGHT_ARROW:
     /* IF rt col->mv to left col ELSE->mv rt */
     if( (grid_item==0)||(grid_item==1)||
         (grid_item==3)||(grid_item==4)||
         (grid_item==6)||(grid_item==7) )
        grid_item++;
     else if(grid_item==2)
        grid_item=0;
     else if(grid_item==5)
        grid_item=3;
     else
        grid_item=6;
     break;
  case LEFT_ARROW:
     /* IF left col->mv to rt col ELSE->mv left */
     if( (grid_item==2)||(grid_item==1)||
         (grid_item==5)||(grid_item==4)||
         (grid_item==8)||(grid_item==7) )
        grid_item--;
     else if(grid_item==0)
        grid_item=2;
     else if(grid_item==3)
        grid_item=5;
     else
        grid_item=8;
     break;
  case DOWN_ARROW:
     /* IF bottom row->mv to top row ELSE->mv down */
     if(grid_item<=5)
        grid_item += 3;
     else if(grid_item==6)
        grid_item=0;
     else if(grid_item==7)
        grid_item=1;
     else
        grid_item=2;
     break;

  case UP_ARROW:
     /* IF top row->mv to bottom row ELSE->mv up */
     if(grid_item>=3)
        grid_item -= 3;
     else if(grid_item==0)
        grid_item=6;
     else if(grid_item==1)
        grid_item=7;
     else
        grid_item=8;
     break;
  case ENTER:
```

Fig. 7-24 continued.

```
            exit=aTRUE;
            break;
        }
    } while(!exit);

/* Remove Lotus Window */
remvWind(GRID);

/* return selected item */
return(grid_item);
}

/****************************/
/*                          */
/* Simple Style Window      */
/*                          */
/* Receives: nothing        */
/* Returns: nothing         */
/*                          */
/* Displays Simple pop up   */
/* information window.       */
/*                          */
/****************************/

/******************************************/
/* Make variables which must retain their */
/* value after the function exits global  */
/******************************************/
int info1_flag=0;

void
info1()
{

/*************************************************************/
/* Initialize grid menu window structure and display window */
/*************************************************************/

if(!info1_flag)
    {
    /* ensure window initialization bypass */
    info1_flag=1;

    /* Allocate memory and return pointer to structure */
    INFORM = setWind(INFORM,12-5,20-5,22-5,49-5);

    /* Set Window Attr - Fore,Back,Intensity,Blink */
    setAttr(INFORM,
            mkAttr(BLACK,CYAN,OFF_INTENSITY,OFF_BLINK));

    /* Set Window Border */
    setBord(INFORM,D_D_D_D);

    /* Set the bottom title */
    setTitle(INFORM," Esoteric Information ");

    /* Display window */
```

Fig. 7-24 continued.

```
   strtWind(INFORM);
   }
else
   dispWind(INFORM);

/* Write menu and exit messages */
wvdWrite(INFORM,1,1,28,
         speed1,
         mkAttr(CYAN,BLACK,OFF_INTENSITY,OFF_BLINK));
wvdWrite(INFORM,2,0,30,speed2,INFORM->attr);
wvdWrite(INFORM,3,1,28,speed3,INFORM->attr);
wvdWrite(INFORM,4,1,28,speed4,INFORM->attr);
wvdWrite(INFORM,5,1,28,speed5,INFORM->attr);
wvdWrite(INFORM,6,1,28,speed6,INFORM->attr);
wvdWrite(INFORM,7,1,28,speed7,INFORM->attr);
wvdWrite(INFORM,8,0,30,speed2,INFORM->attr);
wvdWrite(INFORM,9,1,28,speed8,INFORM->attr);

/* wait for key press */
gtKey();

/* remove window and display original screen information */
remvWind(INFORM);
}

/*****************************/
/*                           */
/* int main(void)            */
/*                           */
/* Receives: nothing         */
/* Returns: nothing          */
/*                           */
/* Sets up the FISRT window  */
/* display and contains the  */
/* scroll bar menu selection */
/* routine.                  */
/*                           */
/*****************************/

int
main(argc,argv)
int argc;
char *argv[];
{
int key;       /* recieves Scan & char key code */
int exit;      /* holds val for main loop check */
int old_row;   /* Tracker for highlight bar      */
int row;       /* Tracker for highlight bar      */
int intense;   /* intensity attribute value      */
int beep_fl;   /* flag for beep on 'Q' keypress */


/*****************************/
/* Initialize VIDIO structure */
/*                           */
/* ALWAYS call at prog start! */
/*****************************/
```

Fig. 7-24 continued.

```
vidInit();

if( (argc == 2)&&(*argv[1]=='+') )
   {
   beep();
   SPARKLE_FLAG = aTRUE; /* turn sparkle control on */
   }

/* Set global attribute intense for inverse video   */
inverse = mkAttr(BLACK,WHITE,OFF_INTENSITY,OFF_BLINK);

/* set global attribute hl_tense for WHITE,WHITE,   */
/* INTENSE,OFF_BLINK                                */
hl_tense = mkAttr(WHITE,WHITE,ON_INTENSITY,OFF_BLINK);

/* Set intense text attribute for this window       */
intense = mkAttr(WHITE,MAGENTA,ON_INTENSITY,OFF_BLINK);

/* Turn off the cursor */
offCur();

/*************************************************************/
/* Initialize main menu window structure and display window */
/*************************************************************/

/* Allocate memory and return pointer to structure */
FIRST = setWind(FIRST,2,4,10,34);

/* Set Window Attr - Fore,Back,Intensity,Blink */
setAttr(FIRST,mkAttr(WHITE,MAGENTA,OFF_INTENSITY,OFF_BLINK));

/* Set Window Border - top, bot, left, right */
setBord(FIRST,D_D_S_S);

/* Set the top and bottom title  */
setTitle(FIRST," TSR 'C'erious (c)1988 ");

/* Display window */
strtWind(FIRST);

/* Write menu name & line below to window */
wvdWrite(FIRST,1,1,29,title,inverse);
wvdWrite(FIRST,2,0,31,i_bar,FIRST->attr);

/* Write menu items to window */
wvdWrite(FIRST,3,1,29,item1,FIRST->attr);
wvdWrite(FIRST,4,1,29,item2,FIRST->attr);
wvdWrite(FIRST,5,1,29,item3,FIRST->attr);
wvdWrite(FIRST,6,0,31,i_bar,FIRST->attr);
wvdWrite(FIRST,7,1,29,item5,FIRST->attr);

/* highlight first letter of item */
wvdAttr(FIRST,3,2,1,intense);        /* L intense */
wvdAttr(FIRST,4,2,1,intense);        /* G intense */
wvdAttr(FIRST,5,2,1,intense);        /* S intense */
wvdAttr(FIRST,7,2,1,intense);        /* Q intense */
```

Fig. 7-24 continued.

```
/* Set highlight trackers to start at item1 (row 3) */
row = 3;
old_row = 3;

/* set default for no beep */
beep_fl = aFALSE;

/* Set loop condition */
exit = aFALSE;

/*****************************************************/
/* Main keyboard loop. Selects: tlotus(), tgrid(),  */
/*                              info1(), & quits     */
/* Up,Down arrow or First letter move highlight bar  */
/*****************************************************/

do
{
/* off highlight bar */
wvdAttr(FIRST,old_row,1,29,FIRST->attr);

/* intense item let */
wvdAttr(FIRST,old_row,2,1,intense);

/* on highlight bar */
wvdAttr(FIRST,row,1,29,inverse);

/* intense HB letter */
wvdAttr(FIRST,row,2,1,hl_tense);

/* YES? beep after  */
if(beep_fl)
   {
   /* Yes-warning beep */
   beep();

   /* reset-> no beep */
   beep_fl=aFALSE;
   }
old_row = row;          /* reset OFF tracker */
key = gtKey();          /* get scan & char   */
switch(key)             /* eval key press    */
   {
   case DOWN_ARROW:
      if(row==7)        /* If bottom row     */
         row=3;         /*   then->top row   */
      else if(row==5)   /* If row 5          */
         row=7;         /*   then skip to 7  */
      else              /* Otherwise         */
         row++;         /*   then down row   */
      break;
   case UP_ARROW:
      if(row==7)        /* If bottom row     */
         row=5;         /*   then skip to 5  */
      else if(row==3)   /* If row 3          */
         row=7;         /*   then->bot row   */
```

```
        else                /* Otherwise      */
            row--;          /*   then up row  */
        break;
case  ENTER:
    switch(row)             /* Eval selection */
        {
        case 3:             /* sel. lotus demo */
            tlotus();
            break;
        case 4:
            tgrid();        /* sel. grid demo */
            break;
        case 5:
            info1();        /* simple demo    */
            break;
        case 7:             /* Exit option    */
            exit=aTRUE;
            break;
        }
    break;
default:                    /* Check ascii val */
    key &=0x00ff;           /* mask scan code  */
    switch(key)             /* which key?      */
        {
        case 'l':           /* L->lotus choice */
        case 'L':
            row=3;
            break;
        case 'g':           /* G->grid choice  */
        case 'G':
            row=4;
            break;
        case 's':           /* S->simple demo  */
        case 'S':
            row=5;
            break;
        case 'q':           /* Q->quit wind    */
        case 'Q':
            row=7;
            beep_fl=aTRUE;  /* set for beep      */
            break;
            }
        break;
    }
} while (!exit);

/* remove window and restore originial screen */
remvWind(FIRST);

/* turn on the cursor */
onCur();
return(0);
}

/*
 * End of source
 ***************/
```

Fig. 7-24 ends.

SUMMARY

Chapter 7 introduced the concept of Windows. It was noted that Windows differed from rectangles, in part, because Windows are referenced by using a local coordinate system, as opposed to the global coordinate system of rectangles.

Windows may be thought of as mini-screens. Routines were presented to treat the Window as a mini-screen. Finally, the comprehensive Window demonstration program, MENU.C, was presented. MENU.C gave concrete coding examples for a variety of Window treatments.

Take a deep breath here, as Chapter 8 takes you into the twilight world of making programs you have created with your TAB library Terminate and Stay Resident. Once again let's return to the land of assembly.

8

Adding TSR Capabilities to your TAB Library

TSR is an industry buzzword for Terminate and Stay Resident programs. Two categories for Terminate and Stay Resident programs could be those programs called with a HOT key and those programs continuously operating underneath user programs. Another consideration for TSR programming is that once a program is RAM resident you will need the capability to detect if the program is currently RAM resident. And lastly, if need be, you will also need the capability of removing the TSR program from memory while restoring the original vector interrupt values.

There are a few ways to snatch hot keys involving DOS interrupt 09h and interrupt 16h. Writing filters for these interrupts are beyond the scope of this text, but using the Print Screen interrupt 05h is not. In fact, the PRTSCRN.C demonstration program will permit you to write TSR programs and have them pop up every time the Print Screen key is pressed. Once the Print Screen is pressed, your TSR program then becomes the foreground program and you can do anything you wish. FIGURE 8-1 shows how PRTSCRN.C operates.

Note in FIG. 8-1 that you can easily modify this program to have as many TSR program branches as you wish. Simply modify the scrolling highlight bar menu to have more choices and away you go. Because you can always leave the print screen option available with the TSR program, you will never need to remove it.

If you do want to remove the PRTSCRN.EXE program from memory, though, the assembly generated program RPS.COM ((R)emove (P)rint (S)creen) will do the trick. The PSDETECT.EXE program will report if PRTSCRN is residing in memory or not. This will prove useful in preventing a PRTSCRN from loading over itself into memory.

Fig. 8-1. Operation of PRTSCRN program.

```
1) Press Print Screen key and
   a Window pops up and gives
   you 2 program options.

2) Move the highlight bar to,
   say, option 1 labeled PRINT
   SCREEN.  Press <ENTER> and
   your text screen will be
   dumped to the printer.

   or...

   Move the highlight bar to
   option 2 labeled SAVE SCREEN.
   Press <ENTER> and you will
   be prompted for a name for your
   text screen. Once given, your
   screen will then be saved in a
   standard DOS text format which
   may be seen using the DOS TYPE
   command or used in any Word
   Processor.
```

To demonstrate the use of a program running continuously under user programs, a Terminate and Stay Resident clock running off the BIOS timer interrupt 0x1c will be demonstrated by CLOCK.EXE. As a small bonus, a blinking ':' between the hours and minutes will embellish the time display.

WRITING A TSR POP-UP WINDOW PROGRAM IN C

Seven new object modules must be added to the TAB library before we can compile and link PRTSCRN.C. FIGURE 8-2 presents the source code to STRENUL.C, the first of the new functions presented. STRENUL(...) replaces ' ' characters at the end of a string with '\0' characters.

Fig. 8-2. The source listing to STRENUL.C.

```
/******************
 * Start Source file
 *
 * File Name:    STRENUL.C
 *
 * Synopsis:     strEnul(string)
 *
 * char *string pointer to string
 *
 * Description: Converts the trailing
 *              bytes of aSPC (0x20)
 *              to aNUL (0)
 *
```

```
 * Returns:      Nothing
 */

/*
 * Include files
 */

#include <tproto.h>

/*
 * Function strEnul
 */

void
strEnul(string)
char *string;
{
char *start;
/* Set pointer to string start       */
start = (char *)string;

/* Set received pointer to string end */
while(*string!=aNUL)
        string++;

/* Set received string to last ASCII  */
/* byte                               */
string--;

/* Change bytes from aSPC to aNUL     */
while( (*string==' ') && (string>start) )
        *string-- = aNUL;
}

/*
 * End of source
 ***************/
```

Fig. 8-2 ends.

The second function added to your library will be RDCHAR. This function uses the BIOS to read a token from the screen at the current cursor location. RDCHAR.C is presented in FIG. 8-3 and RDCHAR.ASM is presented in FIG. 8-4.

WMVCUR.C, shown in FIG. 8-5, is the source code for a function that moves the cursor using the local coordinate system of the Window.

PRCHAR is a function which allows you to send a byte to the printer. The source code for PRCHAR.C is presented in FIG. 8-6 and the source code listing for PRCHAR.ASM is presented in FIG. 8-7.

TSRPS is a function that, when called at the end of the main( ) function, automatically makes your C program a TSR program. Note carefully how the function tsrPS(...) is used in the source listing for the PRTSCRN.C demonstration program. Memory for your C program will be allocated in 16-byte blocks

Fig. 8-3. The source code to RDCHAR.C.

```
/*******************
 * Start Source File
 *
 * File Name:    RDCHAR.C
 *
 * Synopsis:     token = rdChar()
 *
 * int token     screen token returned
 *
 * Description: Screen token returned at
 *              current row and column
 *              location.
 *
 * Returns:      Screen token
 */

/*
 * Include files
 */

#include <dos.h>
#include <tproto.h>

/*
 * Function rdChar
 */

int
rdChar()
{
union REGS ir,or;
/* read token from screen function */
ir.h.ah = 8;

/* which is on page 0              */
ir.h.bh = 0;

/* Invoke int 0x10                 */
int86(0x10,&ir,&or);

/* Return screen token             */
return(or.x.ax);
}

/*
 * End of source listing
 ***********************/
```

called *paragraphs*. That's how the DOS TSR function handles memory. To calculate how many paragraphs your program needs simply divide the program's .EXE file size by 16. That will give you the bare minimum of paragraphs needed. In practice, though, I've always had to allocate 10 to 100 more paragraphs of memory in order to get my program to work properly.

Fig. 8-4. The source code to RDCHAR.ASM.

```
;*******************
; Start Source file
;
; File Name:    RDCHAR.ASM
; Synopsis:     token = rdChar()
;
; int token     screen token returned
;
; Description:  Screen token returned at
;               current row and column
;               location.
;
; Returns:      Screen token


;
; Enable DOS segment-ordering at link time
;

        DOSSEG

;
; Set the memory model for simplified segmentation
; directives
;

        .MODEL SMALL

;
; Make function name visible to linker
;

        PUBLIC _rdChar

;
; Defines the start of the code segment
;

        .CODE

;
; Function name
;
```

```
_rdChar PROC NEAR
;
; Save regs
;

     push BP
     mov  BP,SP

;
; Read screen token function
;

     mov AH,8

;
; On page 0
;

     mov BH,0

;
; Use BIOS int 10h for token read
;

     int  10h

;
; AX now holds screen token
;

     mov  SP,BP
     pop  BP
     ret

_rdChar ENP
     END

;
; End of source listing
;**********************
```

Fig. 8-4 ends.

Fig. 8-5. The source code listing to WMVCUR.C.

```
/******************
 * Start Source file
 *
 * File Name:    WMVCUR.C
 *
 * Synopsis:     wmvCur(W,row,column)
 *
 * WIND *W       pointer to window structure
 *
 * int row       move cursor to this row
 *
 * int column    move cursor to this column
 *
 * Description: wmvCur moves the cursor
 *               to row, column using the
 *               local coordinates of a
 *               window
 *
 * Returns:      Nothing
 */

/*
 * Include files
 */

#include <tproto.h>

/*
 * Function wmvCur
 */

void
wmvCur(W,row,col)
WIND *W;
int row,col;
{
/* Adjust row value from global */
/* coordinate system to local   */
/* coordinate system            */
row += W->ul_row;

/* Adjust row value from global */
/* coordinate system to local   */
/* coordinate system            */
col += W->ul_col;

/* Move the cursor to the       */
/* adjusted row and column      */
mvCur(row,col);
}

/*
 * End of source listing
 ***********************/
```

Fig. 8-6. The source code listing for PRCHAR.C.

```
/*******************
 * Start Source File
 *
 * File Name:    PRCHAR.C
 *
 * Synopsis:     prChar(port,ch)
 *
 * int port      printer port number
 *
 * char ch       character send to printer
 *
 * Description: prChar uses BIOS int 17h,
 *              function 0, to send the
 *              character to the printer
 *
 * Returns:      Nothing
 */

/*
 * Include files
 */

#include <dos.h>
#include <tproto.h>

/*
 * Function prChar
 */

int
prChar(port,ch)
int port;
char ch;
{
union REGS ir,or;
/* Printer int function */
/* send byte to printer  */
ir.h.ah = 0;

/* set printer port      */
ir.x.dx = port;

/* set character to send */
/* to the printer        */
ir.h.al = ch;

/* Invode printer int    */
/* 0x17h                 */
int86(0x17,&ir,&or);

/* return printer status */
return((int)or.h.ah);
}

/*
 * End of Source
 ***************/
```

Fig. 8-7. The source code listing for PRCHAR.ASM.

```
;*******************
; Start Source file
;
; File Name:    PRCHAR.ASM
;
; Synopsis:     prChar(port,ch)
;
; int port      printer port number
;
; char ch       character send to printer
;
; Description:  prChar uses BIOS int 17h,
;               function 0, to send the
;               character to the printer
;
; Returns:      Nothing
;


;
; Small model off defined at 4
; Medium model off defined at 6
;
off  equ  4   ; Small Model offset
;
; set row to parameter 1
; set column to parameter 2
;
port equ  WORD PTR [BP+off]
chr  equ  BYTE PTR [BP+off+2]


;
; Enable DOS segment-ordering at link time
;

    DOSSEG

;

    .MODEL SMALL

;

    PUBLIC _prChar
```

Fig. 8-7 continued.
;

```
     .CODE

;

_prChar PROC NEAR


;
; Save regs
;
     push BP
     mov  BP,SP
;
; Send byte to printer function 0
;
     mov   AH,0

;
; Character to be printer to AL
;

     mov   AL, chr

;
; The port goes to DX
;
     mov   DX,port

;
; Invoke printer int 17h
;

     int 17h

;
; Return printer status in AL
;

     mov   AL,AH
     mov   AH,0

;
```

```
; Restore regs
;
        pop   BP
        ret
;
; End of procedure
;


_prChar ENDP
        END


; End of Source Here
;*******************
```

Fig. 8-7 ends.

The procedure to find how many paragraphs to allocate is simple. First, you compile and link your program. But, do not execute the program. Check the .EXE file's size. Now, go back into the source code, adjust the parameter passed to tsrPS(...), recompile and link the program. If it crashes, allocate more memory, if it doesn't crash, you can allocate fewer paragraphs and see how it goes. This trial and error method required by the procedure described in the text might be a tad cumbersome, but the payoff is that you can find the absolute smallest amount of memory needed to keep your TSR program healthy. Remember, SMALL is a BIG word in TSR programming. The source code for TSRPS.ASM is listed in FIG. 8-8.

Fig. 8-8. The source code to TSRPS.ASM.

```
;*******************
; Source Code Start
;
; File Name:    TSRPS.ASM
;
; Synopsis:     tsrPS(blocks)
;
; int blocks    number of 16 byte paragraph
;               blocks to reserve for the
;               print screen TSR program
;
; Description: This should be the last
;               function called in main().
;               Once called, your program
;               will remain in memory
;               as a Terminate and Stay
;               Resident program and can
;               be invoked with a press
;               of the print screen key.
;
; Returns:      Nothing
```

Fig. 8-8 continued.

```
;
;
; Enable DOS segment-ordering at link time
;

        DOSSEG

;
; Set the memory model for simplified segmentation
; directives
;

        .MODEL SMALL

;
; Make function visible to linker
;

        PUBLIC  _tsrPS

;
; Defines the start of the code segment
;

        .CODE

;
; Set the start of the function
;

_tsrPS PROC NEAR

;
; Save regs
;

        push    BP
        mov     BP,SP

;
; Move number of 16 byte paragraph
; blocks of memory from stack to
; DX
;

        mov     DX,4[BP]

;
; INT 21h Function 49 is TSR
;

        mov     AL,0
        mov     AH,49
        int     21H

;
; restore regs -
;
```

```
        mov     SP,BP
        pop     BP
;
_tsrPS ENDP
;
        END

;
; End of source listing
;**********************
```

Fig. 8-8 ends.

The next object module we need to add to the TAB library will allow us to determine if PRTSCRN has been installed in memory. This feat is accomplished by placing the id number 313 (my lucky number, by the way) in the WORD of memory following directly after the JMP instruction in the new interrupt 5 (set with setPSvec( )). This will be clear when you examine the code for setPSvec( ) shown in FIG. 8-10. The assembly source code listing for PSFIND.ASM is presented in FIG. 8-9. PSFIND's use will be demonstrated in the program PSDETECT presented later in Chapter 8.

Fig. 8-9. The source code listing for PSFIND.ASM.

```
;******************
; Source Code Start
;
; File Name:    PSFIND.ASM
;
; Synopsis:     install = psfind()
;
; int install  Holds info as to PRTSCRN's
;               installation in memory
;               0 => program not installed
;
; Description:
;               1 => PRTSCRN installed
;                    as TSR program
;               0 => PRTSCRN not installed
;                    as TSR program
;
; Returns:      Installation code

;
; Enable DOS segment-ordering at link time
;
        DOSSEG

;
; Set the memory model for simplified segmentation
; directives
;
        .MODEL SMALL
```

Fig. 8-9 continued.

```
;
; Make function name visible to linker
;

        PUBLIC  _psfind

;
; Defines the start of the code segment
;

        .CODE

;
; Function name
;

_psfind PROC NEAR
;
; Save regs
;

        push    BP
        mov     BP,SP
        push    DS
        push    ES
        push    BX
        push    SI


;
; Get int 05h vector
;
        mov     AX,3505h
        int     21h

        mov     AX,ES
        mov     DS,AX


;
; Bypass JMP over data instruction
; at vector address and point
; to PRTSCRN ID
;

        add     BX,3
        mov     SI,BX


;
; Retrieve id value ...
;

        mov     AX,WORD PTR [SI]


;
; ... and compare to received id value
;

        cmp     AX,313
```

```
;
; if equal then return 1 (found)
;
        je      found


;
; if not equal then return 0 (not found)
;
        mov     AX,0
        jmp     findexit

found:

        mov     AX,1

findexit:

;
; restore regs
;
        pop     SI
        pop     BX
        pop     ES
        pop     DS
        mov     SP,BP
        pop     BP
        ret

_psfind ENDP
        END


;
; End of source listing
;**********************
```

Fig. 8-9 ends.

Finally, the last function required by PRTSCRN.EXE is SETPSVEC (FIG. 8-10). As you just saw in FIG. 8-10, this heavily documented routine gets the segment and offset of the default Print Screen vector (0x05). It then moves this

Fig. 8-10. The source code to SETPSVEC.ASM.

```
;*******************
; Source Code Start
;
; File Name:   SETPSVEC.ASM
;
; Synopsis:    setPSvec()
;
; Description: Redirects the print screen
;              key to point to a routine
;              called by default newPS().
;              Note that this print screen
;              int handler also saves and
;              restores the DTA along with
;              the PSP.
```

Fig. 8-10 continued.

```
;
; Returns:      Nothing
;
; Enable DOS segment-ordering at link time
;

        DOSSEG


;
; Set the memory model for simplified segmentatic
; directives
;

        .MODEL SMALL


;
; This extrn MUST be declared in one
; of you other object files.  _newPS
; is the function which will be called
; when the print screen key is pressed.
;

extrn   _newPS:NEAR


;
; Make function visible to linker
;

        PUBLIC  _setPSvec


;
; Defines the start of the code segment
;

        .CODE


;
; The TSR stack has been declared
;

        dw      100h dup (0ffh)
tsrSTACK:


;
; Set the start of the function
;

_setPSvec PROC NEAR


;
; Jump over data declared in the
; CODE segment
;

        jmp     ps1

;

old5    DW      0,0
```

Fig. 8-10 continued.

```
oldDS     DW     0
oldES     DW     0
oldSS     DW     0
oldSP     DW     0
newDS     DW     0
newES     DW     0
newSS     DW     0
newSP     DW     0
tsrPSP    DW     0
curPSP    DW     0
offDTA    DW     0
segDTA    DW     0

;

ps1:

;
; Save Regs
;

          push    BP
          mov     BP,SP

          push    AX
          push    BX
          push    CX
          push    DX
          push    DS
          push    ES

          mov     AX,@DATA
          mov     oldDS,AX

          mov     oldES,ES
          mov     oldSS,SS
          mov     oldSP,SP

          mov     AX,@CODE
          mov     DS,AX

;
; Get the segment and register of
; the existing INT 05h vector...
;

          mov     AX,3505h ; get int 5 vec
          int     21h

;
; ... and store it in memory
;

          mov     old5,BX
          mov     old5+2,ES

;
```

Fig. 8-10 continued.

```
; Set new INT 05h vector to
; ANEWPS
;

        mov     DX,offset ANEWPS
        mov     AX,2505h
        int     21H

;
; Relocate vector info data
; in code segment
;

        call    rem_vecs

;
; Clear interrupt flag
;

        cli

;
; Get tsr PSP ...
;

        mov     AH,51H
        int     21H

;
; ... and save in memory
;

        mov     tsrPSP,BX

;
; Enable interrupts
;
        sti

;
; Pop REGS from stack
;

        pop     ES
        pop     DS
        pop     DX
        pop     CX
        pop     BX
        pop     AX

        mov     SP,BP
        pop     BP

;
; Return to caller
;
```

Fig. 8-10 continued.

```
          ret
_setPSvec ENDP


;
; Far call for new int 05h
;

ANEWPS PROC FAR
;
; Jump over data in code segment
;

          jmp       byp ; uses 3 bytes
;
; The data here is accessed by psremv()
; and rps.com to restore the old print
; screen vector and free the memory
;

id        DW        0   ; uses 2 bytes
o5        DW        0,0 ; uses four bytes
oldCS     DW        0
progon    DB        0

;

byp:
;
; Save regs
;

          push      BP
          mov       BP,SP

          push      AX
          push      BX
          push      CX
          push      DX
          push      DI
          push      SI
          push      DS
          push      ES


;
; Restore NON-INTERRUPT reg values
;

          mov       newSS,SS
          mov       newSP,SP

          mov       DS,oldDS
          mov       ES,oldES
          mov       SS,oldSS
          mov       SP,oldSP


;
; find current PSP
```

Fig. 8-10 continued.

```
;

        mov     AH,51H
        int     21H
        mov     curPSP,BX

;
; set PSP to original tsrPSP
;

        mov     BX,tsrPSP
        mov     AH,50H
        int     21H

;
; set original DTA
;

        mov     AH,2fH
        int     21H
        mov     offDTA,BX
        mov     segDTA,ES
        push    DS
        mov     DS,tsrPSP
        mov     DX,80H
        mov     AH,1aH
        int     21H
        pop     DS

;
; Is busy flag on?
;

        cmp     progon,1

;
; Jump on YES to prevent re-entering
; currently executing 05h code
;

        je      nops

;
; Set busy flag ON
;

        mov     progon,1

;
; Call C function
;

        call    _newPS

;
; C function has returned so
; clear the busy flag
;
```

Fig. 8-10 continued.

```
                mov       progon,0

nops:

;
; reset PSP
;

                mov       BX,curPSP
                mov       AH,50H
                int       21H


;
; reset DTA
;

                push      DS
                push      AX
                mov       AX,offDTA
                mov       DX,AX
                mov       AX,segDTA
                mov       DS,AX
                mov       AH,1aH
                int       21H
                pop       AX
                pop       DS


;
; restore regs
;

                mov       SS,newSS
                mov       SP,newSP

                pop       ES
                pop       DS
                pop       SI
                pop       DI
                pop       DX
                pop       CX
                pop       BX
                pop       AX

                mov       SP,BP
                pop       BP
                iret
ANEWPS ENDP

;
; relocate seg data -
; for future use
;

rem_vecs PROC NEAR
                mov       AX,old5
                mov       o5,AX
                mov       AX,old5+2
```

```
        mov     o5+2,AX

        mov     AX,CS
        mov     oldCS,AX
        ret
rem_vecs ENDP
        END


;
; End of source listing
;***********************
;
```

Fig. 8-10 ends.

information to a specific offset from the address of the new Print Screen routine. This is done so that the program to remove PRTSCRN.EXE (RPS.COM) will have the information to restore the original vector Print Screen Vector. PRTSCRN's code segment is then saved at a specific offset from the new Print Screen routine.

This code segment is used by the RPS.COM program to remove PRTSCRN and to free PRTSCRN's memory for other uses. Lastly, the new Print Screen Routine's address (ANEWPS) is placed in the PC's int vector table.

The new Print Screen routine (ANEWPS) calls a C function with the name newPS( ). It's your job to declare a function in your C source file called newPS ( ). In other words, after setPSvec( ) is called and PRTSCRN is Terminated and Staying Resident, pressing the Print Screen key calls your newPS( ) function.

It is now time to begin presenting the source for the modules that will provide the underpinning of PRTSCRN.EXE and CLOCK.EXE.

Finally, the source code to the test and demonstration program PRTSCRN is listed in FIG. 8-11.

Fig. 8-11. The source code listing to PRTSCRN.C.

```
/********************
 * Source Code Start
 *
 * File Name:    PRTSCRN.C
 *
 * Description: Demonstration program of
 *              a Terminate and Stay Resident
 *              program written in C using the
 *              TAB library
 */

/*
 * Include files
 */

#include <stdio.h>
#include <dos.h>
#include <fcntl.h>
```

Fig. 8-11 continued.

```
#include <io.h>
#include <sys\types.h>
#include <sys\stat.h>
#include <string.h>
#include <ctype.h>

#include <tproto.h>

/*
 * Prototypes
 */

void newPS(void);
void setPSvec(void);
void tsrPS(int);
void strEnul(char *);
void save_screen(void);
void print_screen(void);
void s_screen(void);


/*
 * To Set FILE_SIZE
 * ----------------
 * 1) Compile and Link your TSR program
 * 2) Get .EXE program size
 * 3) Set FILE_SIZE to program size
 * 4) Compile and link again
 */

#define FILE_SIZE 15000

/*
 * Global pointer to WIND structures
 */

WIND *S_SCRN;
WIND *I_PS;

/*
 * window text for file
 * save pop up
 */

char saveit1[28] = "         Screen  Save        ";
char saveit2[28] = "                             ";
char saveit3[28] = "   Save File:                ";
char saveit4[28] = "                             ";
char saveit5[28] = "  Press ENTER to Save        ";
char saveit6[28] = "  Press ESC to exit          ";

char drop11[14]  = " Print Screen ";
char drop12[14]  = " Save Screen  ";
char drop13[14]  = " Mini - DOS   ";
char drop14[14]  = "              ";

/*
```

Fig. 8-11 continued.

```
 * Global data
 */

char file_name[12];
int key;    /* scan and char value   */
int attr;  /* highlight attribute   */
int ps_exit;
int old_row,row;
int inverse;

/*
 * Function s_screen
 *
 * Description:
 *   Save the screen to disk
 */

void
s_screen()
{
int row, column, handle, length, token;
char buffer[81];

/* OPEN a file named in file_name buffer */
handle = open(file_name,
              O_CREAT|O_TRUNC|O_RDWR|O_TEXT,
              S_IREAD|S_IWRITE);

/* word on screen row by row             */
for(row=0; row<25; row++)
   {
   /* clear buffer with NULLS            */
   memset(buffer,aNUL,81);

   /* get character byte                 */
   for(column=0; column<80; column++)
      {
      /* move cursor to row, column      */
      mvCur(row,column);

      /* use BIOS to get screen token    */
      token = rdChar();

      /* Mask off scan code              */
      token &= 0x00ff;

      /* cast INT token to CHAR and move */
      /* to buffer column location       */
      buffer[column] = (char)token;
      }

   /* Convert all trailing spaces (aSPC  */
   /* or 0x20) to aNUL (0)               */
   strEnul(buffer);

   /* determine the length of the ASCII  */
```

Fig. 8-11 continued.

```
    /* bytes in buffer                 */
    length = strlen(buffer);

    /* Append a Carriage Return to the  */
    /* last ASCII byte in buffer ...     */
    buffer[length++] = aCR;

    /* ... followed by a Line Feed char  */
    /* to make the file a DOS text format */
    /* file.                             */
    buffer[length++] = aLF;

    /* Finally, write the string in      */
    /* buffer to disk.                   */
    write(handle,buffer,strlen(buffer));
    }

/* close the file                        */
close(handle);
}

/*
 * Function print_screen
 *
 * Description:
 *   print the screen
 */
void
print_screen()
{
int row, column, counter, length, token;
char buffer[81];

/* Print the screen row by row          */
for(row=0; row<25; row++)
    {
    /* Clear buffer with aNUL            */
    memset(buffer,aNUL,81);

    /* Relocate screen bytes to buffer   */
    /* column by column.                 */
    for(column=0; column<80; column++)
        {
        /* Move the cursor to row, column */
        mvCur(row,column);

        /* Read the token from the screen */
        /* via BIOS                       */
        token = rdChar();

        /* Mask off SCAN byte from token  */
        token &= 0x00ff;

        /* Cast INT token to char and     */
        /* relocate to buffer             */
        buffer[column] = (char)token;
```

Fig. 8-11 continued.

```
    }
    /* Change all training spaces to aNUL */
    strEnul(buffer);

    /* Determine the string length in    */
    /* buffer                            */
    length = strlen(buffer);

    /* Append a Carriage Return to the   */
    /* last ASCII byte in buffer ...     */
    buffer[length++] = aCR;

    /* ... followed by a Line Feed char  */
    /* to make the file a DOS text format */
    /* file.                             */
    buffer[length++] = aLF;

    /* Print the ASCII character byte by */
    /* byte until done.                  */
    for(counter=0; counter<length; counter++)
        /* Port and character passed to  */
        /* prchar.                       */
        prChar(0,buffer[counter]);
    }

}

/*
 * Function save_screen
 *
 * Description:
 *  Save the screen as a DOS
 *  text file.  If a file
 *  of the file_name currently
 *  exists you are querried
 *  as to whether you wish to
 *  over write the file or
 *  not.
 */

/*
 * Global flag used to
 * determine if strtWind(...)
 * or dispWind(...) should be
 * used to display the Print
 * Screen Window
 */

int first_save = 0;

void
save_screen()
{
int handle;
int val,exit;

/* Use strtWind(...) the first time the  */
```

Fig. 8-11 continued.

```
/* the print screen key is pressed      */
if(!first_save)
    {
    /* Display previously allocated       */
    /* window                             */
    strtWind(S_SCRN);

    /* Set flag to use dispWind(...) all  */
    /* other times Print Screen is        */
    first_save = aTRUE;
    }
else
    /* Display window after strtWind      */
    /* called                             */
    dispWind(S_SCRN);

do
    {
    /* Write menu and exit messages */
    wvdWrite(S_SCRN,1,1,28,saveit1,
            mkAttr(CYAN,
                   BLACK,
                   OFF_INTENSITY,
                   OFF_BLINK));
    wvdWrite(S_SCRN,2,1,28,saveit2,S_SCRN->attr);
    wvdWrite(S_SCRN,3,1,28,saveit3,S_SCRN->attr);
    wvdWrite(S_SCRN,4,1,28,saveit4,S_SCRN->attr);
    wvdWrite(S_SCRN,5,1,28,saveit5,S_SCRN->attr);
    wvdWrite(S_SCRN,6,1,28,saveit6,S_SCRN->attr);

    /* Turn on the cursor                 */
    onCur();

    /* Move the cursor within the window  */
    /* for file name data entry location  */
    wmvCur(S_SCRN,3,15);

    /* Clear the fine_name buffer with 0s */
    memset(file_name,'\0',12);

    /* Get file name string               */
    if(!prompt(file_name,12))
        /* On ESC key preess exit from    */
        /* prompt(...) remove the Window  */
        remvWind(S_SCRN);

    /* ENTER key press terminated prompt  */
    else
        {
        /* Open the file named in         */
        /* file_name                      */
        handle = open(file_name,
                      O_RDWR|O_TEXT,
                      S_IREAD|S_IWRITE);

        /* If file named already exists... */
        if(handle>=0)
```

Fig. 8-11 continued.

```
{
/* Print file exists warning to */
/* the screen               */
wvdWrite(S_SCRN,3,1,28,
        "  File Already Exists      ",
        S_SCRN->attr);
wvdWrite(S_SCRN,4,1,28,
        "  Press (Y)es to overwrite ",
        S_SCRN->attr);
wvdWrite(S_SCRN,5,1,28,
        "                           ",
        S_SCRN->attr);

/* Wait and get key press    */
/* response                  */
val = gtKey();

/* Mask out INT's scan code   */
val &= 0x00ff;

/* Trun ASCII key to cap      */
val = toupper(val);

/* If 'Y' the yes overwrite the */
/* file with the same name      */
if(val=='Y')
    {
    /* Close open file          */
    close(handle);

    /* Remove save screen window */
    /* and restore previous      */
    /* screen image              */
    remvWind(S_SCRN);

    /* Save the restored screen  */
    /* to disk                   */
    s_screen();

    /* Set flag to terminate     */
    /* loop                      */
    exit = aTRUE;
    }

/* Another key had been pressed */
else
    {
    /* Close the open file       */
    close(handle);

    /* Remove the window from     */
    /* the screen                 */
    remvWind(S_SCRN);

    /* Terminate the loop         */
    exit = aTRUE;
    }
}
```

290

Fig. 8-11 continued.

```
                /* File name does not currently    */
                /* exist in active directory       */
                else
                    {
                    /* Close the open file         */
                    close(handle);

                    /* Remove the window from the    */
                    /* screen and restore the orig-  */
                    /* inal screen image             */
                    remvWind(S_SCRN);

                    /* Save the screen image to      */
                    /* disk in DOS text file format  */
                    s_screen();

                    /* Terminate loop                */
                    exit = aTRUE;
                    }
                }
        } while(!exit);

}

/*
 * Function newPS
 *
 * Description:
 *  This function uses
 *  a default name EXTRNed
 *  in the assembly file
 *  SETPSVEC.ASM. This is
 *  the new print screen
 *  routine.
 */

/*
 * Global flag used to
 * determine if strtWind(...)
 * or dispWind(...) should be
 * used to display the Print
 * Screen Window
 */

int first_time = 0;

void
newPS()
{
int c_row, c_col;

/* Get current cursor location */
gtCur(&c_row, &c_col);

/* Turn cursor off */
offCur();
```

Fig. 8-11 continued.

```
/* Use strtWind(...) the first time the  */
/* the print screen key is pressed       */
if(!first_time)
    {
    /* Display previously allocated       */
    /* window                             */
    strtWind(I_PS);

    /* Set flag to use dispWind(...) all  */
    /* other times Print Screen is        */
    /* pressed                            */
    first_time = aTRUE;
    }
else
    /* Display window after strtWind      */
    /* called                             */
    dispWind(I_PS);

/* Write menu and exit messages          */
wvdWrite(I_PS,1,1,14,drop11,I_PS->attr);
wvdWrite(I_PS,2,1,14,drop12,I_PS->attr);
wvdAttr(I_PS,1,1,1,attr);
wvdAttr(I_PS,2,1,1,attr);

/* Set highlight bar to TOP item in MENU */
/* window                                */
row = 1;
old_row = 1;
ps_exit = aFALSE;

/* Pop Up window keyboard loop           */
do
    {
    /* Off highlight bar                  */
    wvdAttr(I_PS,old_row,1,14,I_PS->attr);

    /* On highlight of menu item first    */
    /* letter                             */
    wvdAttr(I_PS,old_row,1,1,attr);

    /* Inverse the new menu item's row    */
    wvdAttr(I_PS,row,1,14,inverse);
    old_row = row;

    /* wait for key press                 */
    key = gtKey();

    /* Filter key press                   */
    switch(key)
        {
        /* ESC key pressed                */
        case ESCAPE:
            /* Remove Print Screen Window  */
            /* and restore original screen */
            /* image which was under window */
            remvWind(I_PS);
```

Fig. 8-11 continued.

```
                                /* Set flag to exit from TSR     */
                                /* and return to DOS program     */
                                ps_exit = aTRUE;
                                break;
            /* Down Arrow key pressed         */
            case DOWN_ARROW:
                /* If highlight on row 2 then     */
                if(row==2)
                    /* change highlight to row 1 */
                    row=1;
                else
                    /* move from row 1 to row 2  */
                    row++;
                break;

            /* Up Arrow key pressed          */
            case UP_ARROW:
                /* If highlight on row 1 then    */
                if(row==1)
                    /* move highlight to row 2   */
                    row=2;
                else
                    /* move highlight to row 1   */
                    row--;
                break;

            /* ENTER key pressed            */
            case ENTER:
                switch(row)
                    {
                    /* Print screen Menu Item    */
                    /* selected                  */
                    case 1:
                        /* Remove Print Screen   */
                        /* Pop Up Window         */
                        remvWind(I_PS);

                        /* Send the screen image */
                        /* to printer            */
                        print_screen();

                        /* Set flag to exit from */
                        /* TSR and return to DOS */
                        /* program               */
                        ps_exit = aTRUE;
                        break;

                    /* Save the screen image as  */
                    /* a DOS text file selected  */
                    case 2:
                        /* Remove Print Screen   */
                        /* Pop Up Window         */
                        remvWind(I_PS);

                        /* Save the screen text  */
                        /* image to disk         */
                        save_screen();
```

293

Fig. 8-11 continued.

```
        /* Set flag to exit from  */
        /* TSR and return to DOS   */
        /* program                 */
        ps_exit = aTRUE;
        break;


    }
  break;

/* Another key has been pressed    */
default:

  /* Mask off scan byte            */
  key &=0x00ff;

  /* Turn ASCII to cap             */
  key = toupper(key);

  /* Filter key stroke             */
  switch(key)
      {
      /* Letter 'P' pressed        */
      case 'P':
          /* Remove Print Screen Window    */
          /* and restore original screen   */
          /* image which was under window */
          remvWind(I_PS);

          /* Send the screen image   */
          /* to printer              */
          print_screen();

          /* Set flag to exit from   */
          /* TSR and return to DOS   */
          /* program                 */
          ps_exit = aTRUE;
          break;

      case 'S':
          /* Remove Print Screen Window    */
          /* and restore original screen   */
          /* image which was under window */
          remvWind(I_PS);

          /* Save the screen text    */
          /* image to disk           */
          save_screen();

          /* Set flag to exit from   */
          /* TSR and return to DOS   */
          /* program                 */
          ps_exit = aTRUE;
          break;

      /* Exit on any key press       */
      default:
```

Fig. 8-11 continued.

```
                /* Remove Print Screen Window    */
                /* and restore original screen   */
                /* image which was under window */
                remvWind(I_PS);

                /* Set flag to exit from  */
                /* TSR and return to DOS  */
                /* program                */
                ps_exit = aTRUE;
                break;
            }
        break;
        }
   } while(!ps_exit);

/* turn cousor on */
onCur();

/* Restore the cursor location */
mvCur(c_row,c_col);
}

/*
 * Function main
 */

void
main()
{
/* Prepare video structure */
/* for all TAB library      */
/* routines.                */
vidInit();

/* make highlight attribute */
attr = mkAttr(WHITE,
              BLUE,
              ON_INTENSITY,
              OFF_BLINK);
inverse = mkAttr(BLUE,
              WHITE,
              OFF_INTENSITY,
              OFF_BLINK);

/*****************************************/
/* Initialize grid menu window structure */
/* and display window. This must be done */
/* in main() because memory for these    */
/* functions is dynamically allocated    */
/* using MALLOC(...) or CALLOC(..). One  */
/* restriction of TSR programming is     */
/* that you are NEVER permitted to       */
/* dynamically allocate memory once the  */
/* program has been made resident. But-  */
/* since the call to make the program    */
/* TSR is made as the very last call in  */
/* main(), all calls before the TSR call */
```

```
/* may dynamically allocate memory.      */
/******************************************/


/* Ensure window initialization bypass    */

/* Allocate memory and return pointer to */
/* structure                             */
I_PS = setWind(I_PS,1+4,0+20,4+4,15+20);

/* Set Window Attr - Fore,Back,Intensity */
/* Blink                                 */
setAttr(I_PS,mkAttr(WHITE,
                    BLUE,
                    OFF_INTENSITY,
                    OFF_BLINK));

/* Set Window Border                     */
setBord(I_PS,S_S_S_S);

/* Set the bottom title                  */
setTitle(I_PS," Screen I/O ");

/* Allocate memory and return pointer to */
/* structure                             */
S_SCRN = setWind(S_SCRN,7,24,7+7,24+29);

/* Set Window Attr - Fore,Back,Intensity */
/* Blink                                 */
setAttr(S_SCRN,mkAttr(BLACK,
                      CYAN,
                      OFF_INTENSITY,
                      OFF_BLINK));

/* Set Window Border                     */
setBord(S_SCRN,D_D_D_D);

/* Set the bottom title                  */
setTitle(S_SCRN," Screen I/O ");

/* Redirect the Print Screen Vector 0x05 */
/* so that the routine newPS() is called */
/* whenever the print screen vector is   */
/* called - ID matches value in PSMANAGE */
/* loader program                        */
setPSvec();

/* Make this program Terminate and Stay  */
/* Resident                              */
tsrPS((FILE_SIZE/16)+10);
}

/*
 * End of source
 ***************/
```

Fig. 8-11 ends.

The program to detect if PRTSCRN has been installed is called PS DETECT and is presented in FIG. 8-12.

Fig. 8-12. The source code listing for PSDETECT.C.

```
/*************
 * Source Code Start
 *
 * File Name:   PSDETECT.C
 *
 * Description: Demonstration
 *              psfind
 */

/*
 * Include files
 */

#include <stdio.h>
#include <process.h>

int psfind(void);

/*
 * Function main
 */

void
main()
{
/* Initialize TAB video routines      */
vidInit();

/* Clear the screen and cursor to 0,0 */
scrnClr();

printf
("+-------------------------------------------------------+|n");

printf
("|           PRTSCRN Program Detection Program            |\n");

printf
("+-------------------------------------------------------+\n");
```

```
/* Is PRTSCRN installed in memory?              */
if(psfind())
      /* Yes - installed in memory               */
      printf
    ("\nPRTSCRN is currently Installed in memory.\n");
else
      printf
      ("\nPRTSCRN is not currently installed in memory.\n");
}

/*
 * End of source listing
 **********************/
```

Fig. 8-12 ends.

Now that you have PRTSCRN installed as a TSR and have detected its presence in memory, it's time to remove PRTSCRN and restore the old Print Screen vector using the code listed in PRS.ASM. The steps to remove and restore are:

1. Get the segment and offset to the PRTSCRN redirected 0x05 vector.
2. This segment and offset point to the address of the new Print Screen routine. This new routine begins with a JMP over data held in the code segment. This data contains the original Print Screen segment, the original Print Screen offset, and the original code segment. Change the offset of the PRTSCRN to point into PRTSCRN's data (held after the JMP in the code segment) and set to the original Print Screen offset.
3. Get original Print screen offset.
4. Adjust offset pointer to point to original Print Screen segment.
5. Get original Print Screen offset.
6. Use BIOS to reset Print Screen vector (0x05) to original segment and offset values.
7. Adjust offset pointer to point to code segment for PRTSCRN.
8. Subtract 16 bytes (one paragraph) from segment value.
9. Use BIOS to free memory which had been previously assigned to PRTSCRN.

The code to implement the above procedure is called RPS.ASM. The RPS (Remove PrtScrn) is assembly code which will be assembled as usual, but then linked into a .COM file. The .COM files are far more compact than .EXE files and RPS.ASM is given as an example. The source code for RPS.ASM is listed in FIG. 8-13.

Fig. 8-13. The source code to RPS.ASM.

```
;********************
; Source Code Start
;
; File Name:   RPS.ASM
;
; Synopsis:    rps <ENTER>
;
; Description: RPS.COM is run from the
;              command line, disables
;              the print screen
;              PRTSCRN.EXE program and
;              restores the original print
;              screen vector.  The memory
;              used for PRTSCRN.EXE is then
;              freed.
;
; Returns:     Nothing


;
; Enable DOS segment-ordering at link time
;

        DOSSEG


;
; Set the memory model for simplified segmentation
; directives
;

        .MODEL SMALL

;
; Defines the start of the code segment
;

        .CODE

;
; Make the program RPS.COM
;

        org     100h

;
; Jump over data in code segment
;

ProgStart:
        jmp     ps1
;
saveBX  DW      0
saveDS  DW      0
;
ps1:

;
```

Fig. 8-13 continued.

```
; Get the address of the int 05h
; vector which operates the
; PRTSCRN program
;

        mov     AX,3505h ; ps vector
        int     21h


;
; The ES register holds the
; segment information of the
; PRTSCRN program and BX holds
; the offset information
;
; Relocate segment to DS
;

        mov     AX,ES
        mov     DS,AX


;
; Bypass JMP instruction and
; WORD (3 bytes + 2 bytes) and
; set BX pointing to WORD holding

; offset for old print screen
; vector.
;

        add     BX,5 ; addr of old vec 5 offset


;
; Save BX and DS registers
;

        mov     saveBX,BX
        mov     saveDS,DS


;
; Move offset of old print screen vector
; to DX register
;

        mov     SI,BX ; offset points to int 5
        mov     DX,WORD PTR [SI]


;
; Adjust SI pointer
;

        inc     SI
        inc     SI      ; segment ·points to int 5


;
; Move segment information of old print
; screen vector to DS register
;
```

```
        mov     AX,WORD PTR [SI]
        mov     DS,AX

;
; restore old print screen vector
;

        mov     AX,2505h ; old ps vector restored here
        int     21h

;
; Restore old BX and DS register values
;

        mov     BX,saveBX
        mov     DS,saveDS

;
; Bypass offset and segment of old
; print screen and get code segment
; for the new PRTSCRN.EXE program.
; Pointer adjusted by 4 bytes (2 words)
;

        add     BX,4        ; move BX 4 bytes to oldCS
        mov     SI,BX       ; offset of old CS

;
; Put PRTSCRN code segment into
; AX register, subtract 10h (one
; 16 byte paragraph) from value
; and relocate to ES register
;

        mov     AX,WORD PTR [SI]
        sub     AX,10h
        mov     ES,AX

;
; Finally, free the memory which
; holds PRTSCRN.EXE
;

        mov     AX,0
        mov     AH,49h    ; free memory
        int     21h

;
; Return to DOS us DOS
; terminate function
;

        mov     AH,4cH    ; DOS terminate function
        int     21H       ; DOS int

        END ProgStart

;
; End of RPS.COM program listing
;*********************************
```

Fig. 8-13 ends.

To assemble simply type:

a rps

and then press Enter. RPS.ASM will then assemble into RPS.OBJ. To convert RPS.OBJ into RPS.COM using Turbo's linker simply type:

tlink /t rps

and then press Enter. RPS.COM will now appear on your disk. If you own Microsoft's MASM Macro Assembler you will need to first convert RPS.OBJ into RPS.EXE and then use the EXE2BIN utility to then convert the RPS.EXE to RPS.COM. Check your MASM documentation for specific instructions on this procedure.

WRITING A TSR CLOCK ROUTINE IN C

I'm using WordPerfect 4.2 for preparation of this manuscript and use it for all of my nonsource code writing tasks. The WordPerfect 4.2 screen does not display the current time and because I don't have a clock in my office (don't ask why!), I could certainly use one. The CLOCK utility presented in this section of the text provides that needed clock in my office by keeping time in the upper right corner of my WordPerfect 4.2 screen display.

Interrupt 01ch is called by your PC 18.2 times a second. CLOCK.C's new-Timer( ) is updated every minute (18.2 updates x 60 secs) so it will be easy to change the minute ticker. Adding a blinking colon on the second count between the hour and minute display is also implemented. In truth, it's an approximate second, but close enough for the casual observer. Before the source code to CLOCK.C is discussed, FIGS. 8-14 through 8-16 present the utility functions needed to make your clock a TSR program that functions as billed.

Fig. 8-14. The source code listing to SETTIMER.ASM.

```
;******************
; Source Code Start
;
; File Name:    SETTIMER.ASM
;
; Synopsis:     setTimer()
;
; Description: Redirects the timer (0x1c)
;              key to point to a routine
;              called by default newTimer().
;
; Returns:      Nothing
;
;
```

Fig. 8-14 continued.

```
; Enable DOS segment-ordering at link time
;

        DOSSEG


;
; Set the memory model for simplified segmentation
; directives
;

        .MODEL SMALL


;
; This extrn MUST be declared in one
; of you other object files.  _newTimer
; is the function which will be called
; when int 0x1c is operational.
;

extrn   _newTimer:NEAR


;
; Make function visible to linker
;

        PUBLIC  _setTimer


;
; Defines the start of the code segment
;

        .CODE
;
; Data for TSR stack is held
; in the code segment
;

        dw      100h dup (0ffh)              ; stack for TSR register storage
tsrSTACK:


;
; Set the start of the function
;

_setTimer PROC NEAR
;
; Jump over data declared in the
; CODE segment
;

        jmp     ps1
;
old1c   DW      0,0
oldDS   DW      0
oldES   DW      0
oldSS   DW      0
oldSP   DW      0
```

303

Fig. 8-14 continued.

```
newDS    DW      0
newES    DW      0
newSS    DW      0
newSP    DW    · 0
tsrPSP   DW      0
curPSP   DW      0
offDTA   DW      0
segDTA   DW      0
;
ps1:
;
; Save regs
;

        push    BP
        mov     BP,SP

        push    AX
        push    BX
        push    CX
        push    DX
        push    DS
        push    ES

        mov     AX,aDATA
        mov     oldDS,AX

        mov     oldES,ES
        mov     oldSS,SS
        mov     oldSP,SP


;
; As data is now in Code segment
; make DS = CS
;

        mov     AX,aCODE
        mov     DS,AX


;
; Use BIOS to get int 01ch vector
; After int:
; BX holds offset 1ch
; ES holds segment 1ch
;

        mov     AX,351ch ; get int 1c vec
        int     21h


;
; Save int 1ch vec to memory
;

        mov     old1c,BX
        mov     old1c+2,ES


;
```

Fig. 8-14 continued.

```
; Reset 01ch for new timer routine
;
        mov     DX,offset ANEWTIMER
        mov     AX,251ch
        int     21H


;
; Relocate data which will be used in
; the removal of the new 01ch vec and
; restoration of the old 01ch vector
;
        call    rem_vecs


;
; Disable ints
;
        cli

;
; get tsr PSP ...
;
        mov     AH,51H
        int     21H


;
; ...and save in memory
;
        mov     tsrPSP,BX
;
; Enable ints
;
        sti


;
; Restore regs
;
        pop     ES
        pop     DS
        pop     DX
        pop     CX
        pop     BX
        pop     AX

        mov     SP,BP
        pop     BP
        ret
_setTimer ENDP


;
; New 01ch int routine
;
```

Fig. 8-14 continued.

```
ANEWTIMER PROC FAR
;
; Jump over data declared in the
; CODE segment
;
        jmp     byp
;
id      DW      0
o1c     DW      0,0
oldCS   DW      0
progon  DB      0
;
byp:
;
; Enable ints and push flags
; in preparation for call of
; default 01ch
;
        sti
        pushf
        assume ds:nothing
        call    DWORD PTR old1c
;
; If timer is busy bypass to
; prevent code re-entrancy
;

        cmp     progon,1
        je      notimer


;
; Save regs
;
        push    BP
        mov     BP,SP

        push    AX
        push    BX
        push    CX
        push    DX
        push    DI
        push    SI
        push    DS
        push    ES

        mov     newSS,SS
        mov     newSP,SP

        mov     AX,@CODE
        mov     SS,AX
        mov     SP,offset tsrSTACK ; point to new stack

        mov     DS,oldDS
        mov     ES,oldES


;
; Set 01ch busy flag
```

```
;
        mov     progon,1

;
; C routine called here
;
        call    _newTimer

;
; 01ch busy flag off
;
        mov     progon,0        ; clear program flag

;
; restore regs
;
        mov     SS,newSS
        mov     SP,newSP

        pop     ES
        pop     DS
        pop     SI
        pop     DI
        pop     DX
        pop     CX
        pop     BX
        pop     AX

        mov     SP,BP
        pop     BP
notimer:
        iret
ANEWTIMER ENDP


;
; Relocate data
;
rem_vecs PROC NEAR
        mov     AX,old1c
        mov     o1c,AX
        mov     AX,old1c+2
        mov     o1c+2,AX

        mov     AX,@CODE
        mov     oldCS,AX
        ret
rem_vecs ENDP
        END

;
; End of source listing
;***********************
```

Fig. 8-14 ends.

Fig. 8-15. The source code listing to TSRGTIME.ASM.

```
;******************
; Source Code Start
;
; File Name:    TSRGTIME.ASM
;
; Synopsis:     tsrgtime()
;
; Description: gets the current clock time
;              and transfers it into global
;              ints.
;
; Returns:      Nothing
;
;
; Enable DOS segment-ordering at link time
;

        DOSSEG

;
; Set the memory model for simplified segmentation
; directives
;

        .MODEL SMALL

;
; Make labels vidible to linker
;

        PUBLIC _tsrhour,_tsrmin
        PUBLIC _tsrsec,_tsrhun
        PUBLIC _c_fresh,_d_fresh
        PUBLIC _ampm

;
; Data segment using simplified directive
;

        .DATA
_tsrhour DW      0
_tsrmin  DW      0
_tsrsec  DW      0
_tsrhun  DW      0
click    DW      1092 ; 18.2 per second
_c_fresh DW      0
_d_fresh DW      0
_ampm    DW      0

;
; Make functions visible to linker
;

        PUBLIC  _tsrgtime,_adjclock

;
```

Fig. 8-15 continued.

```
; Defines the start of the code segment
;

        .CODE

;
; Set the start of the function
;

_tsrgtime PROC NEAR
;
; Save regs
;

        push    AX
        push    BX
        push    CX
        push    DX


;
; Get the system time and
; set global time variables
;
        mov     AH,2cH      ; get sys time
        int     21H
        xor     AX,AX       ; 0 -> AX
        mov     AL,CH
        mov     _tsrhour,AX ; save hour
        mov     AL,CL
        mov     _tsrmin,AX  ; save minute
        mov     AL,DH
        mov     _tsrsec,AX  ; save second
        mov     AL,DL
        mov     _tsrhun,AX  ; save hundredths


;
; Adjust values from 24 hour clock
; to 12 hour clock
;

        cmp     _tsrhour,0  ; is hour 0?
        je      is12am      ; y -> jmp
        cmp     _tsrhour,12 ; is hour 12?
        je      is12pm      ; y -> jump
        cmp     _tsrhour,12 ; is hour 1 to 11?
        jb      isam        ; y -> jump
        sub     _tsrhour,12 ; hour > 12 so hour -= 12
        mov     _ampm,1     ; _ampm flag set to PM
        jmp     done

is12am:
        mov     _tsrhour,12 ; set to 12
        mov     _ampm,0     ; AM
        jmp     done

is12pm:
        cmp     _ampm,1
```

Fig. 8-15 continued.

```
        je      toam
        mov     _ampm,1      ; set to 12 PM
        jmp     done

toam:
        mov     _ampm,0
        jmp     done

isam:
        mov     _ampm,0      ; set AM flag

done:
;
; Restore regs
;

        pop     DX
        pop     CX
        pop     BX
        pop     AX
        ret
_tsrgtime ENDP


;
; Called every 18.2 times
; a second, adjusts the
; seconds, minutes, and hours
;

_adjclock PROC NEAR
;
; Save regs
;

        push    AX
        push    BX
        push    CX
        push    DX


;
; Adjust gears of clock
;

        inc     click        ; increment counter
        cmp     click,1093   ; 18.2*60 = 1 minute
        jne     doneadj      ; jmp on < 1 minute
        mov     click,0      ; reset counter
        inc     _tsrmin      ; next minute
        cmp     _tsrmin,60   ; hour done
        jne     doneadj      ; jmp on no new hour
        mov     _tsrmin,0    ; 0 minutes on new hour
        inc     _tsrhour     ; new hour
        cmp     _tsrhour,12  ; is hour 12?
        je      is12         ; y -> jump
        cmp     _tsrhour,13  ; Is 1 PM?
        jne     doneadj      ; No -> exit
        mov     _tsrhour,1   ; now 1 PM
```

```
        mov     _ampm,1         ; set PM flag
        jmp     doneadj         ; exit
is12:
        cmp     _ampm,1         ; Is PM flag set?
        je      amswitch        ; y -> jump
        mov     _ampm,1         ; Is AM -> switch to PM
        jmp     doneadj         ; exit
amswitch:
        mov     _ampm,0         ; switch to AM
doneadj:
;
; Restore regs
;

        pop     DX              ; restore regs
        pop     CX
        pop     BX
        pop     AX
        ret
_adjclock ENDP
        END


;
; End of source listing
;***********************
```

Fig. 8-15 ends.

Fig. 8-16. The source listing for TSRTIME.ASM.

```
;*******************
; Source Code Start
;
; File Name:    TSRTIME.ASM
;
; Synopsis:     tsrtime(blocks)
;
; int blocks    number of 16 byte paragraph
;               blocks to reserve for the
;               print screen TSR program
;
;
; Description: This should be the last
;              function called in main().
;              Once called, your program
;              will remain in memory
;              as a Terminate and Stay
;              Resident program and can
;              be invoked with a press
;              of the print screen key.
;
; Returns:      Nothing
;
;
;
; Enable DOS segment-ordering at link time
;

        DOSSEG
```

Fig. 8-16 continued.

```
;
; Set the memory model for simplified segmentation
; directives
;

        .MODEL SMALL

;
; Make function visible to linker
;

        PUBLIC  _tsrtime

;
; Defines the start of the code segment
;

        .CODE

;
; Set the start of the function
;

_tsrtime PROC NEAR

;
; Now terminate and stay resident
;
;
; Save regs
;

        push    BP
        mov     BP,SP

;
; Move number of 16 byte paragraph
; blocks of memory from stack to
; DX
;

        mov     AX,4[BP]

;
; INT 21h Function 49 is TSR
;
        mov     DX,AX
        mov     AL,0
        mov     AH,49
        int     21H

;
; Restore regs
;

        mov     SP,BP
        pop     BP
```

```
                ret
        ;
        _tsrtime ENDP
                END
        ;
        ; End of source listing
        ;**********************
        ;
```

Fig. 8-16 ends.

FIGURE 8-17 shows the source code listing for CLOCK.C. Examine the comments carefully if they don't seem clear at first. The assembly listings plus CLOCK.C give a good look at using the PC's timer for a TSR program.

Now that you've gotten your TSR clock installed, you might need to remove it. For PRTSCRN, the source code to a COM file, was used to remove it from memory. For CLOCK.C, we'll use a functionally similar EXE file. Compare the file size for the REMCLOCK.EXE and RPS.COM files. It'll prove obvious why assembly generated COM files are the choice when size is an issue. FIGURE 8-18 shows the asembly listing for TIMEREMV.ASM and FIG. 8-19 shows the C source code for REMCLOCK.C.

Fig. 8-17. The source code listing to CLOCK.C.

```
/*******************
 * Source Code Start
 *
 * File Name:   CLOCK.C
 *
 * Description: Demonstration program of
 *              a Terminate and Stay Resident
 *              program written in C using the
 *              TAB library. A clock is placed
 *              on row 0 at the right edge of
 *              a video page 0 screen
 */

/*
 * Include files
 */

#include <stdio.h>
#include <dos.h>
#include <time.h>
#include <string.h>
#include <tproto.h>
#include <stdlib.h>

/*
 * Prototypes
 */

void newTimer(void);
```

Fig. 8-17 continued.

```
void setTimer(void);
void tsrtime(int);
void tsrgtime(void);
void adjclock(void);


/*
 * To Set FILE_SIZE
 * ----------------
 * 1) Compile and Link your TSR program
 * 2) Get .EXE program size
 * 3) Set FILE_SIZE to program size
 * 4) Compile and link again
 */

#define FILE_SIZE 4000
#define UPDATE (182*6)
#define BLINK 0

/*
 * Globals
 */

int    blink = BLINK, clock_attr;
int    min_ctr = UPDATE;

char buffer[80];

time_t time_of_day;
int counter = 0;
int first_time = 0;
int toggle = 0;
int time_row = 0;
int time_col = 60;

/*
 * Declared in assembly bindings
 */

extern int tsrhour,tsrmin,ampm;

/*
 * Function newTimer
 *
 * Description:
 *   This is the function called
 *   18.2 times a second
 */

void
newTimer()
{
char *cptr;
int len;

/* Adjust the gears of the clock */
adjclock();
```

Fig. 8-17 continued.

```
/* Blink ':' approximately once  */
/* a second                      */
if(blink>=18)
   {
   /* Reset blink counter to 0    */
   blink = 0;

   /* It toggle==0 turn ':' on    */
   if(!toggle)
      {
      /* toggle = 1                */
      toggle++;

      /* write ':' to screen       */
      vdWrite(0+time_row,
              4+time_col,
              1,
              ": ",
              clock_attr);

      /* minute counter to 0        */
      min_ctr = 0;

      /* convert min # to ASCII     */
      cptr = itoa(tsrmin,buffer,10);

      /* Length of min ASCII str    */
      len = strlen(cptr);

      /* two digit number           */
      if(len==2)
         {
         /* erase old min number */
         vdWrite(0+time_row,
                 7+time_col,
                 1,
                 " ",
                 clock_attr);

         /* write new min number */
         vdWrite(0+time_row,
                 5+time_col,
                 2,
                 cptr,
                 clock_attr);
         }

      /* If first digit==0          */
      else if(*cptr=='0')

         /* write '00'              */
         vdWrite(0+time_row,
                 5+time_col,
                 2,
                 "00",
                 clock_attr);
      else
```

Fig. 8-17 continued.

```
    {
    /* write single 0        */
    vdWrite(0+time_row,
            5+time_col,
            3,
            "0  ",
            clock_attr);

    /* and follow with       */
    /* single digit number   */
    vdWrite(0+time_row,
            6+time_col,
            1,
            cptr,
            clock_attr);
    }
/* if PM                     */
if(ampm)
    /* print 'pm' sign       */
    vdWrite(0+time_row,
            8+time_col,
            3,
            "pm ",
             clock_attr);

else
    /* print 'am' sign       */
    vdWrite(0+time_row,
            8+time_col,
            3,
            "am ",
            clock_attr);

/* now print the hour        */
/* the same print logic      */
/* as used in minute         */
cptr = itoa(tsrhour,buffer,10);
len = strlen(cptr);
vdWrite(0+time_row,
        1+time_col,
        1,
        "  ",
        clock_attr);
if(len==2)
    vdWrite(0+time_row,
            2+time_col,
            2,
            cptr,
            clock_attr);
else
    {
    vdWrite(0+time_row,
            2+time_col,
            1,
            "  ",
            clock_attr);
    vdWrite(0+time_row,
```

Fig. 8-17 continued.

```
                    3+time_col,
                    1,cptr,
                    clock_attr);
            }
        }
    else
        {
        toggle--;
        vdWrite(0+time_row,
                4+time_col,
                1,
                " ",
                clock_attr);
        }
    }
else
    /* blink counter += 1 */
    blink++;

}

/*
 * Function setClock
 *
 * Description:
 *   receives the row, column
 *   for the clock location
 *   and attribute for the
 *   clock
 */

void
setClock(row,col,attr)
int row;
int col;
int attr;
{
time_row = row;
time_col = col;
clock_attr = attr;
}

void
main()
{
/* Initialize VIDEO structure */
vidInit();

/* Set clock parameters      */
setClock(0,
        69,
        mkAttr(WHITE,
                RED,
                ON_INTENSITY,
                OFF_BLINK));

/* Get current time          */
```

```
tsrgtime();

/* Redirect 01ch vector        */
setTimer();

/* Make CLOCK TSR              */
tsrtime( (FILE_SIZE/16)+10);
}

/*
 * End of source
 ***************/
```

Fig. 8-17 ends.

Fig. 8-18. The source code listing to TIMEREMV.ASM.

```
;*******************
; Source Code Start
;
; File Name:   TIMEREMV.ASM
;
; Synopsis:    timeremv()
;
; Description: Called from C, this
;              function disables the clock
;              by restoring the old 01ch
;              vector and freeing memory.
;
; Returns:     Nothing


;
; Enable DOS segment-ordering at link time
;

        DOSSEG


;
; Set the memory model for simplified segmentation
; directives
;

        .MODEL SMALL


;
; Make function visible to linker
;

        PUBLIC  _timeremv


;
; Defines the start of the code segment
;

        .CODE
```

318

Fig. 8-18 continued.

```
;
; Set the start of the function
;

_timeremv        PROC NEAR
;
; Jump over data declared in the
; CODE segment
;

          jmp      pr1
saveBX  DW       0
saveDS  DW       0
pr1:
;
; Save regs
;

          push     BP
          mov      BP,SP

          push     AX
          push     BX
          push     CX
          push     DX
          push     DS
          push     ES
          push     SI


;
; Get redirected 01ch vector
;

          mov      AX,351ch
          int      21h


;
; ES holds DS for 01ch vector
; DS = ES
;

          mov      AX,ES
          mov      DS,AX


;
; Adjust offset to point to
; original 01ch timer int
;

          add      BX,5


;
; Save regs
;

          mov      saveBX,BX
          mov      saveDS,DS
```

Fig. 8-18 continued.

```
;
; Get old 01ch offset to DX
;
        mov     SI,BX
        mov     DX,WORD PTR [SI]


;
; Next word
;
        inc     SI
        inc     SI


;
; Get old 01ch segment to DS
;
        mov     AX,WORD PTR [SI]
        mov     DS,AX


;
; Restore old 01ch vector
;
        mov     AX,251ch
        int     21h


;
; Restore regs
;
        mov     BX,saveBX
        mov     DS,saveDS


;
; move offset to old CS
;
        add     BX,4
        mov     SI,BX


;
; CS for CLOCK TSR to AX and
; then reduced of 010h
;
        mov     AX,WORD PTR [SI]
        sub     AX,10h


;
; Adjusted CS to ES and free memory
;
        mov     ES,AX
        mov     AX,0
        mov     AH,49h    ; free memory
        int     21h
```

```
;
; Restore regs
;

        pop     SI
        pop     ES
        pop     DS
        pop     DX
        pop     CX
        pop     BX
        pop     AX

        mov     SP,BP
        pop     BP
        ret
_timeremv ENDP
        END
;
; End of source listing
;************************
```

Fig. 8-18 ends.

Fig. 8-19. The source code to REMCLOCK.C.

```
/*******************
 * Source Code Start
 *
 * File Name:   REMCLOCK.C
 *
 * Description: Remove CLOCK TSR program by
 *              restorint old 01ch vector and
 *              then by freeing memory.
 */

/*
 * Include files
 */

#include <tproto.h>

void main(void);
void timeremv(void);

void
main()
{
timeremv();
}

/*
 * End of source listing
 ************************/
```

SUMMARY

Chapter 8 presented the source code with required TAB library source for two Terminate and Stay Resident programs. The first program, PRTSCRN, used the Print Screen key as the hot key and demonstrated how to have multiple function programs available from a scroll bar window menu. The second program, CLOCK, demonstrated how to use the PC's timer to create an on-screen clock. Writing Terminate and Stay Resident program's in C is not a trivial affair, but can certainly be accomplished.

Chapter 9 adds a few more routines to complete your library and presents the listing for a prototype DOS shell. This program has many intrinsic source modules and extrinsic programs, which are called children. TABDOS will prove highly instructive to many readers and seems well placed as the final demonstration program for the TAB library functions.

9

Creating a DOS Shell Using Your TAB Library

What is a DOS shell? A DOS shell is an alternative to the standard A:\ > or
C:\ >. It is basically a new user interface for a Disk Operating System.

My first experience with one type of DOS shell began when I purchased
my first computer, an Atari 800. The DOS interface was named Atari DOS and
consisted of a menu of standard disk operations. The disk operations were
selected by pressing the letter next to the disk operation's description. Some of
Atari DOS's choices were copy file, format disk, delete file, run file, etc. The
operations of this DOS were limited by the choices on the menu and all the
choices were intrinsic to the DOS interface program. Intrinsic DOS commands
are contained in the DOS interface program, as opposed to being an executable
file run from the interface.

The second DOS I came across for the Atari 800 was written by the programmers at Optimized Systems Software. Dubbed OSA +, it tried to replace
the Original Atari DOS. OSA + presented my first experience with a command-
line DOS. Many of the OSA + disk functions were kept in small utility files on
disk. By leaving some functions out of the DOS interface, the designers of
OSA + were able to keep that disk operating system rather compact. OSA +
proved ideal for my Assembler development environment (the MAC65 macro
assembler cartridge also produced by Optimized Systems Software) and I
found myself in programmer's heaven.

Times were a changin' and I migrated to the 68000 Atari 520 ST machine.
The ST's DOS came from Digital Research and its interface was named GEM.
This GEM DOS interface had the menu bar, drop-down window, and the
rodent clicker (I mean mouse, of course) theme that was popularized in Macin-

tosh land. Although I've never really taken to using a mouse driven user interface, there was something very convenient in having disk file names displayed on the screen. Having the disk directory displayed all the time proved wonderfully convenient for all disk operations.

Times changed again and I soon found myself working on a MS-DOS PC clone with that famous command line prompt. After working on the design and co-programming a page composition program called "TypeSetter PC" (it never really took off even though I thought it had a clear place in the market when it was introduced) I meandered to developing the 'C'erious Library.

As previously mentioned, there's no better way to test library functions and to demonstrate their use than to have many demonstration programs—and of such a need TSRDOS was born. TSRDOS is a user interface for MS-DOS with drop-down windows, scrolling highlight bar selection scheme, disk directory files visible, and many of the goodies that the other MS-DOS interfaces sported.

Following the old OSA + scheme, many of TSRDOS functions are extrinsic to TSRDOS. This means that there will be more memory in the PC to run your applications' programs. I finished TSRDOS as the last demonstration program for the 'C'erious library.

Until one afternoon a MIS manager from a Fortune 500 company stood looking at some of our company's product line and TSRDOS appeared on the screen. He said, "Gee, that's a great looking shell. When will it be ready for market?" and the salesman, without blinking, responded "We'll be at alpha test stage within four weeks and we'll have an evaluation copy on your desk soon after that."

So TSRDOS passed from my beloved library development station to our gang of applications programmers (all 1 1/2 of them!). But, the original DOS Shell Interface program remained as a demonstration of the 'C'erious library. And from TSRDOS comes TABDOS which is the final and most comprehensive demonstration program for your TAB library. Although not a completed full-fledged DOS interface, TABDOS nevertheless sports drop-down windows and pop-up windows and dialog boxes.

One final note: remember that TABDOS uses both intrinsic and extrinsic functions. The consequence of this structure dictates that TABDOS (TD.EXE) and all of the extrinsic executable files be placed in a directory included in the PATH. This allows you to change directories from TABDOS and have all the extrinsic programs available for use at all times.

TABDOS is a large program with many source modules. Fortunately, all the compilers mentioned in this text have a MAKE utility which makes program creation and maintenance very easy. (More on MAKE later.)

ADDING THE FINAL OBJECT MODULES TO YOUR TAB LIBRARY

Before the MAKE file and source is presented for TABDOS and the extrinsic programs a few more utility functions must be added to your TAB library in order to get the program to compile and link properly.

FIGURE 9-1 presents the source code listing for CRITERR.ASM. This complex assembly listing steals the BIOS critical error handler and permits the programmer to replace the original interrupt handler, an alternate routine. In CRITERR.ASM, note that after the critical error occurs and the warning message is placed on the screen, the RETRY command is forced into the DOS kernel.

Fig. 9-1. The source code listing for CRITERR.ASM.

```
;******************
; Source Code Start
;
; File Name:   CRITERR.ASM
;
; Synopsis:    setCE()
;
; Description: Called from C, this
;              function steals the
;              critical error handler
;              (0x24) and allows for
;              personalized messages
;              on critical error occurs
;              using DispErr(...) and
;              EraseErr(...).
;
; Returns:     Nothing


;
; Enable DOS segment-ordering at link time
;

        DOSSEG


;
; Set the memory model for simplified segmentation
; directives
;

        .MODEL SMALL


;
; EXTRN's declared on other object
; modules
;

        EXTRN    _mvCur:NEAR
        EXTRN    _DispErr:NEAR
        EXTRN    _ErasErr:NEAR
```

CHAPTER 9

Fig. 9-1 continued.

```
;
; Make function visible to linker
;

        PUBLIC   _setCE


;
; Defines the start of the data segment
;

        .DATA

oldDS   DW      0
oldES   DW      0


;
; Defines the start of the code segment
;

        .CODE


;
; Set the start of the function
;

_setCE  PROC    near
;
; Save regs
;
        push    AX
        push    DX
        push    DS
        push    ES
;
        mov     AX,@DATA
        mov     oldDS,AX
        mov     AX,ES
        mov     oldES,AX
;
; Move CS into DS
;
        push    CS
        pop     DS


;
; Redirect 024h vec
; (critical error handler vector)
;
        mov     DX,offset _TEXT:int24
        mov     AX,2524H
        int     21H
;
; Redirect 00h vec
; (divide by zero)
;
```

Fig. 9-1 continued.

```
        mov     DX,offset _TEXT:int0
        mov     AX,2500H
        int     21H
;
; Restore regs
;

        pop     ES
        pop     DS
        pop     DX
        pop     AX
        ret
_setCE  ENDP


;
; New crit err handler
; is called when citical
; error occurs
;

int24   PROC    far
;
; Save regs
;
        push    BX
        push    CX
        push    DX
        push    SI
        push    DI
        push    BP
        push    DS
        push    ES
;
; Set DS = @DATA and
; ES = DS
;

        mov     AX,@data
        mov     DS,AX
        mov     ES,AX
;
; Move cursor to Row 24
;               Col 66
;
        mov     DH,24       ; row
        mov     DL,66       ; column
        mov     AH,2        ; mvCur func
        mov     BH,0        ; page 0
        int     10h         ; mvCur via BIOS
;
; Call DispErr() on critical error -
; DispErr() is in another object module
;

        call    _DispErr
;
; Wait for key press response ...
```

```
;

        mov     ah,01H ; wait key press
        int     21H
;
; ... and restore screen on key press
;

        call    _ErasErr ; erase message
;
; Force RETRY option into MS-DOS kernel
;

        mov     AL,1

;
; Restore regs
;
;
; Redirect 024h vec
; (critical error handler vector)
;

        pop     ES
        pop     DS
        pop     BP
        pop     DI
        pop     SI
        pop     DX
        pop     CX
        pop     BX
        iret

int24   ENDP

;
; Harmless Divide by 0 error
;

int0    PROC    NEAR
        iret
int0    ENDP
        END
;
; End of source listing
;***********************
```

Fig. 9-1 ends.

FIGURE 9-2 presents the source code listing for DRVNUM.ASM. This assembly ditty was presented to me, in honor of my stupidity, by an assembly wizard. DRVNUM returns the number of drives attached to your PC. It works, and I don't know why! If you understand my buddy's gobble-dee-gook, drop me a line. I'd love to know why this code works.

Fig. 9-2. The source code listing for DRVNUM.ASM.

```
;***********************
;Start of source listing
;
; I received this source from a 'Hacker' (in
; the best sense of the word, that is)
; friend. It returns the number of drives
; available in the AX register. When I asked
; him how it works, he laughed and said:
; "When you grow up little boy, you'll see the
; light!"
;
; Well, I'll be turning 40 in a few days
; and still don't see the light. Hence, there
; are no comments. If any of you have any ideas
; how this works I'd like to hear.
;
        DOSSEG

        .MODEL SMALL

        PUBLIC  _drvnum
        .CODE
_drvnum PROC NEAR
        jmp     dn1
number  DW      0
dn1:
        push    bp
        mov     bp,sp
        mov     si,5Ch
        mov     di,149h
        DB      0c6h,04h
dn2:
        DB      040h
        inc     byte ptr [si]
        mov     byte ptr [si+1],3Ah
        mov     ax,2906h
        int     21h

        mov     si,5Ch
        cmp     al,0FFh
        je      dn3
        inc     number
        mov     cx,3
        rep     movsb
dn3:
        mov     si,5Ch
        cmp     byte ptr [si],5Ah
        jne     dn2
        mov     ax,number
        pop     bp
        ret

_drvnum ENDP
        END
;
; End of source listing
;***********************
```

FIGURE 9-3 presents the source code listing for GETVEC.ASM. This source contains the listings for two functions. One, getvec(...), returns in a long value the segment and offset of any vector. The second function, setvec(...), uses the long value returned by getvec(...) to reset the interrupt vector.

Fig. 9-3. The source code listing for GETVEC.ASM.

```
;******************
; Start Source File
;
; File Name      GETVEC.ASM
;
; Synopsis:      vec = getvec(number)
;
; int number     vector number
;
; long vec       segment and offset of vector
;
; Description    Returns the segment and offset
;                of vector as long
;
;********************************
;
; Synopsis:      setvec(number,vec)
;
; int number     vector number
;
; long vec       segment and offset of vector
;
; Description    Sets the int vector to
;                the segment and offset in
;                vec
;

vec_num equ     BYTE PTR [BP+4]
off_val equ     WORD PTR [BP+6]
seg_val equ     WORD PTR [BP+8]

        .MODEL SMALL

        PUBLIC _setvec,_getvec

        .CODE
;
_getvec PROC NEAR
;
; Save regs
;
        push    BP
        mov     BP,SP
        push    ES
;
        mov     AL,vec_num
        mov     AH,35H
;
        int     21H     ; get int vec
```

```
        mov     DX,ES   ; segment to DX
        mov     AX,BX   ; offset to AX
;
;
;
; Restore regs
;
        pop     ES
        pop     BP
        ret
_getvec ENDP
;
;
;
_setvec PROC NEAR
;
; Save regs
;
        push    BP
        mov     BP,SP
;
        push    ES
        push    DS
;
        mov     DX,off_val
        mov     AX,seg_val
        mov     DS,AX
        mov     AL,vec_num
        mov     AH,25H
        int     21H
;
        pop     DS
        pop     ES
        pop     BP
        ret
_setvec ENDP
;
        END


; End of source
;**************
;
```

Fig. 9-3 ends.

FIGURE 9-4 presents the source code listing for DSYWIND.C. DSYWIND frees up the memory which had previously been allocated for a WIND structure.

FIGURE 9-5 presents the source code listing for DISKINFO.C. DISKINFO fills the DSKINFO structure with disk statistics for the default drive.

FIGURE 9-6 presents the source code listing for DISKFREE.C. This routine uses the statistics returned by diskInfo(...) to calculate the number of free bytes remaining on the default disk drive.

Fig. 9-4. The source code listing for DSYWIND.C.

```
/********************
 * Source Code Start
 *
 * File Name:    DSYWIND.C
 *
 * Synopsis:     dsyWind(W)
 *
 * WIND *W       Pointer to window structure
 *
 * Description: Destroy the Window
 *              structure pointed to
 *              by W and free memory
 *
 * Returns:      Nothing
 */

/*
 * Include Files
 */

#include <alloc.h>
#include <tproto.h>

/*
 * Function dsyWind
 */

void
dsyWind(W)
WIND *W;
{
/* If pointer is not NULL */
if(W->img_ptr!=NULL)

        /* then free memory    */
        free((char *)W->img_ptr);

/* If pointer is not NULL */
if(W->wind_ptr!=NULL)

        /* then free memory    */
        free((char *)W->wind_ptr);

/* If pointer is not NULL */
if(W!=NULL)

        /* then free memory    */
        free(W);
}

/*
 * End of source listing
 ***********************/
```

Fig. 9-5. The source code listing for DISKINFO.C.

```
/******************
 * Start Source file
 *
 * File Name:   DISKINFO.C
 *
 * Synopsis:   DI = diskInfo(DI)
 *
 * DISKINFO *DI pointer to disk information
 *             structure
 *
 * Description: Gets statistics of Disk
 *             via BIOS
 *
 * Returns:    Pointer to DINKINFO structure
 *             which holds the disk statistics
 */

/*
 * Include files
 */

#include <dos.h>
#include <alloc.h>
#include <tproto.h>

#define DSK_SIZE sizeof(DSKINFO)

/*
 * Function diskInfo
 */

DSKINFO
*diskInfo(DI)
DSKINFO *DI;
{
union REGS ir, or;

/* Allocate memory for DISKINFO structure */
DI = (DSKINFO *)calloc(DSK_SIZE,sizeof(char));

/* Prepare the (i)nput (r)egisters for    */
/* BIOS call                              */
ir.h.dl = 0;
ir.h.ah = 0x36;

/* Invoke BIOS int 0x21                   */
int86( 0x21, &ir, &or );

/* Fill elements of structure with        */
/* register information                   */
DI->clust_avail = or.x.bx;
DI->clust_total = or.x.dx;
DI->sec_p_clust = or.x.ax;
DI->bytes_p_sec = or.x.cx;

/* Pointer to DISKINFO structure returned */
```

```
return(DI);
}

/*
 * End of source listing
 ***********************/
```

Fig. 9-5 ends.

Fig. 9-6. The source code listing for DISKFREE.C.

```
/*******************
 * Start Source file
 *
 * File Name:    DISKFREE.C
 *
 * Synopsis:     bytes = diskFree()
 *
 * long bytes    number of free bytes
 *               on default drive
 *
 * Description: The number of free bytes
 *              on the default drive is
 *              returned.
 *
 * Returns:      Free disk bytes
 */

/*
 * Include files
 */

#include <dos.h>
#include <tproto.h>

/*
 * Function diskFree
 */

long
diskFree()
{
DSKINFO *data;
long clust_avail,bytes_p_sec,sec_p_clust,total;

/* Get drive information into */
/* disk data structure        */
data = diskInfo(data);

/* Calculate the free bytes    */
clust_avail = data->clust_avail;
bytes_p_sec = data->bytes_p_sec;
sec_p_clust = data->sec_p_clust;
total = (bytes_p_sec*sec_p_clust)*clust_avail;

/* Return the long total        */
return(total);
```

```
}

/*
 * End of source listing
 ***********************/
```

Fig. 9-6 ends.

EXTRINSIC TABDOS PROGRAMS

There are three extrinsic TABDOS demonstration programs. Once again, these extrinsic programs are called as children through C's spawn process. Upon exit, each of these extrinsic program returns control to its caller.

FIGURE 9-7 presents the source code listing for HELPW1.C. This extrinsic program is a simple text window displaying the first layer of TABDOS keyboard commands. If HELPW1 is called from DOS it will return to DOS on exit. If HELPW1 is called from TABDOS it will return to TABDOS on exit.

Fig. 9-7. The source code listing for HELPW1.C.

```
/****************************
 * Source code start here
 *
 * File Name: HELPW1.C
 *
 * Description: Help window
 *              for TABDOS
 */

/*
 * Include files here
 */

#include <stdio.h>
#include <tproto.h>

WIND *HELP;

/* info1 window data */
char help1[28]  = " Key          Action       ";
char help2[28]  = "  Q   QUIT to DOS          ";
char help3[28]  = "  R   Run Program (.EXE/.COM)";
char help4[28]  = "  S   DOS SYSTEM Prompt     ";
char help5[28]  = "  T   Tag Highlight On/Off  ";
char help6[28]  = "  W   Word Proc. (Misc.) file";
char help7[29]  = "  \\  Go to ROOT Directory  ";
char help8[28]  = "  .   Back one Directory    ";
char help9[28]  = "  H   For MORE HELP         ";
char help10[28] = " ANY other Key to Exit Help ";


/*******************************************/
/* Make variables which must retain their */
/* value after the function exits global  */
/*******************************************/
```

Fig. 9-7 continued.

```
void
helpw1()
{
/* for seperate progtram */
vidInit();

/**************************************************************/
/* Initialize grid menu window structure and display window */
/**************************************************************/

/* Allocate memory and return pointer to structure */
HELP = setWind(HELP,6,24,6+11,24+29);

/* Set Window Attr - Fore,Back,Intensity,Blink */
setAttr(HELP,mkAttr(BLACK,CYAN,OFF_INTENSITY,OFF_BLINK));

/* Set Window Border */
setBord(HELP,D_D_D_D);

/* Set the bottom title */
setTitle(HELP," TAB SHELL HELP ");

/* Display window */
strtWind(HELP);

dispWind(HELP);

/* Write menu and exit messages */
wvdWrite(HELP,1,1,28,help1,
        mkAttr(CYAN,
                BLACK,
                OFF_INTENSITY,
                OFF_BLINK));
wvdWrite(HELP,2,1,28,help2,HELP->attr);
wvdWrite(HELP,3,1,28,help3,HELP->attr);
wvdWrite(HELP,4,1,28,help4,HELP->attr);
wvdWrite(HELP,5,1,28,help5,HELP->attr);
wvdWrite(HELP,6,1,28,help6,HELP->attr);
wvdWrite(HELP,7,1,28,help7,HELP->attr);
wvdWrite(HELP,8,1,28,help8,HELP->attr);
wvdWrite(HELP,9,1,28,help9,HELP->attr);
wvdWrite(HELP,10,1,28,help10,HELP->attr);
wvdAttr(HELP,9,2,3,
        mkAttr(CYAN,
                BLACK,
                OFF_INTENSITY,
                OFF_BLINK));

/* wait for key press */
gtKey();

/* remove window and display original screen information */
remvWind(HELP);
dsyWind(HELP);
}
```

```
void
main()
{
helpw1();
}

/*
 * End of source listing
 ***********************/
```

Fig. 9-7 ends.

FIGURE 9-8 presents the source code listing for QUIT1.C. Upon termination QUIT1 returns a TRUE when the 'Y' or 'y' key has been pressed and a FALSE on any other keypress. The returned value is used by TABDOS to determine whether to return to DOS.

Fig. 9-8. The source code listing for QUIT1.C.

```
/*****************************
 * Source code start here
 *
 * File Name: QUIT1.C
 *
 * Help window for TABDOS
 */

/*
 * Include files here
 */

#include <stdio.h>
#include <tproto.h>

/*
 * Function prototypes
 */

void inform1(void);
int quit1(void);

/*
 * Pointer to WIND structure
 */

WIND *QUIT;

/*
 * Global data
 */

char q_dat1[28]   =
     "       QUIT TAB SHELL        ";

unsigned char q_dat2[30]   =
```

Fig. 9-8 continued.

```
    ( 199,196,196,196,196,196,196,196,196,
      196,196,196,196,196,196,196,196,196,
      196,196,196,196,196,196,196,196,196,
      196,196,182 );

char q_dat3[28]    = "   Quitting TAB's SHELL     ";
char q_dat4[28]    = "   program will clear the   ";
char q_dat5[28]    = "   screen and return you to ";
char q_dat6[28]    = "   the standard DOS Command ";
char q_dat7[28]    = "   Line environment.        ";
char q_dat8[28]    = "     Press (Y)es to QUIT.   ";


/*******************************************/
/* Make variables which must retain their */
/* value after the function exits global  */
/*******************************************/

int
quit1()
{
int key;    /* scan and char value    */

vidInit();

/*************************************************************/
/* Initialize grid menu window structure and display window */
/*************************************************************/

/* Allocate memory and return pointer to structure */
QUIT = setWind(QUIT,7,24,7+10,24+29);

/* Set Window Attr - Fore,Back,Intensity,Blink */
setAttr(QUIT,mkAttr(WHITE,RED,OFF_INTENSITY,OFF_BLINK));

/* Set Window Border */
setBord(QUIT,D_D_D_D);

/* Set the bottom title */
setTitle(QUIT," QUIT ");

/* Display window */
strtWind(QUIT);

dispWind(QUIT);
/* Write menu and exit messages */
wvdWrite(QUIT,1,1,28,q_dat1,
         mkAttr(RED,
                WHITE,
                OFF_INTENSITY,
                OFF_BLINK));
wvdWrite(QUIT,2,0,30,q_dat2,QUIT->attr);
wvdWrite(QUIT,3,1,28,q_dat3,QUIT->attr);
wvdWrite(QUIT,4,1,28,q_dat4,QUIT->attr);
wvdWrite(QUIT,5,1,28,q_dat5,QUIT->attr);
wvdWrite(QUIT,6,1,28,q_dat6,QUIT->attr);
wvdWrite(QUIT,7,1,28,q_dat7,QUIT->attr);
wvdWrite(QUIT,8,0,30,q_dat2,QUIT->attr);
```

```
wvdWrite(QUIT,9,1,28,q_dat8,QUIT->attr);

/* highlight Y for (Y) */
wvdAttr(QUIT,9,12,1,
        mkAttr(WHITE,
               RED,
               ON_INTENSITY,
               OFF_BLINK));

/* wait for key press */
key = gtKey();

/* remove window and display   */
/* original screen information */
remvWind(QUIT);
dsyWind(QUIT);

/* Mask out scan code         */
key &= 0x00ff;

/* Evaluate key press         */
if( (key=='Y')||(key=='y') )
   return(aTRUE);
else
   return(aFALSE);
}

void
main()
{
exit(quit1());
}

/*
 * End of source listing
 ************************/
```

Fig. 9-8 ends.

FIGURE 9-9 presents the source code listing for DSKDEMO.C. DSKDEMO reports the default drive's statistics in a pop-up window. DSKDEMO.C may be called from TABDOS or DOS.

Fig. 9-9. The source code listing for DSKDEMO.C.

```
/*****************************
 * Source code start here
 *
 * File Name: DSKDEMO.C
 *
 * Description:
 *   Demonstration of RECT routines in
 *   concert with the diskInfo function
 */
```

339

Fig. 9-9 continued.

```
/*********************/
/* Include files here */
/*********************/

#include <stdio.h>
#include <dos.h>
#include <stdlib.h>
#include <string.h>
#include <tproto.h>


/***********************/
/* Function declaration */
/***********************/

void main(void);

/************************/
/* Structure declarations */
/************************/

/* pointer to rectangular structure    */
RECT *R;

/* pointer to diskinformation structure */
DSKINFO *data;

/**********************/
/* Global declarations */
/**********************/

/* holds ascii conversion of long */
char num_string[20];

/* text descriptions of drive info */
char box_text[5] [23] = {
        " Default Drive        = ",
        " Clusters available = ",
        " Sectors per cluster = ",
        " Bytes per sector    = ",
        " Free bytes on disk  = " };

/* header at top of rect box */
char header[40] =
{ "        TAB's SHELL Disk Info.        " };

/******************/
/* Function getdrive */
/*                  */
/* Description:     */
/*  Returns default */
/*   disk drive as  */
/*   int, where:    */
/*   0 = A          */
/*   1 = B          */
/*   2 = C          */
/*   3 = D          */
/******************/
```

Fig. 9-9 continued.

```
int
getdrive()
{
union REGS ir,or;

/* DOS get default drive */
ir.h.ah = 0x19;

/* Invoke BIOS int 0x21  */
int86(0x21,&ir,&or);

/* Return default drive  */
return( (int)or.h.al );
}


/****************/
/* Main program */
/****************/

void
main()
{
int g_attr, attr, fill;
int drive;

/*****************************/
/* Initialize Video Structure */
/*                            */
/* Mandatory vidInit call!!!! */
/*****************************/

vidInit();

/***********************/
/* save cursor location */
/***********************/

sCloc();

/******************/
/* Turn cursor off */
/******************/

offCur();

/****************************/
/* Set Rectangular Structure */
/****************************/

R = setRect(R,4,4,12,44);

/**************************************************/
/* create attribute for rectangular area        */
/* fore-WHITE, back-RED,off Intensitym off blink */
/**************************************************/
```

Fig. 9-9 continued.

```
attr = mkAttr(WHITE,RED,OFF_INTENSITY,OFF_BLINK);

/****************************************************/
/* create attribute for disk info report           */
/* fore-BLACK, back-WHITE,off Intensitym off blink */
/****************************************************/

g_attr = mkAttr(BLACK,WHITE,OFF_INTENSITY,OFF_BLINK);

/**************************/
/* Create token for fill */
/**************************/

fill = mkToken(' ',attr);

/***********************************/
/* Save screen image under rectangle */
/***********************************/

saveRect(R);

/********************************/
/* Fill the rectangle with token */
/********************************/

fillRect(R,fill);

/****************************************************/
/* Draw a single line box defined by rectangle *R */
/****************************************************/

boxRect(R,S_S_S_S,attr);

/****************************************************/
/* Write the center justified header to top of box */
/****************************************************/

vdWrite(5,5,38,header,
        mkAttr(BLUE,
               WHITE,
               OFF_INTENSITY,
               OFF_BLINK));

/*********************************************/
/* Get pointer to disk information structure */
/*********************************************/

data = diskInfo(data);

/**************************/
/* Get default drive info */
/**************************/

drive = getdrive();

/***************************************/
```

Fig. 9-9 continued.

```
/* Turn drive number into ascii token */
/**********************************/

drive = mkToken('A'+drive,g_attr);

/***********************/
/* Write text to screen */
/* Inverse three bytes  */
/* Write drive letter   */
/***********************/

vdWrite(6,6,23,box_text[0],attr);
vdAttr(6,6+23,3,g_attr);
vdChar(6,6+24,drive);

/**************************/
/* Clear num_string buffer */
/* Get ascii clust_total  */
/* Write text             */
/* Inverse string len + 2 */
/* Print ascii info       */
/**************************/

memset(num_string,'\0',sizeof(num_string));
itoa(data->clust_total,num_string,10);
vdWrite(7,6,23,box_text[1],attr);
vdAttr(7,6+23,strlen(num_string)+2,g_attr);
vdWrite(7,6+24,strlen(num_string),num_string,g_attr);

/**************************/
/* Clear num_string buffer */
/* Get ascii sec_p_clust   */
/* Write text             */
/* Inverse string len + 2 */
/* Print ascii info       */
/**************************/

memset(num_string,'\0',sizeof(num_string));
itoa(data->sec_p_clust,num_string,10);
vdWrite(8,6,23,box_text[2],attr);
vdAttr(8,6+23,strlen(num_string)+2,g_attr);
vdWrite(8,6+24,strlen(num_string),num_string,g_attr);

/**************************/
/* Clear num_string buffer */
/* Get ascii bytes_p_sec   */
/* Write text             */
/* Inverse string len + 2 */
/* Print ascii info       */
/**************************/

memset(num_string,'\0',sizeof(num_string));
itoa(data->bytes_p_sec,num_string,10);
vdWrite(9,6,23,box_text[3],attr);
vdAttr(9,6+23,strlen(num_string)+2,g_attr);
vdWrite(9,6+24,strlen(num_string),num_string,g_attr);
```

```
/***************************/
/* Clear num_string buffer */
/* Get ascii disk free     */
/* Write text              */
/* Inverse string len + 2  */
/* Print ascii info        */
/***************************/

memset(num_string,'\0',sizeof(num_string));
ltoa(diskFree(),num_string,10);
vdWrite(10,6,23,box_text[4],attr);
vdAttr(10,6+23,strlen(num_string)+2,g_attr);
vdWrite(10,6+24,strlen(num_string),num_string,g_attr);

/**********************/
/* Wait for key press */
/**********************/

gtKey();

/******************************/
/* Restore original screen image */
/******************************/

restRect(R);

/***************************/
/* Restore Cursor location */
/***************************/

rCloc();

/******************/
/* Turn cursor on */
/******************/

onCur();

}

/*
 * End of source listing
 ********************/
```

Fig. 9-9 ends.

FIGURE 9-10 presents the source code listing for TREMOVE.C. This extrinsic program receives a file name and removes it from your directory. It functions in the same manner as the DOS 'DEL' command. Be careful when testing TREMOVE.

Fig. 9-10. The source code listing for TREMOVE.C.

```
/****************************
 * Source code start
 *
 * File Name: TREMOVE.C
 *
 * Description:
 *  Remove a file whose name
 *  has been passed in the DOS
 *  command line string.
 */

/*
 * Inlcude files here
 */

#include <stdio.h>
#include <ctype.h>
#include <process.h>
#include "shell.h"

#include <tproto.h>

/*
 * Function main
 */

void
main(argc,argv)
int argc;
char *argv[];
{
char *cptr;
cptr = argv[1];
remove(cptr);
}

/*
 * End of source listing
 ***********************/
```

YOUR FINAL TAB LIBRARY LISTING

All the TAB Library routines have now been compiled or assembled and added to your TAB_T2S.LIB file. It's time to print the final listing for the content's of your library. FIGURE 9-11 presents the listing of your library. If you forgot how we retrieved our earlier library listing, check your library manager program documentation.

FIGURE 9-11 indicates that there have been 68 routines placed in your TAB library. Because many of the routines are double coded in C and assembly, I suggest (if you own an assembler, which I recommend you do) replacing any C generated object modules with assembly generated object modules. The assembly object modules are smaller than the C generated modules and in most cases will surely execute in less time.

Fig. 9-11. The listing of TAB_T2S.LIB's contents.

```
Publics by module

BEEP       size = 36
  _beep

BOXRECT    size = 428
  _boxRect

CLRRECT    size = 111
  _clrRect

CRITERR    size = 89
  _setCE

DISKFREE   size = 94
  _diskFree

DISKINFO   size = 84
  _diskInfo

DISPWIND   size = 31
  _dispWind

DRVNUM     size = 59
  _drvnum

DSYWIND    size = 49
  _dsyWind

FILLRECT   size = 70
  _fillRect

GETVEC     size = 42
  _getvec                        _setvec

GTCUR      size = 56
  _gtCur

GTKBFLAG   size = 47
  _gtKBflag

GTKBSTAT   size = 21
  _gtKBstat

GTKEY      size = 37
  _gtKey

GTMODE     size = 62
  _gtMode

INPFLT     size = 275
```

Fig. 9-11 continued.

```
        _inpflt

INPNUM      size = 271
  _inpnum

MKATTR      size = 23
  _mkAttr

MKTOKEN     size = 21
  _mkToken

MVCUR       size = 17
  _mvCur

OFFCUR      size = 68
  _offCur

ONCUR       size = 16
  _onCur
PRCHAR      size = 19
  _prChar

PROMPT      size = 215
  _prompt

PSFIND      size = 45
  _psfind

PUTCHR      size = 17
  _putChr

RDCHAR      size = 13
  _rdChar

RDIMG       size = 76
  _rdImg

RDWIND      size = 76
  _rdWind

REMVWIND    size = 31
  _remvWind

RESTRECT    size = 77
  _restRect

SAVERECT    size = 76
  _saveRect

SAVESCRN    size = 4105
  _restScrn                                    _saveScrn

SCLOC       size = 40
  _rCloc                                       _sCloc

SCRNCLR     size = 97
  _scrnClr
```

Fig. 9-11 continued.

```
SETATTR    size = 14
  _setAttr

SETBORD    size = 14
  _setBord

SETPSVEC   size = 823
  _setPSvec

SETRECT    size = 94
  _setRect

SETTIMER   size = 753
  _setTimer

SETTITLE   size = 86
  _setTitle

SETWIND    size = 135
  _setWind

SIZEIMG    size = 48
  _sizeImg

STRENUL    size = 38
  _strEnul

STRTWIND   size = 56
  _strtWind

TIMEREMV   size = 94
  _timeremv

TSRGTIME   size = 231
  _adjclock              _ampm
  _c_fresh               _d_fresh
  _tsrgtime              _tsrhour
  _tsrhun                _tsrmin
  _tsrsec

TSRPS      size = 15
  _tsrPS

TSRTIME    size = 18
  _tsrtime

VDATTR     size = 50
  _vdAttr

VDCHAR     size = 66
  _vdChar

VDHORIZ    size = 58
  _vdHoriz

VDVERT     size = 56
  _vdVert
```

```
VDWRITE     size = 105
  _vdWrite

VIDINIT     size = 110
  _SCRNSEG                              _SPARKLE_FLAG
  _VID_PORT                            _crt
  _vidInit

VRDCHAR     size = 42
  _vrdChar

WMVCUR      size = 33
  _wmvCur

WRBOX       size = 594
  _wb_blank                            _wrBox

WRIMG       size = 77
  _wrImg

WRWIND      size = 77
  _wrWind

WVDATTR     size = 108
  _wvdAttr

WVDHORIZ    size = 79
  _wvdHoriz

WVDVERT     size = 79
  _wvdVert

WVDWRITE    size = 122
  _wvdWrite

WVRDCHAR    size = 82
  _wvrdChar
```

Fig. 9-11 ends.

THE TABDOS PROGRAM

TD.EXE is the executable file for TABDOS. TABDOS is composed of five source files. There is a specialized header file called SHELL.H and a MAKE-FILE used by TURBO's MAKE utility.

TABDOS is designed to demonstrate the power of the TAB library, and not intended as a commercial product. TABDOS demonstrates how to drop down windows, pop up windows, read a directory into memory, sort the files alphabetically, and scroll a highlight bar through the files. You will see individual file statistics and learn how to use C's SPAWN functions to execute programs with your own program. There are just too many goodies to list here.

Although the code is voluminous (for a book, that is), there are many functions that you can lift and use directly in your program. As is the case with virtually all of the programs in the text, instructive documentation is provided.

Finally, TABDOS provides you with a very solid framework for your own DOS interface shell. With a little creative coding you'll be able to say good-bye to the DOS prompt forever.

USING MAKE

MAKE is a wonderful utility that reduces the difficulties of writing large multi-source programs. Simply, MAKE detects every change in a source file. When you decide to create a new version of your program-in-progress MAKE will compile only the files that have been changed and then link the appropriate object files into the executable file.

FIGURE 9-12 presents the listing for MAKEFILE. When you invoke MAKE, by default, the file named MAKEFILE is used to build the new program. After you've typed in the source for MAKEFILE, SHELL.H, TD.C, TD2.C, TD3.C, TD4.C and TD5.C, you can build TD.EXE (TABDOS) by simply typing:

    MAKE

and then pressing Enter. If you decide to modify the program later and, say, make a change in TD3.C, executing MAKE will compile only TD3.C and link the new TD3.OBJ file with the previously created object files. That way you never need to remember which source files you've made changes in. MAKE remembers them all.

Fig. 9-12. The listing for MAKEFILE used in building TD.EXE.

```
td.exe : td.obj td2.obj td3.obj td4.obj td5.obj
 tcc -ms td.obj td2.obj td3.obj td4.obj td5.obj tab_t2s.lib

td.obj : td.c
 tcc -ms -c td.c

td2.obj : td2.c
 tcc -ms -c td2.c

td3.obj : td3.c
 tcc -ms -c td3.c

td4.obj : td4.c
 tcc -ms -c td4.c

td5.obj : td5.c
 tcc -ms -c td5.c
```

The linker will be invoked if the object files used to create TD.EXE have changed. The compiler will be invoked for all source files that have been changed since the last MAKE program building session.

THE SOURCE CODE FOR TABDOS (TD.EXE)

FIGURE 9-13 presents the source code listing for SHELL.H, the header files with function prototypes and definitions particular to TABDOS. FIGURE 9-14 presents the source code listing for TD.C. FIGURE 9-15 presents the source code listing for TD2.C. FIGURE 9-16 presents the source code listing for TD3.C. FIGURE 9-17 presents the source code listing for TD4.C. FIGURE 9-18 presents the source code listing for TD5.C.

Fig. 9-13. The source code listing for SHELL.H.

```
/***************************
 *
 * File Nand: SHELL.H
 *
 * Description:
 *   Defines and function
 *   prototypes for TABDOS
 *   (TD.EXE) are presented.
 */

/*
 * Defines
 */

#define D1_QUIT        0xff
#define DIR_INFO_SIZE  300
#define WIND_HEIGHT    15
#define SUBDIR_MAX     50
#define PROGRAM_MAX    100
#define MISC_MAX       100
#define BATCH          1
#define EXECUTABLE     2
#define NAME_WIDTH     14

/*
 * C function prototypes here
 */

void copy_file(void);

void delete_file(void);
void dir_sort(void);
void draw_screen(void);
void drop_i(void);
void drop_f(void);
void drop_d(void);
int drop_s(void);
void drvdisp(void);
```

Fig. 9-13 continued.

```
void e_load_prog(int,int);

char *f_info(struct ffblk *);

void hi_menu(void);

void info1(void);

void load_prog(int);
void load_vmask(void);
void load_wp(int);

void main(void);

void new_drive(int);
void new_sub(int);

void onclock(void);
void offclock(void);

void path_info(void);
void print_bar(void);
void print_dlet(void);
void print_drive(void);
void print_misc(int);
void print_path(void);
void print_program(int);
void print_subdir(int);

void reset_ctr(void);
void retdrive(void);

void tag_misc(int,int);
void tag_program(int,int);
void tag_subdir(int,int);

struct udate *makedate(unsigned);
struct utime *maketime(unsigned);

void wait_here(void);
/*
 * File Statistics Structures
 */

struct udate
    {
    unsigned numdate;
    unsigned year;
    unsigned month;
    unsigned day;
    char datestring[13];
    };

struct utime
    {
    unsigned numtime;
    unsigned hours;
```

```
      unsigned mins;
      unsigned secs;
      char timestring[9];
      char am_pm;
      };


/*
 * Header file listing ends here
 ******************************/
```

Fig. 9-13 ends.

Fig. 9-14. The source code listing for TD.C.

```
/********************************
 *
 * File Name: TD.C
 *
 * Description:
 *   First source file used in
 *   the creation of TD.EXE
 *   (The program named TABDOS)
 *
 */

/*
 * Include files here
 */

#include <stdio.h>
#include <io.h>
#include <fcntl.h>
#include <sys\stat.h>
#include <sys\types.h>
#include <ctype.h>
#include <dir.h>
#include <process.h>
#include <string.h>

#include <tproto.h>

/*
 * The quotation marks surrounding
 * shell.h tell the compiler that
 * this header file is in the
 * default directory.
 */

#include "shell.h"


/*
 * global variables
 */

int inverse;  /* attribute for inverse    */
```

Fig. 9-14 continued.

```
int bar1;      /* attrtibute for menu bar    */
int back1;     /* attribute for background   */
int scrn_t;    /* screen token               */
int hilite1;   /* highlight atttribute       */
int hi_inv;    /* menu bar hilite & inverse  */
int ctog = 0;  /* clock toggle               */
int bar_ctr = 0;
int old_ctr = 0;
int new_ctr = 0;
int off1ctr = 0;
int off2ctr = 0;
int off3ctr = 0;
int im1ctr = 0;
int im2ctr = 0;
int im3ctr = 0;
int im1_new = 0;
int im2_new = 15;
int im3_new = 30;

/*
 * File selector highligh
 * bar locations
 */

int bar_loc[45][2] = {
    2,1+1,
    3,1+1,
    4,1+1,
    5,1+1,
    6,1+1,
    7,1+1,
    8,1+1,
    9,1+1,
    10,1+1,
    11,1+1,
    12,1+1,
    13,1+1,
    14,1+1,
    15,1+1,
    16,1+1,

    2,14+2,
    3,14+2,
    4,14+2,
    5,14+2,
    6,14+2,
    7,14+2,
    8,14+2,
    9,14+2,
    10,14+2,
    11,14+2,
    12,14+2,
    13,14+2,
    14,14+2,
    15,14+2,
    16,14+2,
```

Fig. 9-14 continued.

```
      2,27+3,
      3,27+3,
      4,27+3,
      5,27+3,
      6,27+3,
      7,27+3,
      8,27+3,
      9,27+3,
     10,27+3,
     11,27+3,
     12,27+3,
     13,27+3,
     14,27+3,
     15,27+3,
     16,27+3 } ;

/*
 * Externs
 */


extern int dr_buff[10];
extern char *dir_info[DIR_INFO_SIZE];
extern char subdir[SUBDIR_MAX][NAME_WIDTH];
extern char program[PROGRAM_MAX][NAME_WIDTH];
extern char misc[MISC_MAX][NAME_WIDTH];
extern char extender[5];
extern char editor[8];

extern WIND *DRVINFO;

/*
 * Menu bar string
 */

char bar_dat[80] =
" Info & Desk   File Operations   Directory Operations   Choices   Help              ";


/*
 * Global structures
 */

RECT *scrnR;

/*
 * Function main
 */

void
main()
{
int key;      /* holds scan and char value   */
int exit;     /* exit flag for key board loop */
int value;    /* temp integer storage        */
int cnt;      /* misc. counter               */
int on_inv;   /* inverse highlight bar        */
```

Fig. 9-14 continued.

```
char *cptr;    /* misc char pointer            */
int handle;    /* io file handle               */
long old24;    /* critical error vector        */
long old0;     /* divide by 0  vector          */
int num;

/* initialize TAB video structure */
vidInit();

/* return how may drives */
retdrive();

/*******************************************/
/* Notice that on the TABDOS display       */
/* there is a place for the current        */
/* time. Use the clock program presented   */
/* earlier in the text to display the      */
/* current time.                           */
/*******************************************/
/*
spawnlp(P_WAIT,"tdclk","tdclk",NULL);
*/

/* save original crit error and divide by */
/* zero vectors to memory                  */
old24 = getvec(0x24);
old0 = getvec(0x00);

/* Install the TABDOS critical error       */
/* handler.                                */
setCE();

/* Initialize dir_info[] to NULL           */
/* This array of pointer will point to     */
/* file status information                 */
for(cnt=0; cnt<DIR_INFO_SIZE; cnt++)
   dir_info[cnt] = '\0';

/* initialize screen sized rectangle       */
scrnR = setRect(scrnR,0,0,25,80);

/* initialize screen token for white       */
/* background                              */
scrn_t = mkToken(' ',mkAttr(BLACK,
                            WHITE,
                            OFF_INTENSITY,
                            OFF_BLINK));

/* initialize text attributes here         */
inverse = mkAttr(BLUE,
                 WHITE,
                 OFF_INTENSITY,
                 OFF_BLINK);
bar1 = mkAttr(WHITE,
              BLUE,
              OFF_INTENSITY,
              OFF_BLINK);
```

Fig. 9-14 continued.

```
hilite1 = mkAttr(WHITE,
                 BLUE,
                 ON_INTENSITY,
                 OFF_BLINK);
hi_inv = mkAttr(WHITE,
                BLUE,
                ON_INTENSITY,
                OFF_BLINK);
on_inv = mkAttr(WHITE,
                BLUE,
                OFF_INTENSITY,
                OFF_BLINK);

/* load tabdos.cfg file                    */
handle = open("tabdos.cfg",
              O_RDWR,
              S_IREAD|S_IWRITE);

/* Beep of file doesnt exist               */
if(handle <0 )
   beep();
else
   {
   /* Read default word processor into     */
   /* memory                               */
   read(handle,extender,5);
   read(handle,editor,8);
   close(handle);
   }

/* Draw the default TABDOS screen          */
draw_screen();

/*****************************************/
/* The main keyboard loop reads key      */
/* presses and then takes the appropriate */
/* action.                               */
/*****************************************/

/* set flag to no exit                     */
exit = aFALSE;

do
   {
   /* Take the file statistic information */
   /* from the appropriate section of     */
   /* allocated memory and print that     */
   /* information on the screen.          */
   /* information below scrolling window  */
   if(new_ctr<15)
      num = (int)subdir[new_ctr+off1ctr][13];
   else if(new_ctr<30)
      num = (int)program[new_ctr+off2ctr-15][13];
   else
      num = (int)misc[new_ctr+off3ctr-30][13];
   vdWrite(21,33,42,
           f_info((struct ffblk *)dir_info[num]),
```

Fig. 9-14 continued.

```
        mkAttr(RED,BLUE,ON_INTENSITY,OFF_BLINK));
vdAttr(21,33+12,1,mkAttr(BLACK,
                         WHITE,
                         OFF_INTENSITY,
                         OFF_BLINK));
vdAttr(21,33+21,1,mkAttr(BLACK,
                         WHITE,
                         OFF_INTENSITY,
                         OFF_BLINK));
vdAttr(21,33+30,1,mkAttr(BLACK,
                         WHITE,
                         OFF_INTENSITY,
                         OFF_BLINK));

/* turn on clock if off          */
if(ctog)
   onclock();

/* Highlight the file selector bar    */
wvdAttr(DRVINFO,
        bar_loc[old_ctr][0],
        bar_loc[old_ctr][1],
        12,
        DRVINFO->attr);
wvdAttr(DRVINFO,
        bar_loc[new_ctr][0],
        bar_loc[new_ctr][1],
        12,
        on_inv);

/* Adjust highlight location index    */
old_ctr = new_ctr;

/* Wait for key press            */
key = gtKey();

/* Filter returned key value     */
switch(key)
   {
   /* switch to drive A          */
   case ALT_A:
      if(dr_buff[0])
         {
         reset_ctr();
         new_drive(0);
         print_drive();
         }
      else
         beep();
      break;
/* switch to drive B                 */
case ALT_B:
   if(dr_buff[1])
      {
      reset_ctr();
      new_drive(1);
      print_drive();
```

Fig. 9-14 continued.

```
         }
      else
         beep();
      break;

/* switch to drive C                */
case ALT_C:
   if(dr_buff[2])
         {
      reset_ctr();
      new_drive(2);
      print_drive();
         }
      else
         beep();
      break;

/* switch to drive D                */
case ALT_D:
   if(dr_buff[3])
         {
      reset_ctr();
      new_drive(3);
      print_drive();
         }
      else
         beep();
      break;

/* Execute the extrinsic HELP prog  */
case F1:
      spawnlp(P_WAIT,"helpw1","helpw1",NULL);
      break;

/* Tag the file or directory at     */
/* highlight bar.                   */
case SPACE:
   if(new_ctr<15)
         tag_subdir(new_ctr+off1ctr,off1ctr);
      else if(new_ctr<30)
         tag_program(new_ctr+off2ctr-15,off2ctr);
      else
         tag_misc(new_ctr+off3ctr-30,off3ctr);
      break;

/* Return file pointer highlight    */
/* to first sub directory position  */
case HOME:
   if(new_ctr<15)
         {
      new_ctr = 0;
      off1ctr = 0;
      print_subdir(off1ctr);
         }
      else if(new_ctr<30)
         {
      new_ctr = 15;
```

Fig. 9-14 continued.

```
      off2ctr = 0;
      print_program(off2ctr);
      }
   else
      {
      new_ctr = 30;
      off3ctr = 0;
      print_misc(off3ctr);
      }
   break;

/* move file highlight bar 1 column */
/* to the right                     */
case RIGHT_ARROW:
   if(new_ctr<15) /* col 1 */
        {
        im1ctr = off1ctr;
        im1_new = new_ctr;
        new_ctr = im2_new;
        off2ctr = im2ctr;
        }
      else if(new_ctr<30)
        {
        im2ctr = off2ctr;
        im2_new = new_ctr;
        new_ctr = im3_new;
        off3ctr = im3ctr;
        }
      else
        {
        im3ctr = off3ctr;
        im3_new = new_ctr;
        new_ctr = im1_new;
        off1ctr = im1ctr;
        }
   break;

/* move highlight bar 1 column to   */
/* the left                         */
case LEFT_ARROW:
   if(new_ctr<15)
        {
        im1ctr = off1ctr;
        im1_new = new_ctr;
        new_ctr = im3_new;
        off3ctr = im3ctr;
        }
      else if(new_ctr<30)
        {
        im2ctr = off2ctr;
        im2_new = new_ctr;
        new_ctr = im1_new;
        off1ctr = im1ctr;
        }
      else
        {
        im3ctr = off3ctr;
```

Fig. 9-14 continued.

```
        im3_new = new_ctr;
        new_ctr = im2_new;
        off2ctr = im2ctr;
        }
   break;

/* move highlight bar down one item */
/* or scroll column up              */
case DOWN_ARROW:
   if( (new_ctr!=14)&&
       (new_ctr!=29)&&
       (new_ctr!=44) )
      {
      if(new_ctr<14)
         {
         if(subdir[new_ctr+off1ctr+1][0]!='\0')
            new_ctr++;
         }
      else if(new_ctr<29)
         {
         if(program[new_ctr+off2ctr+1-15][0]!='\0')
            new_ctr++;
         }
      else
         {
         if(misc[new_ctr+off3ctr+1-30][0]!='\0')
            new_ctr++;
         }
      }
   else
      {
      if(new_ctr==44)
         {
         if(misc[new_ctr+off3ctr+1-30][0]!='\0')
            off3ctr++;
         print_misc(off3ctr);
         }
      else if(new_ctr==29)
         {
         if(program[new_ctr+off2ctr+1-15][0]!='\0')
            off2ctr++;
         print_program(off2ctr);
         }
      else
         {
         if(subdir[new_ctr+off1ctr+1][0]!='\0')
            off1ctr++;
         print_subdir(off1ctr);
         }
      }
   break;

/* move file highlight bar 1 up or  */
/* scroll column down if necessary  */
case UP_ARROW:
   if( (new_ctr!=0)&&
       (new_ctr!=15)&&
```

Fig. 9-14 continued.

```
        (new_ctr!=30) )
      new_ctr--;
   else
      {
      if(new_ctr==30)
         {
         if(off3ctr>0)
            {
            off3ctr--;
            print_misc(off3ctr);
            }
         }
      else if(new_ctr==15)
         {
         if(off2ctr>0)
            {
            off2ctr--;
            print_program(off2ctr);
            }
         }
      else
         {
         if(off1ctr>0)
            {
            off1ctr--;
            print_subdir(off1ctr);
            }
         }

      }
   break;

/* Select highlighted item          */
case ENTER:
   if(new_ctr<15)
      {
      new_sub(new_ctr+off1ctr);
      reset_ctr();
      }
   if( (new_ctr>=15)&&(new_ctr<=29) )
      {
      offclock();
      e_load_prog(new_ctr+off2ctr-15,
                  EXECUTABLE);
      reset_ctr();
      }
   if(new_ctr>=30)
      {
      cptr = (char *)
            strstr(misc[new_ctr+off3ctr-30],
                  ".BAT");
      if(cptr!=NULL)
         {
         offclock();
         e_load_prog(new_ctr+off3ctr-30,
                     BATCH);
         reset_ctr();
         }
```

Fig. 9-14 continued.

```
            }
        break;
/* function keys have been tried    */
/* - on to the alphanumeric keys    */
default:

    /* mask off scan code           */
    key &= 0x00ff;

    /* turn val to upper case        */
    key = toupper(key);

    /* Filter key val                */
    switch(key)
        {
        /* Drop Info window           */
        case 'I':
            offclock();
            vdAttr(0,1,11,hi_inv);
            drop_i();
            print_bar();
            hi_menu();
            break;

        /* Drop File window           */
        case 'F':
            offclock();
            vdAttr(0,15,15,hi_inv);
            drop_f();
            print_bar();
            hi_menu();
            break;

        /* Drop Info window           */
        case 'D':
            offclock();
            vdAttr(0,33,20,hi_inv);
            drop_d();
            print_bar();
            hi_menu();
            break;

        /* Drop Choice window         */
        case 'C':
            offclock();
            vdAttr(0,56,18,hi_inv);
            value = drop_s();
            if(value=='A')
                {
                new_ctr = 0;
                off3ctr = 0;
                }
            print_bar();
            hi_menu();
            break;

        /* HELP!                      */
```

Fig. 9-14 continued.

```
case 'H':
   offclock();
   spawnlp(P_WAIT,
           "helpw1",
           "helpw1",
            NULL);
   break;

/* quit!                    */
case 'Q':
   offclock();
   if(spawnlp(P_WAIT,
              "quit1",
              "quit1",
               NULL))
      exit=aTRUE;
   break;

/* Command Line prompt       */
case 'S':
   offclock();
   e_load_prog(MISC_MAX-1,BATCH);
   reset_ctr();
   break;
/* Run executable program     */
case 'R':
   offclock();
   if( (new_ctr>=15)&&(new_ctr<=29) )
      {
      load_prog(new_ctr+off2ctr-15);
      reset_ctr();
      }
   break;

/* Word process the text file */
case 'W':
   offclock();
   if(new_ctr>=30)
      {
      load_wp(new_ctr+off3ctr-30);
      reset_ctr();
      }
   break;

/* Go to root directory      */
case 92:
   chdir("\\");
   reset_ctr();
   draw_screen();
   break;

/* Go back 1 level of dir     */
case '.':
   chdir("..");
   reset_ctr();
   draw_screen();
   break;
```

Fig. 9-14 continued.

```
            /* non function key - beep     */
            default:
                beep();
                break;
            }
        }
    } while(!exit);

/* Exit from TABDOS                        */
/* Remove your TSR clock!                  */

/*
spawnlp(P_WAIT,"remclock","remclock",NULL);
*/

/* restore original critical error vector */
setvec(0x24,old24);
setvec(0x00,old0);

/* clear the screen                        */
scrnClr();

/* turn cursor on                          */
onCur();

}

/*
 * Function: print_bar
 *
 * Description:
 *  Print the menu bar
 */

void
print_bar()
{
vdWrite(0,0,80,bar_dat,bar1);
}

/*
 * Function: hi_menu
 *
 * Description:
 *  Highlight the menu
 */

void
hi_menu()
{
vdAttr(0,1,1,hilite1);
vdAttr(0,15,1,hilite1);
vdAttr(0,33,1,hilite1);
vdAttr(0,56,1,hilite1);
vdAttr(0,66,1,hilite1);
}

/*
```

Fig. 9-14 continued.

```
 * Function: draw_screen
 *
 * Description:
 *   Draw the TABDOS screen
 */

void
draw_screen()
{
/* clear the screen */
scrnClr();

/* inverse screen */
fillRect(scrnR,scrn_t);

/* turn cursor off */
offCur();

/* print menu bar */
print_bar();

/* highlight first letters of menu */
hi_menu();

/* print the drive configurarion */
print_drive();
}

/*
 * Function: offclock
 *
 * Description:
 *   Turn the clock off
 *   by removing it from
 *   memory.
 */

void
offclock()
{
ctog = 1;
/*
spawnlp(P_WAIT,"remclock","remclock",NULL);
*/
}

/*
 * Function: onclock
 *
 * Description:
 *   Turn the clock on by
 *   installing it as TSR
 *   in memory
 */

void
onclock()
```

```
{
ctog = 0;
/*
spawnlp(P_WAIT,"clock","clock",NULL);
*/
}

/*
 * Function: reset_ctr
 *
 * Description:
 *   Set the highlight bar
 *   index to row 0 column 0
 */

void
reset_ctr()
{
new_ctr = 0;
off1ctr = 0;
off2ctr = 0;
off3ctr = 0;
}

/*
 * End of TD.C source listing
 ****************************/
```

Fig. 9-14 ends.

Fig. 9-15. The source code listing for TD2.C.

```
/********************************
 *
 * Source code listing starts here
 *
 * File Name: TD2.C
 */

/*
 * Include files here
 */

#include <dos.h>
#include <sys\types.h>
#include <dir.h>
#include <alloc.h>
#include <string.h>
#include <process.h>
#include <stdlib.h>

#include <tproto.h>
#include "shell.h"

/*
 * Externs
```

Fig. 9-15 continued.
```
 */

extern char subdir[SUBDIR_MAX][NAME_WIDTH];
extern char program[PROGRAM_MAX][NAME_WIDTH];
extern char misc[MISC_MAX][NAME_WIDTH];
extern char *dir_info[DIR_INFO_SIZE];
extern WIND *DRVINFO;

/*
 * Globals arrays
 */

char passed[10][10];
char editor[8] = { 'b',0,0,0,0,0,0,0 };

/*
 * Function load_prog
 *
 * Description:
 *  Load a program from the
 *  directory of .EXE and .COM
 *  programs as a CHILD of
 *  TD.EXE
 */

void
load_prog(offset)
int offset;
{
char buffer[12];
int cnt;

/* Clear the file name buffer */
memset(buffer,'\0',12);

/* Move the file name from program[][] to */
/* buffer                                  */
for(cnt=0; cnt<12; cnt++)
   {
   /* exit loop on '.' or '\0'           */
   if((program[offset][cnt]=='.')||
      (program[offset][cnt]=='\0'))
      break;

   /* Move character of file name to     */
   /* buffer                             */
   buffer[cnt] = program[offset][cnt];
   }

/* Clear the screen                       */
scrnClr();

/* turn on the cursor                     */
onCur();

/* Load the program named in buffer as    */
/* a CHILD using the SPAWN process        */
```

Fig. 9-15 continued.

```
spawnlp(P_WAIT,buffer,buffer,NULL);

/* After exiting the program named in      */
/* buffer turn off the cursor              */
offCur();

/* Wait for key press to return to TABDOS */
wait_here();

/* Redraw the TABDOS main screen           */
draw_screen();
}


void
e_load_prog(offset,choose)
int offset,choose;
{
char buffer[50];
int pos,cnt,b_attr,column;
char cbuffer[50];
char *cwd;
RECT *R;

/* Get the current working directory       */
/* into cbuffer                            */
getcwd(cbuffer,50);

/* Set character pointer cwd to buffer     */
cwd = cbuffer;

/* Set attribute                           */
b_attr = mkAttr(WHITE,
                BLACK,
                OFF_INTENSITY,
                OFF_BLINK);

/* Clear buffer with '\0's                 */
memset(buffer,'\0',50);

/* A .BAT file has been chosed from the    */
/* MISC files                              */
if(choose==BATCH)
   {
   for(cnt=0; cnt<12; cnt++)
     {
     /* If '.' or '\0' in file name is     */
     /* reached then exit                  */
     if((misc[offset][cnt]=='.')||
        (misc[offset][cnt]=='\0'))
        break;

     /* Move file name character           */
     buffer[cnt] = misc[offset][cnt];
     }
   }
else
```

369

Fig. 9-15 continued.

```
    {
    /* Load a .EXE or .COM program        */
    for(cnt=0; cnt<12; cnt++)
        {
        /* If '.' or '\0' in file name is  */
        /* reached then exit               */
        if((program[offset][cnt]=='.')||
           (program[offset][cnt]=='\0'))
           break;

        /* Move file name character        */
        buffer[cnt] = program[offset][cnt];
        }
    }

/* Prepare a RECT structure               */
R = setRect(R,23,0,24,79);

/* Draw a horizontal line at row 23       */
vdHoriz(23,0,80,b_attr);

/* Black out bottom row - row 24 -        */

vdAttr(24,0,80,b_attr);

/* Print psuedo DOS prompt                */
vdWrite(24,0,3," :>",b_attr);

/* Print active drive                     */
vdWrite(24,0,1,cwd,b_attr);

/* get length of char string in buffer    */
column = strlen(buffer);
if(column != 0)
    {
    /* Add aSPC at first aNUL              */
    buffer[column++] = ' ';

    /* Write file name from directory      */
    /* buffer                              */
    vdWrite(24,3,strlen(buffer),buffer,b_attr);
    }
/* Move the cursor to the end of file     */
/* name                                   */
mvCur(24,3+column);

/* Turn on the cursor                     */
onCur();

/* Get a character string using           */
/* prompt(...)                            */
pos = prompt(&buffer[column],80-column);

/* Clear the screen                       */
scrnClr();

/* If ENTER key pressed                   */
if(pos!=0)
```

Fig. 9-15 continued.

```
    /* Then use system() to load program  */
    /* as if it were run directly from DOS */
    system(buffer);

/* Turn off the cursor                     */
offCur();

/* Wait here for key press                 */
wait_here();

/* Redraw the TABDOS screen                */
draw_screen();
}

/*
 * Function: load_wp
 *
 * Description:
 *  Use the default word processor
 *  to load the appropriate program
 *  from the list of file names
 *  held by misc[]
 */

void
load_wp(offset)
int offset;
{
char buffer[12];

/* Clear buffer                            */
memset(buffer,'\0',12);

/* Copy the selected file name to buffer   */
strcpy(buffer,misc[offset]);

/* Clear the screen                        */
scrnClr();

/* Turn on the cursor                      */
onCur();

/* Load the default editor with the name   */
/* of the file to be edited passed as a    */
/* parameter                               */
spawnlp(P_WAIT,editor,editor,buffer,NULL);

/* Turn off the cursor                     */
offCur();

/* Wait here for key press                 */
wait_here();

/* Redraw the screen                       */
draw_screen();
}
```

Fig. 9-15 continued.

```
/*
 * Function: load_vmask
 *
 * Description:
 *  Load memory map display program
 */

void
load_vmask()
{
/* Clear the screen                 */
scrnClr();

/* Use system command to load vmask     */
/* Source for vmask not provided in this */
/* text...sorry!                         */
/*
system("vmask /m");
*/

/* Wait here for key press           */
wait_here();

/* Redraw the TABDOS screen          */
draw_screen();
}

/*
 * Function: wait_here
 *
 * Description:
 *  Print the message and wait for
 *  key press
 */

void
wait_here()
{
int row,col;
/* Get the current cursor location   */
gtCur(&row,&col);

/* Move down two rows below message  */
if(row<23)
    row += 2;

/* Turn off the cursor               */
offCur();

/* Print the message                 */
vdWrite(row,
        0,
        31,
        "Press any key to continue...   ",
        mkAttr(WHITE,
               BLACK,
               ON_INTENSITY,
```

```
                         OFF_BLINK));

/* Wait for key press                        */
gtKey();
}

/*
 * End of TD2.C source listing
 *****************************/
```

Fig. 9-15 ends.

Fig. 9-16. The source code listing for TD3.C.

```
/********************************
 *
 * Source code listing starts here
 *
 * File Name: TD3.C
 */

/*
 * Include files here
 */

#include <stdio.h>
#include <dos.h>
#include <sys\types.h>
#include <dir.h>
#include <alloc.h>
#include <string.h>
#include <process.h>
#include <stdlib.h>

#include <tproto.h>
#include "shell.h"

/*
 * Externs
 */

extern WIND *DRVINFO;

/*
 * Globals
 */

RECT *RPD;
RECT *TD;
static int drv_number;

char subdir[SUBDIR_MAX][NAME_WIDTH];
char program[PROGRAM_MAX][NAME_WIDTH];
char misc[MISC_MAX][NAME_WIDTH];

char *dir_info[DIR_INFO_SIZE];
int dr_buff[10] = { 0,0,0,0,0,0,0,0,0,0 };
```

Fig. 9-16 continued.

```
char extender[5] = { '.','*',0,0,0 };
char tag = '*';

/*
 * Function maketime
 *
 * Description: Unpacks the
 *   file time data into standard
 *   form
 */


char format[80];

struct utime
*maketime(packedtime)
unsigned packedtime;
{
unsigned hour12set;
static struct utime today;

/* move packed data to structure */
today.numtime = packedtime;
today.hours = packedtime;

/* set seconds in structure     */
today.secs = today.hours & 0x001f;

/* set hours in structure       */
today.hours >>= 5;

/* set minutes in structure     */
today.mins = today.hours & 0x003f;

/* adjust hours                 */
today.hours >>= 6;
/* adjust seconds              */
today.secs *= 2;

/* set am/pm flag               */
today.am_pm = (today.hours >= 12) ?
             'p' : 'a';

/* convert 24 hour to 12 hour   */
hour12set = today.hours % 12;
hour12set = (hour12set==0) ?
           12 : hour12set;

/* Prepare time string to be    */
/* printed                      */
sprintf(today.timestring,
      "%2u:%02u %cm",
      hour12set,
      today.mins,
      today.am_pm);
return(&today);
}
```

Fig. 9-16 continued.

```
/*
 * Function makedate
 *
 * Description: Unpacks the
 *  file date data into standard
 *  form
 */

struct udate
*makedate(packeddate)
unsigned packeddate;
{
static struct udate filedate;
static char *months[] =
    {
    "???",
    "Jan",
    "Feb",
    "Mar",
    "Apr",
    "May",
    "Jun",
    "Jul",
    "Aug",
    "Sep",
    "Oct",
    "Nov",
    "Dec"
    } ;

/* set the file day and month    */
filedate.numdate = packeddate;
filedate.day = filedate.numdate & 0x001f;

/* set the file month            */
filedate.month = (filedate.numdate >> 5) &
                0x000f;
filedate.year = (packeddate >> 9) +
                1980;
sprintf(filedate.datestring,
        "%2u %3s %u",
        filedate.day,
        months[filedate.month],
        filedate.year);
return &filedate;
}

/*
 * Function f_info
 *
 * Description: Use the
 *  information for the
 *  file statistics to
 *  derive the date, time, etc...
 */

char
*f_info(ffblk)
```

Fig. 9-16 continued.

```
struct ffblk *ffblk;
{
struct utime *today;
struct udate *dod;
char nbuff[13],
     dbuff[13],
     tbuff[13],
     sbuff[13];
char *cptr;

/* clear buffers with 0s   */
memset(nbuff,0,13);
memset(dbuff,0,13);
memset(tbuff,0,13);
memset(sbuff,0,13);

/* convert the time and    */
/* date information        */
today = maketime(ffblk->ff_ftime);
dod = makedate(ffblk->ff_fdate);

/* prepare buffers for     */
/* print                   */
sprintf(nbuff,"%s",ffblk->ff_name);
sprintf(sbuff,"%8Lu",ffblk->ff_fsize);
sprintf(tbuff,"%s",today->timestring);
sprintf(dbuff,"%s",dod->datestring);

/* place ' 's in format    */
memset(format,' ',80);

/* relocate file stat info */
memcpy(&format[0],nbuff,strlen(nbuff));
memcpy(&format[13],sbuff,strlen(sbuff));
memcpy(&format[22],tbuff,strlen(tbuff));
memcpy(&format[31],dbuff,11);

/* terminate string with 0 */
format[43] = 0;

/* set pointer to file     */
/* time and date formatted */
/* information             */
cptr = format;

/* and return the pointer  */
return cptr;
}


/*
 * Function print_drive
 *
 * Description: Prints the
 *   default drive with
 *   attendant display
 */
```

Fig. 9-16 continued.

```
void
print_drive()
{
union REGS ir, or;
int attr;

/* set attribute byte     */
attr = mkAttr(WHITE,
              RED,
              ON_INTENSITY,
              OFF_BLINK);

/* print the drive letter */
print_dlet();

/* get the default drive   */
ir.h.ah = 25;
int86(33,&ir,&or);

/* filter drive number     */
/* to highlight button     */
switch(or.h.al)

    {
    /* drive a             */
    case 0:
       vdAttr(3,2,3,attr);
       break;

    /* drive b             */
    case 1:
       vdAttr(3+3,2,3,attr);
       break;

    /* drive c             */
    case 2:
       vdAttr(3+6,2,3,attr);
       break;

    /* drive d             */
    case 3:
       vdAttr(3+9,2,3,attr);
       break;
    }
drvdisp();
path_info();
print_path();
}

/*
 * Function: print_dlet
 *
 * Description: draws the buttons
 *    and drive letter
 */

void
print_dlet()
```

Fig. 9-16 continued.

```
{
int number, plain, attrb;

number = drv_number;

/* set attributes          */
plain = mkAttr(BLUE,
               WHITE,
               OFF_INTENSITY,
               OFF_BLINK);
attrb = mkAttr(BLACK,
               WHITE,
               OFF_INTENSITY,
               OFF_BLINK);

if(number >= 1)
   {
   dr_buff[0] = 1;
   RPD = setRect(RPD,2,1,4+1,5+1);
   boxRect(RPD,S_S_S_S,attrb);
   vdWrite(3,2,3," A ",plain);
   }
else
   return;

if(number >= 2)
   {
   dr_buff[1] = 1;
   RPD = setRect(RPD,5,1,7+1,5+1);
   boxRect(RPD,S_S_S_S,attrb);
   vdWrite(6,2,3," B ",plain);
   }
else
   return;

if(number >= 3)
   {
   dr_buff[2] = 1;
   RPD = setRect(RPD,8,1,10+1,5+1);
   boxRect(RPD,S_S_S_S,attrb);
   vdWrite(9,2,3," C ",plain);
   }
else
   return;

if(number >= 4)
   {
   dr_buff[3] = 1;
   RPD = setRect(RPD,11,1,13+1,5+1);
   boxRect(RPD,S_S_S_S,attrb);
   vdWrite(12,2,3," D ",plain);
   }
else
   return;

}
```

Fig. 9-16 continued.

```
/*
 * Function new_drive
 *
 * Description: Use BIOS
 *  to select a new default
 *  disk drive
 */

void
new_drive(drive)
int drive;
{
union REGS ir, or;
ir.h.dl = drive;
ir.h.ah = 14;
int86(33,&ir,&or);
}


/*
 * Function: path_info
 *
 * Description:
 *  Path_info reads the directory
 *  information fromm the current
 *  path into newly opened mallocs
 */

void
path_info()
{
int done;
struct ffblk ffblk;
struct ffblk *direntp;
int cnt,cnt1,cnt2,cnt3;
char *cptr;

/* clear the file info buffers   */
for(cnt=0; cnt<SUBDIR_MAX; cnt++)
    memset(&subdir[cnt][0],'\0',NAME_WIDTH);
    for(cnt=0; cnt<PROGRAM_MAX; cnt++)
    memset(&program[cnt][0],'\0',NAME_WIDTH);
    for(cnt=0; cnt<MISC_MAX; cnt++)
    memset(&misc[cnt][0],'\0',NAME_WIDTH);

/* free previously allocated     */
/* memory no longer needed       */
for(cnt=0; cnt<DIR_INFO_SIZE; cnt++)
    {
    if(dir_info[cnt]==NULL)
        break;
    free(dir_info[cnt]);
    dir_info[cnt] = NULL;
    }

/* Read the default directory    */
/*   while dynamically allocating */
```

Fig. 9-16 continued.

```
/* memory to hold the infor      */
cnt = 0;
done = findfirst("*.*",&ffblk,FA_DIREC);
while(!done)
   {
   dir_info[cnt] = (char *)
                   malloc(sizeof(struct ffblk));
   memcpy(dir_info[cnt],
          &ffblk,
          sizeof(struct ffblk));
   cnt++;
   done = findnext(&ffblk);
   }

/* sort ptrs to files by name    */
dir_sort();

/* move the file name and        */
/* pointer index to proper 2 dim */
/* arrays                        */
for(cnt=0,cnt1=0,cnt2=0,cnt3=0;
    cnt<DIR_INFO_SIZE;
    cnt++)
   {
   if(dir_info[cnt]==NULL)
      break;
   direntp = (struct ffblk *)
             dir_info[cnt];
   /* Is SUB DIR subdirectory */;
   if(direntp->ff_attrib==FA_DIREC)
      {
      /* index to complete file info */
      subdir[cnt1][13] = cnt;
      memcpy(subdir[cnt1++],
      direntp->ff_name,12);
      }
   else
      {
      cptr = (char *)
             strstr(direntp->ff_name,
             ".COM");
      /* Is PROGRAM .COM file */
      if(cptr!=NULL)
         {
         /* index to complete file info */
         program[cnt2][13] = cnt;
         memcpy(program[cnt2++],
                direntp->ff_name,12);
         }
      else
         {
         cptr = (char *)
         strstr(direntp->ff_name,
         ".EXE");
         /* Is PROGRAM .EXE file */
         if(cptr!=NULL)
            {
```

Fig. 9-16 continued.

```
                    /* index to complete file info */
                    program[cnt2][13] = cnt;
                    memcpy(program[cnt2++],
                    direntp->ff_name,
                    12);
                    }
                else
                    {
                    cptr = (char *)
                            strstr(".*",extender);
                    if(cptr!=NULL)
                        {
                        /* index to complete file info */
                        misc[cnt3][13] = cnt;
                        /* Is MISC file */
                        memcpy(misc[cnt3++],
                                direntp->ff_name,
                                12);
                        }
                    else
                        {
                        cptr = (char *)
                                strstr(direntp->ff_name,
                                extender);
                        /* Is PROGRAM .EXE file */
                        if(cptr!=NULL)
                            {
                            /* index to complete file info */
                            misc[cnt3][13] = cnt;
                            /* Is MISC file */
                            memcpy(misc[cnt3++],
                                    direntp->ff_name,
                                    12);
                                            }
                                        }

                                    }
                                }
                            }
                        }
                    }

            /*
             * Function: tag_subdir
             *           tag_program
             *           tag_misc
             *
             * Description: Tag the file
             *   for each of the three
             *   file catagories
             */

            void
            tag_subdir(val,offset)
            int val;
            int offset;
            {
            /* toggle tag on  */
            if(subdir[val][12] == 0)
```

Fig. 9-16 continued.

```
    subdir[val][12] = 1;
else
/* toggle tag off */
    subdir[val][12] = 0;

/* print sub dir  */
print_subdir(offset);
}

void
tag_program(val,offset)
int val;
int offset;
{
/* toggle tag on  */
if(program[val][12] == 0)
    program[val][12] = 1;

/* toggle tag off */
else
    program[val][12] = 0;

print_program(offset);
}

void
tag_misc(val,offset)
int val;
int offset;
{
if(misc[val][12] == 0)
    misc[val][12] = 1;
else
    misc[val][12] = 0;
print_misc(offset);
}

/*
 * Function: print_path
 *
 * Description:
 *  Print sub directory
 *  information to the screen
 */

void
print_path()
{
int cnt;
int len;

/* Print file into to screen */
for(cnt=0; cnt<WIND_HEIGHT; cnt++)
    {
    if(subdir[cnt]=='\0')
        break;
    len = strlen(subdir[cnt]);
```

Fig. 9-16 continued.

```
   if(len>12)
      len=12;
   wvdWrite(DRVINFO,
            cnt+2,
            1+1,
            len,
            subdir[cnt],
            DRVINFO->attr);
   if(subdir[cnt][12])
      wvdWrite(DRVINFO,
               cnt+2,
               1,
               1,
               &tag,
               DRVINFO->attr);
   else
      wvdWrite(DRVINFO,
               cnt+2,
               1,
               1," ",
               DRVINFO->attr);

   }
for(cnt=0; cnt<WIND_HEIGHT; cnt++)
   {
   if(program[cnt]=='\0')
      break;
   len = strlen(program[cnt]);
   if(len>12)
      len=12;
   wvdWrite(DRVINFO,
            cnt+2,
            14+2,
            len,
            program[cnt],
            DRVINFO->attr);
   if(program[cnt][12])
      wvdWrite(DRVINFO,
               cnt+2,
               14+1,
               1,
               &tag,
               DRVINFO->attr);
   else
      wvdWrite(DRVINFO,
               cnt+2,
               14+1,
               1,
               " ",
               DRVINFO->attr);
   }
for(cnt=0; cnt<WIND_HEIGHT; cnt++)
   {
   if(misc[cnt]=='\0')
      break;
   len = strlen(misc[cnt]);
   if(len>12)
```

Fig. 9-16 continued.

```
        len=12;
    wvdWrite(DRVINFO,
            cnt+2,
            27+3,
            len,
            misc[cnt],
            DRVINFO->attr);
    if(misc[cnt][12])
        wvdWrite(DRVINFO,
                cnt+2,
                27+2,
                1,
                &tag,
                DRVINFO->attr);
    else
        wvdWrite(DRVINFO,
                cnt+2,
                27+2,
                1,
                " ",
                DRVINFO->attr);
    }

}


/*
 * Function: print_subdir
 *           print_program
 *           print_misc
 *
 * Description: Print the
 *  file name information
 *  for each of the three
 *  columns
 */

void
print_subdir(offset)
int offset;
{
int cnt,len;
for(cnt=0; cnt<WIND_HEIGHT; cnt++)
    wvdWrite(DRVINFO,
            cnt+2,
            1,
            13,
            "            ",
            DRVINFO->attr);

for(cnt=0; cnt<WIND_HEIGHT; cnt++)
    {
    if(subdir[cnt+offset]=='\0')
        break;
    len = strlen(subdir[cnt+offset]);
    if(len>12)
        len=12;
    wvdWrite(DRVINFO,
```

Fig. 9-16 continued.

```
                    cnt+2,
                    1+1,
                    len,
                    subdir[cnt+offset],
                    DRVINFO->attr);
        if(subdir[cnt][12])
           wvdWrite(DRVINFO,
                    cnt+2,
                    1,
                    1,
                    &tag,
                    DRVINFO->attr);
        else
           wvdWrite(DRVINFO,
                    cnt+2,
                    1,
                    1,
                    " ",
                    DRVINFO->attr);
    }
}

void
print_program(offset)
int offset;
{
int cnt,len;
for(cnt=0; cnt<WIND_HEIGHT; cnt++)
   wvdWrite(DRVINFO,
            cnt+2,
            14+1,
            13,
            "             ",
            DRVINFO->attr);

for(cnt=0; cnt<WIND_HEIGHT; cnt++)
   {
   if(program[cnt+offset]=='\0')
      break;
   len = strlen(program[cnt+offset]);
   if(len>12)
      len=12;
   wvdWrite(DRVINFO,

            cnt+2,
            14+2,
            len,
            program[cnt+offset],
            DRVINFO->attr);
        if(program[cnt][12])
           wvdWrite(DRVINFO,
                    cnt+2,
                    14+1,
                    1,
                    &tag,
                    DRVINFO->attr);
        else
           wvdWrite(DRVINFO,
```

Fig. 9-16 continued.

```
                cnt+2,
                14+1,
                1,
                " ",
                DRVINFO->attr);
    }
}

void
print_misc(offset)
int offset;
{
int cnt,len;
for(cnt=0; cnt<WIND_HEIGHT; cnt++)
    wvdWrite(DRVINFO,
                cnt+2,
                27+2,
                13,
                "              ",
                DRVINFO->attr);

for(cnt=0; cnt<WIND_HEIGHT; cnt++)
    {
    if(misc[cnt+offset]=='\0')
        break;
    len = strlen(misc[cnt+offset]);
    if(len>12)
        len=12;
    wvdWrite(DRVINFO,
                cnt+2,
                27+3,
                len,
                misc[cnt+offset],
                DRVINFO->attr);
    if(misc[cnt][12])
        wvdWrite(DRVINFO,
                    cnt+2,
                    27+2,
                    1,
                    &tag,
                    DRVINFO->attr);
    else
        wvdWrite(DRVINFO,
                    cnt+2,
                    27+2,
                    1,
                    " ",
                    DRVINFO->attr);
    }
}

/*
 * Function: new_sub
 *
 * Description: aA new sub
 *  directory has been
 *  selected and the screen
```

Fig. 9-16 continued.

```
 *  is redrawn and updated
 */

void
new_sub(offset)
int offset;
{
char buffer[12];
memset(buffer,'\0',12);
strcpy(buffer,subdir[offset]);
chdir(buffer);
draw_screen();
}


/*
 * Function: dir_sort
 *
 * Description:
 *   Sort the directory
 *   acording to name
 */

void
dir_sort()
{
struct date today;
register int f;
register int b;
int pos,count;
struct ffblk *temp, *d1, *d2;
char num_string[80];


/***************************/
/* Clear num_string buffer */
/* Get ascii date          */
/* Write text              */
/* Print ascii info        */
/***************************/
TD = setRect(TD,16,0,21,32);

getdate(&today);
memset(num_string,' ',sizeof(num_string));
sprintf(num_string,
        " Today's Date is:    %d/%d/%d ",
        today.da_mon,
        today.da_day,
        today.da_year);
vdWrite(17,1,30,num_string,
    mkAttr(WHITE,
           BLUE,
           OFF_INTENSITY,
           OFF_BLINK));
boxRect(TD,
        S_S_S_S,
        mkAttr(BLACK,
```

Fig. 9-16 continued.

```
                WHITE,
                OFF_INTENSITY,
                OFF_BLINK));
vdWrite(18,
        1,
        30,
        " The Current Time:              ",
        mkAttr(WHITE,
               BLUE,
               OFF_INTENSITY,
               OFF_BLINK));

/* get dir entry count */
count=0;
while(dir_info[count]!=NULL)
    count++;

pos = 3;
do
    {
    /* forward sort switch loop */
    for(f=1; f<count; f++)
        {
        /* backward sort switch loop */
        for(b=count-1; b>=f; b--)
            {
            /* get pointers to dir structs */
            d1 = (struct ffblk *)
                dir_info[b-1];
            d2 = (struct ffblk *)
                dir_info[b];
            /* compare & switch on TRUE */
            if( d1->ff_name[pos] >
                d2->ff_name[pos] )
                {
                temp = (struct ffblk *)
                        dir_info[b-1];
                dir_info[b-1] = (char *)
                                dir_info[b];
                dir_info[b] = (char *)temp;
                }
            }
        }
        pos--;
    } while(pos>=0);

/***************************/
/* Clear num_string buffer */
/* Get ascii disk free     */
/* Write text              */
/* Inverse string len + 2  */
/* Print ascii info        */
/***************************/

memset(num_string,'\0',sizeof(num_string));
ltoa(diskFree(),num_string,10);
vdWrite(19,
```

```
            1,
            30,
            " Free Bytes on Disk:           ",
            mkAttr(WHITE,
                   BLUE,
                   OFF_INTENSITY,
                   OFF_BLINK));
    vdWrite(19,
            1+21,
            strlen(num_string),
            num_string,
            mkAttr(WHITE,
                   BLUE,
                   OFF_INTENSITY,
                   OFF_BLINK));
}

/*
 * Function: retdrive
 *
 * Description: Return the
 *  number of active drives
 */

void
retdrive()
{
drv_number = drvnum();
}

/*
 * End of the source listing for TD3.C
 ************************************/
```

Fig. 9-16 ends.

Fig. 9-17. The source code listing for TD4.C.

```
/********************************
 *
 * Source code listing starts here
 *
 * File Name: TD4.C
 */

/*
 * Include files here
 */


#include <ctype.h>
#include <stdio.h>
#include <io.h>
#include <fcntl.h>
#include <sys\stat.h>
#include <sys\types.h>
#include <process.h>
#include <string.h>
```

Fig. 9-17 continued.

```
#include <dir.h>

#include <tproto.h>
#include "shell.h"

/*
 * Global pointers
 */

WIND *I_DROP;
WIND *F_DROP;
WIND *D_DROP;
WIND *S_DROP;
RECT *R_ch;

/* drop_i window data */
char drop11[11]    = "Help Info  ";
char drop12[11]    = "Memory Info";
char drop13[11]    = "Disk Info  ";
char drop14[11]    = "TSR Info   ";

char fd21[15]    = "Delete File    ";
char fd22[15]    = "Erase * Files  ";
char fd23[15]    = "Copy File      ";
char fd24[15]    = "Move * Files   ";
char fd25[15]    = "Tag File(s)    ";
char fd26[15]    = "Rename File    ";
char fd27[15]    = "Alter Attribute";

char dd31[20]    = "Change to Root Dir  ";
char dd32[20]    = "Go Back One Dir     ";
char dd33[20]    = "--------------------";
char dd34[20]    = "Make New Directory  ";
char dd35[20]    = "Remove Directory    ";

char ds41[20]    = "Alter Default .EXT  ";
char ds42[20]    = "Choose New Word Proc";
char ds43[20]    = "--------------------";
char ds44[20]    = "Display Cur. Setting";
char ds45[20]    = "Save Current Setting";

extern char editor[8];
extern char extender[5];

/*
 * Function drop_i
 *
 * Description: Drop down
 *   information window
 */

void
drop_i()
{
int key;    /* scan and char value   */
int attr;   /* highlight attribute   */
int exit;
```

Fig. 9-17 continued.

```
int old_row,row;
int inverse;
/* make highlight attribute */
attr = mkAttr(WHITE,
              BLUE,
              ON_INTENSITY,
              OFF_BLINK);
inverse = mkAttr(BLUE,
                 WHITE,
                 OFF_INTENSITY,
                 OFF_BLINK);

/****************************************/
/* Initialize grid menu window structure /
/* and display window                   */
/****************************************/

/* ensure window initialization bypass  */
/* Allocate memory and return pointer    */
/* to structure                          */
I_DROP = setWind(I_DROP,1,0,6,12);

/* Set Window Attr -                     */
/*    Fore,Back,Intensity,Blink          */
setAttr(I_DROP,mkAttr(WHITE,
                      BLUE,
                      OFF_INTENSITY,
                      OFF_BLINK));

/* Set Window Border                     */
setBord(I_DROP,S_S_S_S);

/* Set the bottom title                  */
setTitle(I_DROP,"            ");

/* Display window                        */
strtWind(I_DROP);

dispWind(I_DROP);

/* Write menu and exit messages          */
wvdWrite(I_DROP,1,1,11,drop11,I_DROP->attr)
wvdWrite(I_DROP,2,1,11,drop12,I_DROP->attr)
wvdWrite(I_DROP,3,1,11,drop13,I_DROP->attr)
wvdWrite(I_DROP,4,1,11,drop14,I_DROP->attr)
wvdAttr(I_DROP,1,1,1,attr);
wvdAttr(I_DROP,2,1,1,attr);
wvdAttr(I_DROP,3,1,1,attr);
wvdAttr(I_DROP,4,1,1,attr);

row = 1;
old_row = 1;
exit = aFALSE;

do
   {
   /* off highlight bar                  */
```

Fig. 9-17 continued.

```
wvdAttr(I_DROP,old_row,1,11,I_DROP->attr
wvdAttr(I_DROP,old_row,1,1,attr);
wvdAttr(I_DROP,row,1,11,inverse);
old_row = row;

/* wait for key press              */
key = gtKey();
switch(key)
   {
   case ESCAPE:
      remvWind(I_DROP);
      exit = aTRUE;
      break;
   case DOWN_ARROW:
      if(row==4)
         row=1;
      else
         row++;
      break;
   case UP_ARROW:
      if(row==1)
         row=4;
      else
         row--;
      break;
   case ENTER:
      switch(row)
         {
         case 1:
            remvWind(I_DROP);
            spawnlp(P_WAIT,
                    "helpw1",
                    "helpw1",
                    NULL);
            exit = aTRUE;
            break;
         case 2:
            remvWind(I_DROP);
            load_vmask();
            exit = aTRUE;
            break;
         case 3:
            remvWind(I_DROP);
            spawnlp(P_WAIT,
                    "dskdemo",
                    "dskdemo",
                    NULL);
            exit = aTRUE;
            break;
         case 4:
            remvWind(I_DROP);
            spawnlp(P_WAIT,
                    "info1",
                    "info1",
                    NULL);
            exit = aTRUE;
            break;
```

Fig. 9-17 continued.

```
                    }
                break;
            default:
                key &=0x00ff;
                key = toupper(key);
                switch(key)
                    {
                    case 'H':
                        remvWind(I_DROP);
                        spawnlp(P_WAIT,
                                "helpw1",
                                "helpw1",
                                NULL);
                        exit = aTRUE;
                        break;
                    case 'M':
                        remvWind(I_DROP);
                        load_vmask();
                        exit = aTRUE;
                        break;
                    case 'D':
                        remvWind(I_DROP);
                        spawnlp(P_WAIT,
                                "dskdemo",
                                "dskdemo",
                                NULL);
                        exit = aTRUE;
                        break;
                    case 'T':
                        remvWind(I_DROP);
                        spawnlp(P_WAIT,
                                "info1",
                                "info1",
                                NULL);
                        exit = aTRUE;
                        break;
                    }
                break;
            }
    } while(!exit);
dsyWind(I_DROP);
}

/*
 * Function: drop_f
 *
 * Description: Drop down
 *  File management window
 */

void
drop_f()
{
int key;   /* scan and char value       */
int attr;  /* highlight attribute       */
int exit,inverse;
int old_row,row;
```

Fig. 9-17 continued.

```
/* make highlight attribute */
inverse = mkAttr(BLUE,
                 WHITE,
                 OFF_INTENSITY,
                 OFF_BLINK);
attr = mkAttr(WHITE,
              BLUE,
              ON_INTENSITY,
              OFF_BLINK);

/* Allocate memory and return pointer to  */
/*    structure                           */
F_DROP = setWind(F_DROP,1,14,9,30);

/* Set Window Attr -                      */
/*   Fore,Back,Intensity,Blink            */
setAttr(F_DROP,mkAttr(WHITE,
                      BLUE,
                      OFF_INTENSITY,
                      OFF_BLINK));

/* Set Window Border                      */
setBord(F_DROP,S_S_S_S);

/* Set the bottom title                   */
setTitle(F_DROP,"                ");

/* Display window                         */
strtWind(F_DROP);

dispWind(F_DROP);

/* Write menu and exit messages           */
wvdWrite(F_DROP,1,1,15,fd21,F_DROP->attr);
wvdWrite(F_DROP,2,1,15,fd22,F_DROP->attr);
wvdWrite(F_DROP,3,1,15,fd23,F_DROP->attr);
wvdWrite(F_DROP,4,1,15,fd24,F_DROP->attr);
wvdWrite(F_DROP,5,1,15,fd25,F_DROP->attr);
wvdWrite(F_DROP,6,1,15,fd26,F_DROP->attr);
wvdWrite(F_DROP,7,1,15,fd27,F_DROP->attr);
wvdAttr(F_DROP,1,1,1,attr);
wvdAttr(F_DROP,2,1,1,attr);
wvdAttr(F_DROP,3,1,1,attr);
wvdAttr(F_DROP,4,1,1,attr);
wvdAttr(F_DROP,5,1,1,attr);
wvdAttr(F_DROP,6,1,1,attr);
wvdAttr(F_DROP,7,1,1,attr);

exit = aFALSE;
row = 1;
old_row = 1;

do
   {
   /* off highlight bar                   */
   wvdAttr(F_DROP,old_row,1,15,F_DROP->attr);
   wvdAttr(F_DROP,old_row,1,1,attr);
```

Fig. 9-17 continued.

```
wvdAttr(F_DROP,row,1,15,inverse);
old_row = row;

/* wait for key press */
key = gtKey();
switch(key)
    {
    case ESCAPE:
        remvWind(F_DROP);
        exit = aTRUE;
        break;
    case DOWN_ARROW:
        if(row==7)
            row=1;
        else
            row++;
        break;
    case UP_ARROW:
        if(row==1)
            row=7;
        else
            row--;
        break;
    case ENTER:
        switch(row)
            {
            case 1:
                remvWind(F_DROP);
                delete_file();
                exit = aTRUE;
                break;
            case 2:
                remvWind(F_DROP);
                exit = aTRUE;
                break;
            case 3:
                remvWind(F_DROP);
                copy_file();
                exit = aTRUE;
                break;
            case 4:
                remvWind(F_DROP);
                exit = aTRUE;
                break;
            case 5:
                remvWind(F_DROP);
                exit = aTRUE;
                break;
            case 6:
                remvWind(F_DROP);
                exit = aTRUE;
                break;
            case 7:
                remvWind(F_DROP);
                exit = aTRUE;
                break;
            }
```

Fig. 9-17 continued.

```
            break;
        default:
            key &=0x00ff;
            key = toupper(key);
            switch(key)
                {
                case 'D':
                    remvWind(F_DROP);
                    delete_file();
                    exit = aTRUE;
                    break;
                case 'E':
                    remvWind(F_DROP);
                    exit = aTRUE;
                    break;
                case 'C':
                    remvWind(F_DROP);
                    copy_file();
                    exit = aTRUE;
                    break;
                case 'M':
                    remvWind(F_DROP);
                    exit = aTRUE;
                    break;
                case 'T':
                    remvWind(F_DROP);
                    exit = aTRUE;
                    break;
                case 'R':
                    remvWind(F_DROP);
                    exit = aTRUE;
                    break;
                case 'A':
                    remvWind(F_DROP);
                    exit = aTRUE;
                    break;
                }
            break;
        }
    } while(!exit);
dsyWind(F_DROP);
}

/*
 * Function: drop_d
 *
 * Description: Drop down directory
 *   operations window
 */

void
drop_d()
{
int attr;  /* highlight attribute      */

/* make highlight attribute          */
attr = mkAttr(WHITE,
```

Fig. 9-17 continued.

```
                BLUE,
                ON_INTENSITY,
                OFF_BLINK);

/*******************************************/
/* Initialize grid menu window structure  */
/* and display window                      */
/*******************************************/


/* Allocate memory and return pointer to  */
/*   structure                             */
D_DROP = setWind(D_DROP,1,32,7,53);

/* Set Window Attr -                       */
/* Fore,Back,Intensity,Blink               */
setAttr(D_DROP,mkAttr(WHITE,
                      BLUE,
                      OFF_INTENSITY,
                      OFF_BLINK));

/* Set Window Border                       */
setBord(D_DROP,S_S_S_S);

/* Set the bottom title                    */
setTitle(D_DROP,"                  ");

/* Display window                          */
strtWind(D_DROP);

dispWind(D_DROP);

/* Write menu and exit messages            */
wvdWrite(D_DROP,1,1,20,dd31,D_DROP->attr);
wvdWrite(D_DROP,2,1,20,dd32,D_DROP->attr);
wvdWrite(D_DROP,3,1,20,dd33,D_DROP->attr);
wvdWrite(D_DROP,4,1,20,dd34,D_DROP->attr);
wvdWrite(D_DROP,5,1,20,dd35,D_DROP->attr);
wvdAttr(D_DROP,1,1,1,attr);
wvdAttr(D_DROP,2,1,1,attr);
wvdAttr(D_DROP,4,1,1,attr);
wvdAttr(D_DROP,5,1,1,attr);

/* wait for key press */
gtKey();

/* remove window and display original      */
/* screen information                      */
remvWind(D_DROP);
dsyWind(D_DROP);
}

/*
 * Function: drop_s
 *
 * Description: Alter default
 *   word processor settings
 */
```

Fig. 9-17 continued.

```
int
drop_s()
{
int key;    /* scan and char value   */
int value; /* value to be returned  */
int attr;  /* highlight attribute   */
int cnt,b_attr, handle;

/* make highlight attribute           */
attr = mkAttr(WHITE,
              BLUE,
              ON_INTENSITY,
              OFF_BLINK);
b_attr = mkAttr(WHITE,
                BLACK,
                ON_INTENSITY,
                OFF_BLINK);

/***************************************** */
/* Initialize grid menu window structure */
/* and display window                    */
/*****************************************/

/* Allocate memory and return pointer to  */
/* structure                              */
S_DROP = setWind(S_DROP,1,54,7,75);

/* Set Window Attr -                      */
/* Fore,Back,Intensity,Blink              */
setAttr(S_DROP,mkAttr(WHITE,
                      BLUE,
                      OFF_INTENSITY,
                      OFF_BLINK));

/* Set Window Border                      */
setBord(S_DROP,S_S_S_S);

/* Set the bottom title                   */
setTitle(S_DROP,"              ");

/* Display window                         */
strtWind(S_DROP);

dispWind(S_DROP);

/* Write menu and exit messages           */
wvdWrite(S_DROP,1,1,20,ds41,S_DROP->attr);
wvdWrite(S_DROP,2,1,20,ds42,S_DROP->attr);
wvdWrite(S_DROP,3,1,20,ds43,S_DROP->attr);
wvdWrite(S_DROP,4,1,20,ds44,S_DROP->attr);
wvdWrite(S_DROP,5,1,20,ds45,S_DROP->attr);
wvdAttr(S_DROP,1,1,1,attr);
wvdAttr(S_DROP,2,1,1,attr);
wvdAttr(S_DROP,4,1,1,attr);
wvdAttr(S_DROP,5,1,1,attr);

 /* wait for key press                    */
```

Fig. 9-17 continued.

```
key = gtKey();

/* remove window and display original      */
/* screen information                      */
remvWind(S_DROP);
dsyWind(S_DROP);
key &=0x00ff;
key = toupper(key);
switch(key)
   {
   case 'C':
      R_ch = setRect(R_ch,21,1,23+1,78+1);
      saveRect(R_ch);
      boxRect(R_ch,S_S_S_S,b_attr);
      vdWrite(22,
              2,
              76,
              " Select WP: Ex. Word Perfect's 'wp.exe' is entered 'wp'. >                ",b_attr);
      vdWrite(22,61,strlen(editor),editor,b_attr);
      mvCur(22,61);
      onCur();
      prompt(&editor[0],8);
      offCur();
      restRect(R_ch);
      value = 'C';
      break;
   case 'A':
      R_ch = setRect(R_ch,21,1,23+1,78+1);
      saveRect(R_ch);
      boxRect(R_ch,S_S_S_S,b_attr);
      vdWrite(22,2,76,
 " Select File Extender for MISC Files. Current Setting:                ",b_attr);
      vdWrite(22,
              57,
              strlen(extender),
              extender,b_attr);
      mvCur(22,58);
      onCur();
      if(!prompt(&extender[1],3))
         {
         offCur();
         restRect(R_ch);
         }
      else
         {
         for(cnt=1; cnt<4; cnt++)
            {
            if(extender[cnt] == ' ')
               extender[cnt] = '\0';
            }
         }
      strupr(&extender[1]);
      offCur();
      restRect(R_ch);
      draw_screen();
      value = 'A';
      break;
```

```
    case 'S':
        /* load tabdos.cfg file */
        handle = open("tabdos.cfg",
                            O_CREAT |
                            O_TRUNC |
                            O_RDWR,
                            S_IREAD |
                            S_IWRITE);
        if(handle <0 )
            beep();
        else
            {
            write(handle,extender,5);
            write(handle,editor,8);
            close(handle);
            }
        break;
    }
return(value);
}

/*
 * End of source code listing for TD4.C
 ***********************************/
```

Fig. 9-17 ends.

Fig. 9-18. The source code listing for TD5.C.

```
/********************************
 *
 * Source code listing starts here
 *
 * File Name: TD5.C
 */

/*
 * Include files here
 */

#include <stdio.h>
#include <sys\types.h>
#include <ctype.h>
#include <process.h>
#include <string.h>
#include <dir.h>
#include <alloc.h>

#include <tproto.h>
#include "shell.h"

/*
 * Externals
 */

extern int bar_ctr;
```

Fig. 9-18 continued.

```
extern int old_ctr;
extern int new_ctr;
extern int off1ctr;
extern int off2ctr;
extern int off3ctr;
extern int im1ctr;
extern int im2ctr;
extern int im3ctr;
extern int im1_new;
extern int im2_new;
extern int im3_new;

extern char subdir[SUBDIR_MAX][NAME_WIDTH];
extern char program[PROGRAM_MAX][NAME_WIDTH];
extern char misc[MISC_MAX][NAME_WIDTH];

/*
 * Pointers to WIND structures
 */

WIND *F_DELETE;
WIND *F_COPY;

WIND *DRVINFO;

char drvdat1[41]   =
"   SUB DIR     PROGRAMS       MISC.    ";

/* file delete window data */
char delete1[28]    = "        File Delete        ";
char delete2[28]    = "                           ";
char delete3[28]    = " Delete File:              ";
char delete4[28]    = "                           ";
char delete5[28]    = " Press (Y)es to Delete     ";
char delete6[28]    = " Press (N)o to exit        ";

/* copy file window data */
char copy1[28]     = "         Copy File         ";
char copy2[28]     = "                           ";
char copy3[28]     = " Copy File:                ";
char copy4[28]     = " To Drive:                 ";
char copy5[28]     = "                           ";
char copy6[28]     = "ENTER to Copy / ESC to Exit ";


char in_name[14];
char out_name[14];

/*
 * Function: DispErr
 *
 * Description: Function called
 *  by default by the critical
 *  error handler. Prints message
 *  prompting user response.
 */
```

Fig. 9-18 continued.

```
void
DispErr()
{
beep();
beep();
beep();
beep();
vdWrite(24,
        10,
        61,
"*ERROR* Drive Not Ready! Insert Disk in Drive & Press ANY KEY",
        mkAttr(WHITE,
               BLACK,
               OFF_INTENSITY,
               OFF_BLINK));
vdAttr(24,10,7,mkAttr(WHITE,
                      BLACK,
                      ON_INTENSITY,
                      OFF_BLINK));
vdAttr(24,35,36,mkAttr(WHITE,
                       BLACK,
                       ON_INTENSITY,
                       OFF_BLINK));
vdAttr(24,10,7,mkAttr(WHITE,
                      BLACK,
                      ON_INTENSITY,
                      ON_BLINK));
}

/*
 * Function: ErasErr
 *
 * Description: removes the Critical error
 *   message after the default retry is entered
 *   into the DOS kernel
 */

void
ErasErr()
{
vdWrite(24,10,61,
 "                                                              ",
          mkAttr(BLACK,
                 WHITE,
                 OFF_INTENSITY,
                 OFF_BLINK));
}

/*****************************************/
/* Make variables which must retain their */
/* value after the function exits global  */
/*****************************************/

void
delete_file()
{
int key;   /* scan and char value   */
```

Fig. 9-18 continued.

```c
char *cptr;
char far *fptr;

/*******************************************/
/* Initialize grid menu window structure   */
/*   and display window                     */
/*******************************************/

if(new_ctr<15)
   cptr = subdir[new_ctr+off1ctr];
else if(new_ctr<30)
   cptr = program[new_ctr+off2ctr-15];
else
   cptr = misc[new_ctr+off3ctr-30];

fptr = (char far *)cptr;

/* Allocate memory and return pointer to */
/*   structure                           */
F_DELETE = setWind(F_DELETE,7,24,7+7,24+29);

/* Set Window Attr -                      */
/* Fore,Back,Intensity,Blink              */
setAttr(F_DELETE,mkAttr(BLACK,
                        CYAN,
                        OFF_INTENSITY,
                        OFF_BLINK));

/* Set Window Border                      */
setBord(F_DELETE,D_D_D_D);

/* Set the bottom title                   */
setTitle(F_DELETE," File Operations ");

/* Display window                         */
strtWind(F_DELETE);

dispWind(F_DELETE);

/* Write menu and exit messages */
wvdWrite(F_DELETE,1,1,28,delete1,
        mkAttr(CYAN,
               BLACK,
               OFF_INTENSITY,
               OFF_BLINK));
wvdWrite(F_DELETE,2,1,28,delete2,F_DELETE->attr);
wvdWrite(F_DELETE,3,1,28,delete3,F_DELETE->attr);
wvdWrite(F_DELETE,4,1,28,delete4,F_DELETE->attr);
wvdWrite(F_DELETE,5,1,28,delete5,F_DELETE->attr);
wvdWrite(F_DELETE,6,1,28,delete6,F_DELETE->attr);
wvdWrite(F_DELETE,3,16,strlen(cptr),cptr,
        mkAttr(WHITE,
               BLACK,
               ON_INTENSITY,
               OFF_BLINK));

/* wait for key press */
```

Fig. 9-18 continued.

```
key = gtKey();
key &= 0x00ff;
key = toupper(key);
if(key=='Y')
    {
    spawnlp(P_WAIT,"tremove","tremove",fptr,NULL);
    draw_screen();
    }

/* remove window and display original scrn info */
remvWind(F_DELETE);
dsyWind(F_DELETE);
}

/*
 * Function: copy_file
 *
 * Description: Copy file
 *   window
 */

void
copy_file()
{
int key;    /* scan and char value    */
int inverse,exit;
char *cptr;

inverse = mkAttr(WHITE,
                 BLACK,
                 ON_INTENSITY,
                 OFF_BLINK);

/* get the file name */
if(new_ctr<15)
    cptr = subdir[new_ctr+off1ctr];
else if(new_ctr<30)
    cptr = program[new_ctr+off1ctr-15];
else
    cptr = misc[new_ctr+off1ctr-30];
/* Allocate memory and return pointer to */
/*   structure                           */
F_COPY = setWind(F_COPY,7,24,7+7,24+29);

/* Window Attr - Fore,Back,Intensity,Blink */
setAttr(F_COPY,mkAttr(BLACK,
                      CYAN,
                      OFF_INTENSITY,
                      OFF_BLINK));

/* Set Window Border */
setBord(F_COPY,D_D_D_D);

/* Set the bottom title */
setTitle(F_COPY," File Operations ");

/* Display window */
```

Fig. 9-18 continued.

```
strtWind(F_COPY);

dispWind(F_COPY);

/* Write menu and exit messages */
wvdWrite(F_COPY,1,1,28,copy1,
        mkAttr(CYAN,
               BLACK,
               OFF_INTENSITY,
               OFF_BLINK));
wvdWrite(F_COPY,2,1,28,copy2,F_COPY->attr);
wvdWrite(F_COPY,3,1,28,copy3,F_COPY->attr);
wvdWrite(F_COPY,4,1,28,copy4,F_COPY->attr);
wvdWrite(F_COPY,5,1,28,copy5,F_COPY->attr);
wvdWrite(F_COPY,6,1,28,copy6,F_COPY->attr);
wvdWrite(F_COPY,3,16,strlen(cptr),cptr,inverse);
onCur();
wmvCur(F_COPY,4,13);
out_name[0] = ' ';

exit = aFALSE;
do
   {
   wvdWrite(F_COPY,4,13,1,out_name,inverse);
   /* wait for key press */
   key = gtKey();
   switch(key)
      {
      case ENTER:
         exit = aTRUE;
         break;
      case ESC:
         exit = aTRUE;
         break;
      default:
         key &= 0x00ff;
         key = toupper(key);
         switch(key)
            {
            case 'A':
            case 'B':
            case 'C':
            case 'D':
               out_name[0] = key;
               break;
            default:
               beep();
               break;
            }
         break;
      }
   } while(!exit);

offCur();

/* remove window and display original screen information */
remvWind(F_COPY);
```

Fig. 9-18 continued.

```
dsyWind(F_COPY);
}



/*********************************************/
/* Make variables which must retain their */
/* value after the function exits global  */
/*********************************************/

int drvdisp_flag=0;

/*
 * Function: drvdisp
 *
 * Description: Prints heading info
 * for file display
 */

void
drvdisp()
{
char *cwd;
char bott=193;
char buffer[50];

if(drvdisp_flag)
    {
    dsyWind(DRVINFO);
    drvdisp_flag = 0;
    }

if(!drvdisp_flag)
    {
    drvdisp_flag=1;

    DRVINFO = setWind(DRVINFO,3,32,20,74);

    setAttr(DRVINFO,mkAttr(BLACK,
                           WHITE,
                           OFF_INTENSITY,
                           OFF_BLINK));

    setBord(DRVINFO,S_S_S_S);


    getcwd(buffer,50);
    cwd = buffer;
    setTitle(DRVINFO,cwd);

    strtWind(DRVINFO);
    }
else
    dispWind(DRVINFO);

wvdWrite(DRVINFO,1,1,41,drvdat1,
         mkAttr(RED,
```

```
                        BLACK,
                        ON_INTENSITY,
                        OFF_BLINK));
        wvdVert(DRVINFO,2,14,15,
                DRVINFO->attr);
        wvdVert(DRVINFO,2,27+1,15,
                DRVINFO->attr);
        wvdWrite(DRVINFO,2+15,14,1,&bott,
                DRVINFO->attr);
        wvdWrite(DRVINFO,2+15,27+1,1,&bott,
                DRVINFO->attr);

}


/*
 * End of source file TD5.C
 **************************/
```

Fig. 9-18 ends.

SUMMARY

The source code listing for TABDOS has provided you with a wealth of programming information. Many TABDOS's functions can be considered separate source modules and may be applied to your own programs without modifications.

This text started out by describing why C libraries are important. Once that fact had been established, a method for selecting library functions and library building was presented. Following our own advice, the creation of the TAB library began in earnest.

We discovered that many library object modules could be coded in either C or assembly. Although assembly coding is a tad more esoteric than C programming, assembly modules often took up far less space and ran faster than C generated modules. By including as many of the assembly generated modules as possible in the TAB library, the programs created with the TAB library will be a hybrid of C and assembly.

As the theme of this text is Menus, Windows, and User Interfaces, the many library demonstration programs conformed to our theme. LOTUS, GRID, DROP DOWN, SCROLLING BAR menus and user interfacers were all presented.

TABDOS demonstrates the deep power of the TAB library and how it may be used to present professional looking programs.

Index

Index

A

A.BAT, 50
accumlator register (AX), 38
AH register, 37, 38
AL register, 37
ALLOC.H, 141
Alt key, 87
ANEWPS, 284
ASCII, 9, 25, 87, 108
  borders with characters from, 170
  keyboard codes for, KEY-
    BOARD.H, 13
  keyboard definition program for,
    ASCII.H, 12
ASCII.H header file, 12, 25
attribute byte
  bit arrangement for, 57
  make, MKATTR.C, 58
AX register, 37, 38

B

BAR1.C, 130-132, 203
BAR1.EXE, 132
BAR2.C, 138-141
BAR3.C, 160, 162-166
BAR4.C, 203, 204-210
base pointer register (BX), 38-40
beep(), 93
BEEP.C, 93-94
BH register, 37

BIOS, 37
  keyboard handling routines and,
    87-117
  peripheral access with, universal,
    56
  register values for cursor move,
    44
  screen access with, 56
BL register, 37, 38
Blaise C Tools + Library, 4, 5, 6
borders, 9, 170-194
  predefined, 216
  window, SETBORD.C, 221
boxRect(), 170, 174, 211
BOXRECT.ASM, 174, 175, 178-188
BOXRECT.C, 175-178
BP register, 39, 40
BX register, 37, 38

C

'C' erious library, 4-8
CASE, 91, 92
case sensitivity, 50
CC.BAT, 29, 31-34, 45
CGA, 56
CH register, 37, 38
CHAR, 25
CL register, 37, 38
clock, TSR routine in C, 302-321
CLOCK.C, 302, 313-318

CLOCK.EXE, 264, 284
clrRect(), 170, 190
CLRRECT.C, 190-191
code model, 43
code segment register, 39, 40
colors (see screens, colors)
Control key, 87
coordinate systems, global vs. local,
  213
count register (CX), 38
CRITERR.ASM, 325-328
CS register, 39, 40
cursor, 44
  cursor routines, 22
  disable/enable, 156-160
  location of, GTCUR.C, 92
  location of, structure for (CURLO-
    CATION), 19
  movement of, C or assembly,
    MVCUR.C, 44-56
  register values for BIOS, 44
  restore location, 141, 142
  save location, 132, 141
  test movement of, TESTCUR.C,
    45-46
  turn off after vidInit(), 132
CX register, 37, 38, 39

D

data model, 43

411

Other Bestsellers of Related Interest

ASSEMBLER LANGUAGE FOR APPLICATION PROGRAMMING—Revised Edition—Don H. Stabley

In this revised edition of his bestselling guide, Don Stabley gives you a sound basis in the fundamentals of Assembler Language and a better understanding of high-level languages. The book's organization by function helps you to make clear distinctions among similar operations, allowing you to select the specific operation needed to solve a programming problem. Step-by-step illustrations and a wealth of diagrams, tables, review exercises, and code samples add still more to its usefulness. 448 pages, 418 illustrations. Book No. 3354, $36.95 hardcover only

HARD DISK MANAGEMENT WITH DOS—2nd Edition—Dan Gookin

". . . a comprehensive guide to hard-disk management under MS-DOS." —*ALA Booklist*

". . . a valuable part of any computer user's reference tools." —**The Midwest Book Reviews**

This valuable resource of utilities, applications, and management tips takes you from day-to-day basics to your system's most advanced capabilities. Designed to streamline your use of hard disk computers, this comprehensive sourcebook covers. . .file organization, batch file programming, menu generating, backing up procedures, solutions to hard disk/data security, and performance enhancements. 384 pages, 66 illustrations. Book No. 3490, $19.95 paperback, $29.95 hardcover

MS-DOS BEYOND 640K: Working with Extended and Expanded Memory—James Forney

Find out how some relatively inexpensive hardware and software enhancements can give your 8088, 80286, or 80386-based computer the ability to run larger applications, create multiple simultaneous work environments, maintain larger files, and provide all the memory you need. This book provides a clear picture of all the alternatives and options available, even up-to-the-minute tips and techniques for using Lotus 1-2-3®, Release 3.0, in extended memory! 248 pages, illustrated. Book No. 3239, $22.95 paperback, $31.95 hardcover

80386 MACRO ASSEMBLER AND TOOLKIT—Penn Brumm and Don Brumm

Now you can expand your programming horizons with MASM 5.1. This practical guide to writing and using assembly language on 80386-based computers centers on the Microsoft Macro Assembler (MASM), Version 5.1. It is designed to help you become a proficient programmer—able to write effective code and solve problems efficiently. A collection of useful macros is provided to illustrate the concepts presented. There is also a detailed discussion of MASM syntax and grammar, plus coverage of the options and their usage. 608 pages, 284 illustrations. Book No. 3247, $25.95 paperback, $35.95 hardcover

EXPLORING NATURAL LANGUAGE PROCESSING: Writing BASIC Programs That Understand English—David Leithauser

This book shows how to write interfaces for programs which allow you to communicate with those programs in plainly phrased English. Using familiar words and syntax increases the ease and efficiency of working with your computer. Here are programming methods that allow you to interact with computers in much the same manner we humans direct and instruct one another. 340 pages, 96 illustrations. Book No. 3045, $19.95 paperback only

EXPLORING HYPERTEXT PROGRAMMING: Writing Knowledge Representation and Problem-Solving Programs—Safaa H. Hashim

Designed as a practical guide for designing and writing complete hypertext systems, *Exploring Hypertext Programming* demonstrates two types of AI applications for hypertext: information retrieval and problem-solving. Presented as complete working programs, these applications will not only show you the principles of hypertext programming, but also form useful models for your own applications development. 368 pages, 145 illustrations. Book No. 3208, $22.95 paperback only

HIGH-SPEED ANIMATION AND SIMULATION FOR MICROCOMPUTERS—Lee Adams

Create realistic simulations, high-speed animation, and exciting 3-dimensional computer graphics with BASIC! Using 40 professional-caliber programs, Adams demonstrates advanced animation techniques for all of the IBM PC® family of computers—including PCs, XTs, ATs, and PCjrs. He shows you how to design and direct lifelike animation and simulations or create 3-dimensional animated images. 406 pages, 370 illustrations. Book No. 2859, $20.95 paperback only

HIGH PERFORMANCE INTERACTIVE GRAPHICS: Modeling, Rendering, and Animating for IBM PCs® and Compatibles—Lee Adams

This comprehensive reference contains over 6000 lines of available source code and 44 breathtaking demonstration programs. Author Lee Adams helps you understand the concepts behind the programs. You'll learn modeling, rendering, and animation on IBM-compatible microcomputers in the context of a modular programming environment and properly structured BASIC code. 480 pages, 229 illustrations, 8 color pages. Book No. 2879, $22.95 paperback only

---

Look for These and Other TAB Books at Your Local Bookstore

To Order Call Toll Free 1-800-822-8158

(in PA and AK call 717-794-2191)

or write to TAB BOOKS, Blue Ridge Summit, PA 17294-0840.

Title	Product No.	Quantity	Price

Subtotal $ _____

☐ Check or money order made payable to TAB BOOKS

Charge my ☐ VISA ☐ MasterCard ☐ American Express

Acct. No. _____ Exp. _____

Signature: _____

Name: _____

Address: _____

City: _____

State: _____ Zip: _____

Postage and Handling
($3.00 in U.S., $5.00 outside U.S.) $ _____

Please add appropriate local
and state sales tax $ _____

TOTAL $ _____

TAB BOOKS catalog free with purchase; otherwise send $1.00 in check or money order and receive $1.00 credit on your next purchase.

Orders outside U.S. must pay with international money order in U.S. dollars.

TAB Guarantee: If for any reason you are not satisfied with the book(s) you order, simply return it (them) within 15 days and receive a full refund. **BC**

Prices Subject to Change Without Notice.

Get 'C'erious
The Complete Library and Source

If you are fascinated by the power and flexibility of the programs in *Building C Libraries: Windows, Menus and User Interfaces*, you should definitely consider investing in the TSR Systems 'C'erious Tools Library routines on disk (see *Dr. Dobbs*, 'Examining Room' column April 1989 for a review).

'C'erious contains a comprehensive manual, all the source and executable programs in the book, plus additional functions with source and demonstration programs. All told, there are over 125 functions in the 'C'erious library, including Hot Key terminate and stay resident functions.

If you're a novice programmer just writing your first C program, or a savvy professional looking to spice up your application's user interface, using a high-performance library such as 'C'erious will make the task dramatically easier.

The software is guaranteed to be free of manufacturer's defects. (If you have any problems just return the disks to TSR Systems within 30 days and we'll happily send you a replacement. Also, our technical support is responsive and friendly.) Purchasing 'C'erious will save you the time and effort of typing in and debugging all the functions and sample programs, along with many useful functions which have not been included in the book. Interested?

'C'erious Toolkit regularly sells for $99.95 but with this coupon you'll get the entire toolkit (Manual, Source, and Demo programs) for just $59.95. There is no better deal available for a high-performance TSR, windowing, and menu creation C library.